The Gbandes

The Gbandes

A People of the Liberian Hinterland

Benjamin G. Dennis
University of Michigan
Flint

PROFESSIONAL-TECHNICAL SERIES
NELSON-HALL COMPANY ■ CHICAGO

ISBN: 0–911012–50–8

Library of Congress Catalog Card No.: 72–88580

Copyright © 1972 by Benjamin G. Dennis

Manufactured in the United States of America

Contents

Acknowledgments

I STARTED WRITING *The Gbandes: A People of the Liberian Hinterland* in 1965, the year I became chairman of the Department of Sociology and Anthropology at Ohio University, Athens, Ohio. The unfinished manuscript more or less lay around while I learned more and became involved in a variety of university responsibilities and research. There was an enormous advantage to putting the book aside at this time. During this period of waiting I was able to meet with a number of Gbandes who helped clarify obscure points in the manuscript.

Probably one must write a book about his society in order to really understand what change is, in society and in one's self. Something else happens when one writes a book about which he feels deeply: he becomes a creature of his book, for as he pours ideas and emotion into it the process shapes him, so that he can never be the same again. Writing it is the author's contention, clarifies his positions and commits his soul—often far beyond what he ever imagined possible. If you would remain placid and uncommitted, never write a book that has a deep meaning for you.

In writing this book I have been helped greatly by my wife, Anita K., whose unfettered originality, meaningful inquisitiveness and personal involvement in the writing of this book has been a constant inspiration to me. She proofread

every chapter and made subtle and cogent suggestions
which helped improve the manuscript. She and her cousin,
Mrs. Jane Paine, typed the entire manuscript, not simply as a
job to be done but with a sense of contributing to something
worthwhile. I am indebted to both of them for their help. I
want to thank my children, Winona and Benjamin II, whose
very presence made me sensitive to the study of the
Gbandes, in a sense, as this is a written record of their ancestors—the Gbandes and all the peoples of Lofa County,
Liberia, which is referred to as "the Liberian Hinterland." I
am grateful to Dr. Louise Spindler for having read the entire
first draft of the manuscript and having made the most useful
suggestions which led me to rewrite the book. My thanks go
to Dr. John Messenger who also read the first draft and offered critical and professional advice which contributed to
the improvement of the book.

I want to thank Ohio University for a number of things:
first, for providing the climate for this type of academic ex-
position; secondly, for the "small grant" made by the African
Language and Area Studies of the International Studies
Center of Ohio University—Athens, Ohio. I also want to
thank the University of Michigan—Flint for the fine facilities
which hastened the completion of the book. I want also to
thank Mrs. Jane Desser for the illustrations illuminating the
text, and Rose Brabbs for helping with the final corrections,
particularly those concerned with Gbande terms.

I am deeply indebted to Professor O. Anthony Bates for
the transcription, arrangement, and analysis of Gbande
terms as they appear in this work. (See the Appendix.) His
linguistic contribution is indeed the beginning of scientific
breakthrough in the study and understanding of my people—
the Gbandes. Notwithstanding, the author assumes all responsibility for any errors or omissions.

Finally, I want to thank my people, the Gbandes and
their neighbors—the Gissies, Mendes, Lomas, and Belles—the
people of Lofa County, whose way of life made possible the

writing of this book. I am indebted to them beyond my capacity to repay for letting us in on their way of life. Thanks also to the unnoted number of individuals who contributed to the preparation of this book—friends, colleagues, students, and secretaries.

Introduction

IN RECENT YEARS, Africa has come to acquire a new meaning for itself and for its peoples. The continent is becoming an increasingly significant part of the modern world. In many respects, however, it remains the most enigmatic continent. There are several reasons why Africa appears enigmatic, and chief among them is the lack of knowledge about its peoples, their cultural history, their social structure, and their social organizations. Since most of what has been written about the continent, up until a few years ago, was written by non-Africans, these works were, to a great extent, a reflection of the writers' cultures rather than Africa's culture. Today, the number of non-Africans who are interested in Africa is increasing. Likewise, the number of trained Africans and those Africans who are interested in writing about their continent is growing. The works of these indigenous Africans are already on the market in America and in Europe. These works are done either on the region or on the tribe of which their authors are a part. The work of Jomo Kenyatta, *Facing Mt. Kenya*, first published in 1938 in Great Britain, and that of Victor C. Uchendu, *The Igbo of Southeast Nigeria* (1965), are cases in point. Truly, we are fast approaching the day in which the statement "Anthropology begins at home" is becoming a reality.

Since it is neither possible nor desirable to study every

tribe in Africa at once, but since we cannot truly understand Africa and Africans without such a study, it becomes imperative that we focus upon a core tribe in each sub-region. This will permit some knowledge and understanding of four or more groups beside the core group. The present study is an attempt in this direction. It is concerned with a group of people whose way of life, although very rich, has remained in obscurity, as is the case with most African peoples. There are countless reasons for the obscurity of this people's way of life, three of which will be considered at this point.

The first two reasons may be attributed to their size and location. There are approximately 30,000 Gbandes [8, p. 260], and they are located in the extreme northwestern hinterland of Liberia. Although the size of a population is not always the most important criteria for research, it cannot be ignored, especially in the case of the Gbandes. It is exceedingly difficult, if not impossible, to obtain a grant to conduct a study of a relatively unknown group of people. The Gbandes' small number has thus made them undesirable for study, particularly since they pose no problem politically or otherwise. Second, the Gbandes do not occupy any strategic location that would warrant investigation. Foundations which can afford the funds for such research are reluctant to do so for purely scientific inquiry. For the Gbandes of Liberia the problem has been their inaccessibility. For example, before and during the early part of President Tubman's administration, which began in 1944, the only way to get to the Gbandes was to walk. Communication facilities in those days were such that Sierra Leone, which was a British colony, was much closer to the Gbandes than Monrovia, the capital of Liberia. Anyone wishing to go to the Gbandes on foot, especially from Monrovia, would go via Sierra Leone rather than spending a week or more on foot enroute from Monrovia. Third, there are few, if any, significant anthropological and/or sociological studies about any group in this area of Liberia or perhaps any area of the hinterland.

For me, the life of this people poses a special interest and challenge for at least two reasons. First, they are closely related to my own group, the Mendes, and any serious and conscientious study of the Gbandes would significantly contribute to and facilitate the understanding of their neighbors, particularly the Mendes. Second they have a rich way of life. My familiarity with this people and their neighbors has made it possible for me to illuminate facets of Gbande life which would otherwise have been difficult, if not impossible, to examine.

The Gbandes

Chapter 1
Geography

GEOGRAPHICALLY, WITH RESPECT to their neighbors, the Gbandes are centrally located: the Gissies to the north and northwest; the Lomas to the east and southeast; the Belles to the south; and the Mendes to the west. The north and the northeast territory where the Gbandes merge with the Gissies is made up of flat semi-grassland. As one moves from the northwest to the north, the forest gives way to grassland. The peoples in this area are marginally productive. They are small farmers and herders with no strong attachment to either group. In the east and southeast where the Lomas meet the Gbandes the land is timbered. As one moves from east to southeast, the forest becomes thicker. The peoples in this area are primarily farmers, although they do keep cattle, goats, and sheep. Rice is their principal crop. In the south, the territory is shared by the Gbandes and the Belles and is characterized by high forests which extend westward. Villages or *tɛi* are usually built at considerable distances from each other. At first sight, the area gives the appearance of being populated by hunters instead of farmers. Although the people are farmers for the most part, the size of their farms is small in comparison to other sections of Gbandeland. One of the many factors contributing to this is the difficulty in clearing the high forests and the relatively small size of their families. Since these two conditions are often prerequisites

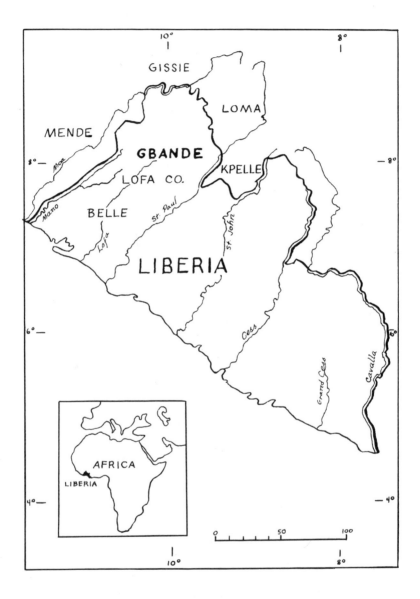

Gbandeland

for farm work in the absence of machinery, they cannot be overlooked. Finally, in the west, the Gbandes are separated from the Mendes by a narrow strip of forest belt. This belt is an extension of the southern forests which separate the Belles from the Gbandes. Villages are built much closer together, and farms are considerably larger in this section than those in the south. As is quite apparent, the same livestock is in abundance. The Islamic religion is well entrenched in this section of Gbandeland, more so than in any other section.

With regard to climate and topography, the Gbandes are favored with two distinctive climatic seasons, rainy and dry. The rainy season, which begins in June and ends in October, reaches its high point around the latter part of June and extends through the first part of October. The month of October is called *vōndōngi*, which means "trace" or "track-leaver," because most tracks made by men and animals during this month remain until the next rainy season when they are finally washed away. During the months of July, August, and September, the heavy rains prevent most activities, such as farming and hunting. The rainy season also brings a severe shortage of food because it is close to the time of harvest when the food supply is lowest. The rainy weather permits very little time for outdoor activities which are necessary for replenishing the depleted food supply. This is also the season in which the wild or uncultivated food supplies are scarce. They are scarce and hard to find because everybody is searching for the same wild foods at the same time, and one has to travel great distances in order to find them. The distance factor hinders the conveyance of large and sufficient quantities to the village storehouse. This tends to be a period in which most fruit-bearing trees are dormant. Consequently, this is also a dormant period for the Gbande people. After these five months—June, July, August, September, and October—the remaining seven months, beginning at the end of October, constitute the months of the dry

season. They are November, December, January, February,
March, April, and May. However, only the months of February and March are really dry and March is the hottest
month. During the months of November, December, and
January, and the first part of February, the temperatures of
day and night are in sharp contrast. In these months, the
maximum temperature usually ranges from 75° to 80° or
even 90° during the day. It starts rising about 10:00 A.M. and
reaches its highest point at about 2:00 P.M. From this point,
it tends to drop gradually until about 4:00 P.M.; then it com-
mences to drop rapidly until it reaches its lowest point of
about 50° or 60°, or even as low as 45°. The lowest point is
usually reached around 3:00 to 4:00 A.M. This period is characterized by a dry, dusty type of wind that blows across the
Atlantic coast and is known as the Harmattan Wind. This
dry, cold wind causes lips and skin to crack. It penetrates the
skin and causes it to have a dusty appearance. During this
season, every hut has to keep its fire burning throughout the
night and well into the morning, at least until 10:00 A.M. The
Liberian Republic hinterland, which includes Gbandeland,
is one of the country's coldest regions and has the heaviest
rainfall.

Topography

Topographically, the central portion of Gbandeland is covered with low brush forests and scattered swamps. Here intensive subsistence farming exploits the rich, fertile soil. Although this area does not have many large bodies of water, it
is nevertheless well watered by a number of streams feeding
in and out of several swamps. The southern portion of
Gbandeland is covered with high, dense forests and at least
one hill of considerable size which extends westward. This
belt and hill appear to be a no man's land; the land has never
been exploited in any way, farming or otherwise. This virgin
land contains one of the best supplies of natural timber in
Liberia. It forms the southern and western boundaries be-

tween the Gbandes and the Belles and between the Gbandes and the Mendes. The northernmost section, which the Gbandes share with the Gissies, is characterized by lowland and brush. This is the area in which one finds some herding. The less fertile soil may account for the small farms in this area. As one moves east-southeastward the low brushland becomes mixed with moderate forests. This again is an area of intensive subsistence agriculture. A few cattle, sheep, and goats are raised here. The lowland and brush form a boundary between the Gbandes and the Lomas or Buzies.

There are several rivers in Gbandeland. The Lofa River is the largest one of the southern part near the city of Gondolahum, close to the Belle people. The Moah River is the largest in the west and runs around the city of Vahum through the section occupied by the Mendes. The northeast and southeast have one large river in common. This is the Kiahala River which originates in the east-southeast around the Loma city of Vorjamine and runs northwestward. The city of Kololahum, the Liberian government headquarters where the Gissies and the Gbandes mingle, sits on the northern bank of the Kiahala River. Besides these large rivers, there are many rivers of lesser size throughout Gbandeland. These rivers made Gbandeland an ideal agricultural land. Considerable deposits of iron ore, gold, diamonds, and several other important minerals have also been found in Gbandeland.

In summary, Gbandeland is relatively level with irregular small hills throughout. It is well watered by many rivers, both large and small. The high forest belt is found in the southeast, south, and southwest. The central portion is covered with low to intermediate brush, whereas the east and northeast are predominantly low, flat land with low brush.

Demography

The demographic data of this people, although interesting, are difficult to record and classify when standard

demographic variables are used. The Gbande way of life and
place of residence make effective demographic work nearly
impossible. One problem is that as a rule the Gbandes register neither birth nor death. They firmly believe that children
are the gifts of the ancestor spirits; hence, to tell the number
of one's children is like counting one's blessings. This to them
is a form of bragging. Secondly, the Gbande concept of
children is not congruent with that of the census takers or
with the Western concept. For them the concept of
"children" in the family refers to infants, those who are still
riding on their mother's back and feeding on her milk. It
refers to those who cannot walk or talk clearly. Once an individual begins to walk, talk, and eat adult food, he or she is no
longer included in the concept of "children." The closest
equivalent Gbande word for children is *dulalày* (small child).
Moreover, when the concept is just "children" or *do* it
includes all offspring of one's brothers, sisters, and cousins of
the same generation. This is a common problem for most of
Africa. This point is very crucial in any discussion about population density for the continent as a whole. There can be no
certainty about the actual number or size of Gbande people,
nor can there be any for the African continent under these
conditions. What we have now, in the way of population
figures for the Gbandes and Africa, must be considered a
very crude estimate and therefore grossly inadequate. The
third problem is the inaccessibility of some Gbande villages.
Since census takers never reach such villages, they are not
included in the census, resulting in inaccurate population
reports.

Other important variables to be included in a
demographic description are the standard demographic
characteristics—for example, birth, death, and migration, as
well as morbidity. Problems with these variables, with the
exception of morbidity, are discussed at length in Chapter
13; hence, they will not be treated here. The problem with
morbidity data may be inferred from the discussion of fertil-

ity and mortality. In terms of these latter three variables Gbande demography fits into the category of the "high potential growth demographic model," but it is now tending to move gradually towards the "transitional demographic model [14, p. 7]." This change in Gbande demographic structure may be attributed to many things; a few will be discussed at this point. As far as I know, the prima-facie evidence and subtle moment of change in Gbande demography came with the establishment of the Anglican Episcopalian church, school, and medical center. These institutions were greatly responsible for many changes that are now perceptible among this people.

Although the medical center is not exactly centrally located, it can be reached by all Gbandes in a day and a half, or at most, two days (walking). To some extent, this medical center has both modified and greatly revolutionized Gbande traditional practices. The services which it offers, as minimal as they are, have helped reduce the high infant mortality rate. Before its establishment and during its early years in Gbandeland, childbirth was a major cause of death. Prior to the coming of the medical center, there was no respectable hospital in this section of Liberia. Childbirth was the exclusive affair of the women, with midwives officiating. No man, with the exception of the blacksmith,° was allowed to help with or witness childbirth, no matter what medical training he might have had. The period of childbirth was considered an actual engagement in the war between man and nature. Man became identified with nature through being responsible for bringing about the birth of a child. During childbirth many women often died with their infants. Many of the infants who survived the crisis of birth often died a few days after birth because of injuries received at the

---

°The blacksmith's special importance in Gbande society is explained in Chapter 10 "Gbande Art," subsection "Metal and Leather Work."

time of birth or infection due to the unsanitary conditions of the place of birth, which was usually in the woods.

In those days, for a woman or a man to stand nude before a person of the opposite sex was a matter of great shame and disgrace, and hence this action could not be condoned even if one's life was at stake. This traditional rule of modesty was even stronger if the person of the opposite sex was a stranger. Therefore, when going to the hospital for treatment, if such treatment involved undressing, female patients would often allow themselves to be treated only by female doctors and male patients only by male doctors. Otherwise, they absolutely refused treatment, no matter how drastic the consequence.

Today, most of these practices have changed. Both male and female are now going for medical care with less regard for the sex of the doctor. Perhaps the success of this institution in modifying and revolutionizing Gbande traditional practices stems from the particular approaches used by the first missionaries who went to Gbandeland. One of the first things these missionaries did was to establish a school of instruction for everybody—that is, for both adults and children with little or no regard for cultural groupings. This institution provided new types of work for all those who wanted to work. All such employees were engulfed with benevolence by their employers. They were at first encouraged to try the hospitals whenever they felt sick. Every opportunity was exercised to press this encouragement. When the workers and students became accustomed to hospital treatment, they were asked to bring in their sick relatives and friends for free treatment. They were told that these relatives and friends would have to remain and work for a few months after their discharge so that the hospital doctors could observe them to make sure that they were really healed. During their stay, they were taught the A B C's and how to read simple material, depending on the time that they were willing to remain there.

The missionaries introduced the hospital to the Gbandes. Diseases that used to take months to cure or were perhaps considered incurable were now curable, and people who required surgery received it, if they were willing to go to the hospital. Pretty soon, the news of the powerful hospital-medicine men spread throughout Gbandeland, to the extent that those who were suffering from a hernia, goiter, elephantiasis, tropical ulcers, yaws, ancylostomiasis (hookworm disease), trypanosomiasis (sleeping sickness), or other common maladies came to the hospital. The successful treatment of these maladies and many others convinced the women that they too could be benefited. For the first time, they too used the hospital for childbirth, without regard to the sex of the doctor. The first of these maternity patients were asked by the hospital doctors to bring along their mid-wife or midwives. These midwives were invited into the delivery room. They were told that they too were doctors and that all doctors should work together for the purpose of saving lives. This deference to the midwives and other indigenous doctors had an inestimable and obvious psychological impact on the Gbandes. The concurrent introduction of literacy and medical treatment, in which the Gbande doctors were both consultants and participants, was truly a big breakthrough. These indigenous doctors felt a part of the medical center, and this led to the acceptance and success of this institution. Without this, there would have been some reluctance on the part of the Gbandes to use the hospital or the school. The introduction of literacy and medical treatment simultaneously is one of the chief causes of the shift in the Gbande demographic structure. Through the literacy program the Gbandes were taught first aid and hygienic methods. In turn, the Gbande doctors introduced the hospital doctors to some important herbs. In this way the Gbande doctors were able to maintain their self-esteem and feel that they were contributing significantly to the medical center.

The first white man who came to establish the mission is

described by those who met him as a man having an unusually long neck. Hence he was called *Gbōlō*, the Gbande word for "neck," and the mission he started is called *Gbōlōlāhon*, meaning "necktown." Today it is called Gbololahum Holy Cross Mission of Liberia. This mission is truly a melting pot where Mendes, Lomas, and Gissies meet with Gbandes. One of the largest weekly markets, which meets every Friday, is held in the vicinity of Gbololahum. This market is concerned with the exchange of foodstuffs and other domestic goods.

Regions of Gbandeland

The Gbandes are divided into four or possibly five sub-divisions. These subdivisions are identifiable by dialect: (1) Tahamba; (2) Goolahum or Ngoolahum, closely related to Tahamba; (3) Wawoma or Waoma; (4) Hasala or Vasala; and (5) Yawuyahum or Hembe.

The Tahambas occupy the northcentral portion of Gbandeland. They consider themselves not only the oldest but the purest Gbandes. They are also the most politically active and economically industrious. Among this people, a man's social and political status is enhanced by the size of his cultivated rice farm. Fishing, hunting, carving, singing, storytelling, and other talents enhance one's status, but these are still secondary to having a large rice farm.

Tahamba villages are fairly large, and they are built close enough together that a neighboring village can be reached by walking for about one or two hours. The roads or paths connecting these villages are well maintained by the villagers. Each village has the responsibility of keeping its section of the path in good condition the year round. However, bridges are built and maintained in common by two or more villages. The national political capital for the Gbandes, which is Kololahum, is located in this area. Other important towns are Nyeanwālāhum, Somalahum, and Dianbough.

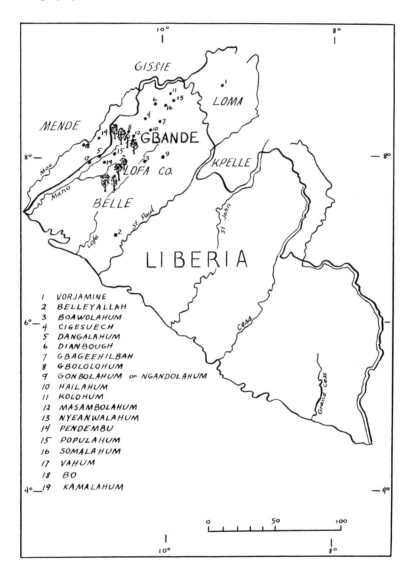

The following cities are numbered on the map:

1. VORJAMINE
2. BELLEYALLAH
3. BOAWOLAHUM
4. CIGESUECH
5. DANGALAHUM
6. DIANBOUGH
7. GBAGEEHILBAH
8. GBOLOLOHUM
9. GONBOLAHUM or NGANDOLAHUM
10. HAILAHUM
11. KOLOHUM
12. MASAMBOLAHUM
13. NYEANWALAHUM
14. PENDEMBU
15. POPULAHUM
16. SOMALAHUM
17. VAHUM
18. BO
19. KAMALAHUM

The cities of Gbandeland

The next subdivision is the Goolahum or Ngoolahum. This group considers itself the purest modern Gbande. There is, however, little or no marked difference between the Goolahums and the Tahambas, except that Goolahum villages are somewhat smaller and farther apart than those of the Tahambas. Their claim of purity lies in the fact that they are surrounded only by other Gbandes; hence their language has been influenced less by other languages and contains only elements of the Gbande language. One can list several important villages in this area, such as Boawolahum and Hailahum.

The third subdivision is the Wawoma or Waoma. The Wawoma are to the northwest and west of the Tahambas. The Gbololahum Holy Cross Mission is in this area. The only large village in the subdivision is called Masambolahum, about a twenty-minute walk from Gbololahum. The Gbandes here are mixed with the Mandingoes who are natives of Guinea, Ivory Coast, and perhaps Senegal. There are also a few Mendes present among them. The Wawomas' rice farms are very small in comparison with those of the Tahambas or the Goolahums. The Islamic religion is well established in this area. This faith was brought in by the Mandingoes, who are staunch adherents of Islam. This may be one reason why the Wawoma have not shown the same enthusiasm as other Gbandes for the Gbololahum Holy Cross Mission, located within their territory.

The fourth subdivision is the Hasala or Vasala. This group is located in the extreme western portion of Gbandeland. This is the subdivision of which I am a part, because this group is mixed with my membership group, the Mendes. Farms in this area are large but few. Distances between villages are considerable. This subdivision tends to identify itself more with the Mendes than with the Gbandes. The large villages are Kamalahum, Popalahum, Dangalahum, and Vahum (my village) in Guma District. The language is a mixture of Mende and Gbande with a heavy

Mende accent. The Islamic religion is more prevalent in this area than in any other part of Gbandeland, with the exception of the Wawoma area.

The fifth and final subdivision is the Yawuyahum or Hembe. This group is located east-southeast of Gbandeland. It is a mixture of Lomas or Buzies and Gbandes. They are identified more with the Lomas than with other Gbandes. Their language is Gbande with Loma pronunciations. Farms are large but sparse. Distances between villages are far and villages are usually small. The towns of Cigesuech and Ngandolahum (Gondolahum) are among the most important. Roads or paths are difficult to maintain because of the considerable distances between villages.

Although there are differences among these subdivisions, these differences are important only in the internal affairs of the Gbandes, regulating social customs and attitudes. Any threat from an external source eliminates these differences and unifies the Gbandes against the common enemy. When a Gbande is away from his homeland, these differences are minimized; he then draws from a deeper and more finding experience—that of being a Gbande.

Chapter 2
The Gbandes and Their Neighbors

THE GBANDES (the name means "human beings") are surrounded by four groups whose cultures, although related, are different enough from the Gbandes' and from each other's to mark them as different groups. However, two of these groups are more closely related to the Gbandes in many aspects of their cultures; the most striking similarity is that of their languages. The first of these related cultural groups is the Lomas or Buzies. The Gbandes, call this group *gbalūwi*, meaning "strong skin." The next group is the Mendes, called *hēgāwèn* by the Gbandes, meaning "people from the low land" or "people from below." The other two groups, although sharing many cultural similarities with the Gbandes and living adjacent to them, speak languages which are remote from each other and from the Gbande language. Language is the great difference between these peoples and the Gbandes. They are the Gissies and the Belles. The relationship of each group to the Gbandes will now be discussed.

Lomas

The Gbandes are greatly influenced by the Lomas' culture, particularly in the areas of religion, medicine, and singing. These three areas are inseparable in both the Gbandes' and the Lomas' cultures. They are usually summed up under the

name of religion. It is in the practice of religion that the
Lomas are held in high esteem by the Gbandes. They are
considered very gifted in the practice of indigenous medicine. The practice of medicine includes diviners, magicians,
sorcerers, healers, and so forth. A person who becomes specialized in one or more of the above is called *zowī* or
"doctor" by the Lomas; the Gbande word for this is *sowì*.
The Loma language is the professional language used by
those who have become *zowī* in their medical and/or
religious practices. A Gbande *sowì* proficient use of Loma
language and adoption of Loma mannerisms in his professional role enhance his status as a powerful doctor. In the
past, Gbande young men of low status aspired to become a
sowì because it was an avenue of social escalation open to
all. Now, young men of low status are attracted to other
goals, such as Western education and vocations. However,
the importance of this aspect of Loma culture on the
Gbandes is obvious even to the casual observer. For example, most of the Gbandes' male secret songs are sung in
the Loma language. Access to most of these songs is limited
to initiated men, those who are graduates of the Poro school
(a Gbande male educational institution). It is, therefore, imperative that all Gbande males learn the Loma language at a
very early age. For this reason most Gbande men speak the
Loma language with little or no accent. On the other hand,
very few Lomas are capable of speaking the Gbande language with equal proficiency.

It can be seen that the Gbandes respect, fear, and suspect the Lomas. The Lomas are respected because of their
assumed medical skills. This respect stems from the belief
that good or bad luck and life or death depend upon the
skills of the Loma *zowī*. Moreover, since the ambition of
every Gbande young man is to acquire knowledge of Loma
songs, religion, and medicine, and since the fulfillment of this
ambition depends upon his acceptance by a Loma doctor,
young men and their parents must accord these *zowī* the

highest respect. Very often, Gbande young men who want to become a *sowì* give themselves or are given by their parents in apprenticeship to a professional Loma *zowī*. These young men are willing to humble themselves entirely in order to become *zowī*. For example, once a young man becomes an apprentice, he remains an apprentice until the death of his teacher, provided of course he outlives him. It is only then that he can become a full doctor of *sowì* by inheriting both the medicines and power associated with the honors of his teacher. This requirement is based upon the widespread belief among these peoples that there are areas of medical knowledge which the Loma *zowī* cannot disclose to anyone until his death is imminent. For this reason, it is a common practice, and perhaps a desirable one, for an apprentice to attach himself to an old *zowī*. (Let me point out here that the attachment of an apprentice to an old *zowī* serves at least two full purposes: first, and perhaps most obvious, is that the apprentice is expected to outlive his teacher; second is that the rule of seniority is observed, because old age is a standard criterion of social stratification in both the Gbande and Loma societies. It is believed that the older the *sowì* is, the greater his powers, and because of these qualities, he is more feared, honored, and respected by everybody including his colleagues.)

The professional Loma *zowī* is generally feared by all Gbandes since his behavior cannot be predicted because he has little or no control over it—that is, he follows the dictates of his medicines most of the time. Consequently, it is an absolute necessity to exercise extreme caution in dealing with such a *zowī* however insignificant he may look. His assets are his medical skills, and he might be forced by the power of these medicines to use his skills against anyone at the least provocation. At times, it is claimed, these medicines are not to be satisfied with anything less than the highest penalty for an offender. It is also believed that the *zowī* is a carrier of both good and bad omens, either one of which may be used depending on the situation. The powers of the *zowī* are thought to be unlimited in that they are unrestricted by space. That is, he can have his omens fulfill his wishes without the physical presence of those for whom they are designed. Because of this, a *zowī* is an object of suspicion in time of crisis.

There is a bit of ethnocentrism in Gbande thought with reference to the Lomas as a whole, and especially with regard to the *zowī* and Loma men. A Loma *zowī* is said to be raw, crude, and perhaps unpolished in most of his behavior. This type of behavior, however, is admired and sought after by Gbande apprentices, because it is said to be the trademark of the medical profession. There is an even more important reason why Gbandes are interested in engaging in behavior considered less desirable by Gbande standards. Since the Lomas are said to be extremists and there is no limit to their love or hatred, the Gbandes want to make every effort to become friends with the Loma *zowī* and his family. Gbande ethnocentrism is more pronounced with respect to the type of relationship between the sexes of the two groups. Gbande males tend to marry Loma females freely, but very few if any Loma males marry Gbande females. Loma males are said to be rough, but their women are said to be industrious.

Mendes

The Gbandes are very much influenced by the Mende culture. Mende manners of dressing and speaking and their traditional intellectual discourse are greatly admired. Mende dances are considered classical, but their songs (unlike the Loma songs) are considered love songs and consequently reserved for women. Although it is a truism that love is a matter which concerns both male and female, and the Gbandes also believe this, they are convinced that the act of loving is primarily a feminine affair. Only women really

know how to love, because love is indisputably the most for-
midable asset they have to compensate for their lack of physical courage and strength. The Mendes, according to the
Gbandes, approximate women in these attributes. They lack
courage, strength, and other masculine attributes, and this
lack of masculine attributes is exhibited by the Mendes in
their songs. For this reason, very few Gbande males sing
Mende songs. On the whole, the Mendes are viewed with
mixed feelings, such as admiration, respect, suspicion, and
disgust. These mixed feelings stem from the belief that
Mendes are lazy and cunning. As a result, the Gbandes consider them unreliable and selfish.

   Most Mendes are followers of the Islamic religion.
Those who have embraced this religion are able to read and
write Arabic. Being able to read and write Arabic is greatly
admired by the Gbandes, but being a Muslim goes far
beyond the ability to read and write. It is identified with the
ability to manipulate circumstances in favor of or against
whomever one wishes. Therefore, it is believed that Mende
Muslims have the power to make good luck charms or talismans for almost anything. For example, there are talismans
for getting a choice position, passing an examination successfully, or being popular with the opposite sex or with important persons, and there are talismans which protect one
against witchcraft, sorcery, and so forth. These talismans
consist of secret writings selected from the Koran. (The
Koran is equivalent to the Christian Bible.) These talismans
are prepared by the leading Mende Muslims who have
achieved the title of *kamān*, which is equivalent to the Loma
zowī or Gbande *sowì*. All Muslims are called *m>le*, the term
kamān, which means "master," is reserved for those who
have so distinguished themselves. Strangely enough, these
talismans are always good and valid even when they have
failed to bring about the desired results. Such failure in
producing the expected result is almost always the fault of
the user, who has not been scrupulous enough. Whether or

not the user gets what he wants, the *kamān* gets his pay
because he is always right. For these, among other reasons,
the Mendes are respected and admired.

As mentioned before, the Mendes are also viewed with
suspicion and disgust. They are considered manipulators
because they are perfectly willing to work for or against a
particular person, depending on the offer made to them.
They are said to be more interested in rewards than human
beings. Therefore, once they get set against or for anyone for
large rewards, the only thing that can possibly change their
minds are counter rewards, larger than the first. Mendes are
also considered characterized by an ability to hide their
anger. Therefore, it is thought desirable to treat the *kamān*
with kindness whenever possible, because it is difficult to
know their intentions.

Although Mende women are much desired as status
symbols, it appears that more Mende males marry Gbande
females than Gbande males marry Mende females. Mende
women are said to be knowledgeable in all social affairs on
the one hand, and expensive and demanding on the other
hand. With respect to language, here again we find that the
Gbandes exhibit great ability to speak the Mende language,
whereas the Mendes, like the Lomas, have less ability or
perhaps lack motivation to speak the Gbande language.
Gbande women are desired by the Mendes for their characteristic of being hardworking. Mende modes of dress are
desired by both Gbande males and females. They are said to
be clean, but so much of their time is spent on etiquette that
they have little or no time for anything else. This is why they
are considered lazy. Nonetheless, the Gbandes are
influenced by the Mendes as much as they are by the Lomas.

Gissies

Although the Gissies are as close as the Lomas and Mendes
are in space to the Gbandes, they are culturally far removed

from them, at least in language. Unlike the Lomas and the
Mendes, whose influence on the Gbandes has been indicated, the Gissies show no distinct influence on the
Gbandes. Undoubtedly there must be some reciprocal influences because the two groups have long lived in close proximity and had frequent interactions. Nevertheless, the cultural differences between the Gissies and the Gbandes tend
to be considerably greater than those between the Gbandes
and the Lomas or the Mendes. The great difference between
the Gbandes and the Gissies stems from the language barrier
between them. Very few Gbandes are able or bother to speak
the Gissies' language. To them, the sound of the Gissies' language tends to be repugnant as contrasted with the language
of the Lomas or the Mendes. Furthermore, the Gbandes
would prefer having an interpreter rather than a Gissie
speak Gbande because the Gissie are thought to be worse
speakers of the Gbande language than any of their
neighbors. The subtle mutual disparagement implied by the
lack of a common means of communication is all too obvious.
Since language is one of the main vehicles of culture, impedi-
ments to its sharing will often result in extreme ethnocentrism, especially in the case of peoples in close proximity. In
the following discussion, this ethnocentrism is exemplified by
the Gbandes' relationship with the Gissies.

The Gbandes exercise great caution in their relationship
with the Gissies, because they firmly believe that although
the Gissies are intelligent and brave, they are very emotional
and irrational in most of their behavior. The Gissies are said
to be impatient and jealous over women. Like the Lomas,
they are considered extremists. For example, when they love,
nothing is too good or too hard to accomplish for their loved
ones; likewise, when they hate or when they are angry, they
are said to be capable of killing. Their sanitary practices, although not too different from those of the Gbandes, are said
to be poor. They are said to be prone to commit suicide at
the least provocation. Nevertheless, the Gissies are said to be

good workers when they are well fed. They are considered honest people and good athletes. Gambling is said to be a characteristic way in which Gissies spend their leisure time. Gissie women are said to be as beautiful as Mende women but less expensive. Gissie women are considered as intelligent as Gissie men but much milder and kinder. For these reasons, Gissie women are much desired.

Belles

This brings us to the fourth and last neighbor of the Gbandes, the Belles. The Belles are the southernmost neighbors of the Gbandes and they are perhaps the least familiar to the Gbandes. This lack of knowledge about the Belles' way of life stems from many sources.

One of these sources is probably the selective residential isolationism of the Belles. The Belles live in the deep forest areas which separate their territory from the southcentral portion of the hinterland inhabited by the Gbandes. In this area, most Belle villages are well concealed deep in the forest belt. There are no roads or paths to their villages. The only access to them is by way of natural creeks or streams, because the Belles believe that their residence should be as secret as their religion. Therefore, in most instances, only a Belle knows where to find Belle villages. This kind of isolation, of course, is not conducive to promoting an understanding between people of different cultures. The Belle language itself also creates barriers. It is, perhaps, the most difficult language not only in this area but in all of Liberia. It is even more difficult than the Gissie language, which is by no means an easy language. As a matter of fact, I know of no Gbande or any other person who is able to speak the Belle language. Another source of the Belles' isolation is their ability to speak the languages of their neighbors fluently without accent. These languages are those of the Lomas, Kpelles (northeastern neighbor of the Lomas), and Gbandes. By mastering these languages, the Belles do not allow their neighbors an opportunity to learn their language. Linguistically, the Belles can pass for any of these groups. But the Belle women seldom leave home; they tend to be overprotected. The only point which might betray a Belle is physical appearance. Belles have distinctive features which are uniquely Belle. They are one of the most beautiful peoples known to me in this part of Africa.

A Gbande myth or ethnocentrism concerning the Belles is that they were considered cannibals in the remote past, and that this is the reason they are ashamed to speak their language among non-Belles. The myth of past cannibalism is also the reason given for the location of the Belle villages in the heart of the deep forest. These beliefs are strengthened by the fact that the Liberian detention camp for punishment of criminals is located in the heart of Belle country in the city of Belleyallah. This is a city where it is believed that prisoners disappear. It appears here as elsewhere that what a people cannot explain by factual information and experience is accounted for by myth.

Chapter 3
The Gbande Mode of Making a Living

THE ECONOMIC ACTIVITIES of the Gbande people are of two types: subsistence occupations and cash-producing occupations. By and large, the former is much more important than the latter. Subsistence activities engage all able-bodied persons—men, women, and children. At least eight months of the year are devoted to production of basic subsistence crops; the remaining four months are spent earning cash and growing lesser subsistence crops.

Subsistence Crops

The basic subsistence crop is rice, grown on dry land. Success in dry rice farming depends on the full participation of the whole family, except for the very young or old. The work is well defined with division of labor by sex and by age. The men are responsible for the strenuous and hazardous work. The farming site is usually selected on the outskirts of the village by the male head of the extended family. Once he has done this, the decision about the size of the farm is made by him and his oldest son. This decision depends upon the number of males in the family who are able to contribute to the clearing of the area selected for the farm. The women are then informed of the location of the area. The men make the farm site known to other members of the community by clearing small spots of land beside a path or road where they can easily be seen and by placing a bunch of leaves in the fork of a stick in the center of the cleared spots. This sign indicates the selection of the spot as well as the size of the farm without indicating who the owner shall be. Farms are usually made together in one general area by the inhabitants of a village, so that the people can work the land together conveniently. Each year a new group of farm sites is selected in order to let the other areas renew themselves. After an area has been used it is given at least five or six years to renew itself. Some areas may stand idle ten or fifteen years before they are used again. Thus the farm sites are rotated each year around the village site. The outer boundaries of these farms are understood by all, and a certain amount of land around each village is considered the village's own to supply its people.

At about the beginning of February the men begin to clear the underbrush on the farm site. This is done with a type of machete called a *ɓolobáy*, a heavy, steel, unifacial, sharp-edged instrument usually made by the village blacksmith but also available from traders. Usually, the men wear a pair of self-made leather gloves called $k > l\bar{u}$ on both hands, and each worker carries a long, carefully shaped stick which enables him to move the thick brush back to make the cutting easier. The work usually starts around 6:00 A.M. and continues until dark.

At about noon, the women bring a lunch of cooked rice soaked in palm oil to the men, calling out the name of the youngest male worker as they arrive. Upon hearing his name, this worker goes to meet the women and conducts them to the spot where the noon meal will be eaten. This is necessary because while the site is being cleared, no particular place is designated for eating or resting. The selection of such a place depends on where the men happen to be working at noon. When the women arrive at a good spot close to the workers, the youngest man calls out the name of the oldest male worker. The oldest man then tells the others that the women and food are here and shows them the spot that has been chosen for the meal. He also asks them to bring their tools with them. The youngest man meanwhile has remained with the women to boast of how hard they have been working and of his own contribution. At the eating place the oldest women greet the oldest men first, then they greet the rest of the workers, and finally they admire and praise the men for their hard work. All the workers wash their hands and eat from the same bowl or dish even if there are two or more dishes. In case there are two or more dishes, the oldest woman will uncover the one she wants the workers to eat from first. After eating, the oldest male will retire first, followed by the next senior member, and so on. The youngest, being last to retire, must wash the dishes. The youngest also has the distinctive task of dividing the meat during the meal, no one is allowed to pick any piece he wants. The oldest male is served first with the best and biggest piece of meat, followed by the next senior member and so on down the line. It usually takes about thirty minutes to eat. The women do not eat at this time; they eat in the village. When the men are through eating, the women pack the dishes and return to the village. After the women have departed, the men spend twenty minutes repairing and resharpening their tools on a special polished stone called a $k>t\bar{u}$ which is always kept by their side. The men discuss how far they should reach before the sun sets. They are likely to work harder and to clear a larger area if it is covered with low brush. Such areas are usually inhabited by small animals such as rats, frogs, possums, and raccoons. In such a case, the men usually decide to combine hunting with farming by making a large circle around a low brush area. As the uncut brush area becomes smaller, the animals will start jumping out into the cleared areas. Very few of these animals are able to escape the eyes of the men, for they are skillful hunters.

The young boys are excused about thirty minutes before
the work is finished for the day, in order to gather dry sticks
for firewood. At quitting time each man, with the exception
of the oldest male, will look for a dry log to take with him to
the village to serve as a base for the fire. The oldest male
carries the game they have killed. He is assisted by the next
oldest male if necessary.

This goes on for three or four weeks, after which the
most hazardous work in farm-making starts. This is the
felling of the large trees which the lighter tools for brush
clearing have left untouched. Homemade axes or $k\!\!>\!\!n\!\!>$ are
used for this job. Usually many small and middle-sized trees
have been cut into, but not enough to fell them. The larger
trees are cut down in the direction of these smaller trees in
order to knock them down. This phase of the clearing continues for about a week and a half. At about the middle of
the last week in March, fire is set to the new farm site to do
the final clearing. The setting of the fire may be postponed
for several hours or even days if the direction of the wind is
wrong. March is the hottest month of the dry season, and
there are usually strong variable winds in this month. When
the spot has been burned and the fire has died out, the
members of the family will comb the whole area in search of
any animal that may have been trapped by the fire. If the fire
missed any spots, the men will carefully use their cutlasses or
the small tools used in cutting underbrush to clear them.
This is the end of the men's exclusive work. Contrary to popular belief, this method of clearing the farm site by fire rarely
leads to forest fires. In fact, I have never heard of any such
case.

Although rice or *mbáy* is the basic crop, many other
crops grow at the same time, such as cassava, corn, peppers,
potatoes, pineapples, okra, tomatoes, bananas, various types
of greens such as bitter leaves (similar to spinach or collard
greens), cabbage, and other cultivated and wild greens. (See
the Glossary for Gbande terms.) Pineapples, bananas, okra,

peppers, eggplant, and bitter leaves, and other greens grow wild abundantly during this season and are not necessarily planted from year to year. Cassava, cabbage, potatoes, tomatoes, eggplant, okra, and peppers may be grown in little patches right behind the huts in the village. This is basically women's work but the men and children may help. Lima beans and other beans are planted near the burned-out stumps in the rice fields. Some corn and cotton seeds are mixed in small proportions with the rice seed as it is planted. The corn is harvested first from the field and the cotton is harvested last. Moreover, the felled trees which have been scorched by the fire have many types of mold and fungi growing on them which are used to augment the food supply. They are usually referred to as *falèy,* the English equivalent of which is "mushrooms." The family owns all of these crops until the rice is harvested. Then whatever is left of the farm becomes public property, available to anyone who happens to be passing through the farm area.

The actual planting of the rice crop is done by all able-bodied persons—men, women, and children. They use home-made hoes or *kalī* to scratch the earth. Those for the men are much larger with longer handles than those for the women and children. The hoe handles are from two and a half to three feet long, which means that the planters have to stoop down to work. The corner of the farm containing the richest soil is sectioned off first and this area is divided into as many smaller plots as there are workers. The size of these individual plots depends upon the condition of the soil—that is, how difficult it is to hoe and how much could be covered in half an hour (the time usually allotted for each section). Those areas of the section in which the thickest new grass has sprung up since the fire are worked by the men. One or two of the men tuck large baskets of rice grains under their arms and scatter the seed over the area first. Then the men hoe the earth, removing the grass and loosening the topsoil at the same time that they cover the seeds. The women and children do the same in their smaller plots. Anyone who fails to do this properly is considered a lazy person. If a worker completes his plot ahead of time he can rest until the last person finishes and the new plots are sectioned off. This process is repeated until the whole farm is planted. Depending upon the size of the farm, this can take anywhere from four to six weeks or more. The old women who cannot do the more strenuous work of planting follow behind the workers, lifting the loose grass over the visible seeds to hide them from birds and other pests. This process, done with a digging stick, also serves the purpose of knocking the soil from the roots of the grass so it won't grow again. Since the planting covers a span of weeks, the men later take over the planting completely as the grass grows thicker and taller, and all of the women then follow behind with digging sticks.

Before the planting has started, a temporary hut called a *gbɛbèy* or "kitchen" is erected in the center of the farm providing shelter from rain or unfavorable weather. Cooking is done there and rest periods are spent there. The shelter serves as a community center where the men talk, work, tell jokes and stories of adventure, and even play games. It becomes the center of family union at the noon break. Even the evening meals are prepared there by the old women who cannot work with the planters. From here on, everyone from the village except the very old goes out to the farm each morning and returns each evening to their huts. The babies are also kept in the *gbɛbèy* and are taken care of by the younger children of the family who are not old enough to plant rice. They also help the old women get firewood and water.

At the sight of the first rice sprouts while the planting is still going on, the young boys who had been helping the planters are assigned another job—that of protecting the rice sprouts from birds and other pests. During this period, the young boys have to go to the farm very early, usually at dawn. Very often these boys have to carry torches to see their way. When it rains, they either use flashlights or walk the paths in the dark. Flashlights are a luxury they cherish.

When the rice planting is finished and the young rice plants are well entrenched, the men and boys turn the farm over to the women for at least a month. During this time the women pull all the weeds from the rice fields by hand. This is referred to as *gulu wūla mbáy hon* and means, literally, "pulling the sticks out of the rice." When the women have finished weeding, the whole family takes a short vacation from farming except for periodic visits by the men to see that everything is going well. This vacation lasts until the rice starts bursting into grains.

The boys are the first to return to work. Each day at dawn they leave home in order to reach the farm in time. In strategic places, the men build scaffolds twelve to fifteen feet high with a platform six by eight feet on top. A roof is built over half of the platform, and the floor beneath it is packed with dirt so that a small fire can be built. The boys use the fire to warm themselves or to roast corn or other food. From the scaffold platforms the men construct a network of ropes

Kelēn̄ggē

and rattles which extend to all parts of the farm. The boys
shake these networks of ropes and loud rattles to scare
intruders away. They themselves are provided with
noisemakers and a musical instrument called a *kelēn̄ggē* that
resembles a xylophone. Since after a while the birds and
monkeys become somewhat accustomed to the noise created
by the boys, each boy is provided with three or four
slingshots to drive the pests away. Piles of small rocks are accumulated under each of the scaffolds. These rocks are taken
as needed to the top in a round, rigid, rattan basket called a
kembān̄ggī, designed especially for this job. These baskets
are constructed from the entire rattan vine, whereas other
flexible baskets are made from only the outer covering of the
vine. Sometimes monkeys will run to another area of the
field, squatting down and hiding to escape the boys; they
wait until the noise stops and then go on nibbling until they
are discovered by the boys again. They are then bombarded
with a volley of rocks. The noisemakers and rattles, however,
are effective in frightening larger game such as deer or wild
hogs. The boys continue this work until the rice is ready for
harvesting.

During the period prior to harvesting there is a scarcity
of cultivated food for at least a month; therefore, the men
must turn to gathering wild yams and other wild food. The
corn or *ñ>n̄ggī* and other foodstuffs are harvested first, at
least two months before the rice.

The rice harvest starts in September and ends in October; all those old enough to do so participate. It is done by
using a small knife or *ßowain* to cut the stalks of rice one by
one. When each worker gets a handful cut, he ties them into
a small bundle with rice straw and places them in a pile
where they are later picked up and carried to the *gbebèy*
(kitchen), where they are stacked into large heaps and then
transferred to the village. In carrying them to the village, the
men use a cylindrical basket called a *kas>y* strapped on
their backs by means of a special bark from a tree called the

ndɛndēy. The rice is then stored in these bundles in the attics of two separate huts. The rice to be used by the family for food is in the big hut where the women live. The finest grains of rice are stored in the attic of the oldest male's hut. These are reserved for planting the following year's crop. Once the rice is stored, it is attacked by a host of rats who live in the attic. These are some of the best-fed rats in the world.

Rice Preparation

Preparing the rice for cooking is a tedious task performed daily by the women, especially the young girls. It is assigned to them by the female head of the family. The rice is first threshed from the husks by trampling on it on a mat or *sabày* made from a tall tropical grass of the sugar cane family called *salèy.* After the rice has been separated from the husks, the next step is the process of hulling. Hulling is done by pounding the husked rice in a wooden receptacle called a *kondày* with a specially prepared slender stick called a *gɛtèy.* (The English equivalents for these instruments are a mortar and a pestle.) The mortars in which the initial hulling is done usually have wide shallow bowls. When the rice is hulled in this mortar, the chaff is meticulously fanned or *gafɛ̄* away by an instrument called a *dafɛ̄,* the Gbande word for "fan." It is made from a fiber of the rattan family which the Gbandes call *balúwi.* The process is repeated in mortars with narrower and deeper bowls. The chaff is again fanned away and the process is repeated for the third and final time, after which the rice is ready for cooking. In each of the three steps described above the mortar may be filled several times, because the mortars are not big enough to hold the large quantities of rice needed for a day's meals.

The cooking or *gundēñgḡī* of the rice, as indicated elsewhere, is done in the big hut (the women's hut). The fire is kept going in the center of this hut almost continually. At the time of cooking the fire is kindled with several dry sticks or

k>$\bar{vi}$ which have been specially collected and prepared by the young boys as described earlier in this chapter. These pieces of wood are placed between three or four large logs or k>vi _botòy_ brought in by the men. Three large pots or _fɛ_ are simultaneously filled with water and balanced over the fire upon these logs and against each other.

The cooking is now begun. The largest of the three pots is the rice pot. Okra, peppers, eggplant, and other foods are immediately put into the rice pot. When the water boils the rice is added, having been washed in cold water. It is tested from time to time by pressing a few grains firmly between the thumb and index finger. If the grains are sufficiently soft to be crushed, the rice is said to be ready for steaming. The steaming is done by covering the rice with okra, cassava, or banana leaves, or some other soft leaves, and a lid is placed over it. The pot is then removed from the open flame to live coals by a specially prepared cooking stick called a _kambáŋggí_, which is about twelve inches long with two hooks at one end. This stick is also used to stir the contents of the rice and the other pots.

While the rice is cooking the two remaining pots are also filled with water. One is selected to cook the meat and the other to cook the vegetables. Meat, birds, and fish are generically called _suwáy_ or "meat." A combination of two or three of the above may be cooked by boiling them until they are almost dry, with palm oil added along with other seasoning. Popular among the animals used for meat, because of their abundance, are rats, squirrels, opossums, wild hogs, raccoons, and deer. The meat for the meal may be fresh, dried, or salted. For dried meat, the men cut up the game into pieces of about two pounds each and string them over the fire for three to five days. The women then put the rock-hard pieces in a large earthenware pot in the attic sitting directly over the fire, and they cover it tightly to keep out the rats. Each week, the week's supply of meat is brought down and packed tightly in another pot filled with palm oil.

All newly dried meat goes up to the attic pot so the oldest meat is always used first. Salted meat can likewise be used. The bottom of an earthenware pot is first covered with a lot of salt; then a layer of fresh meat is added and covered with salt again. This is repeated until the pot is full, and it is then covered tightly. Dried or salted meat can be stored for as much as a year if necessary. Even the meat of animals dead from unknown causes is not repugnant to this people. In this case the meat is cooked by boiling it all day with lots of hot peppers, after which it is thought to be safe for eating.

The third pot is likewise filled with water. In this pot are put mushrooms and leaves such as potato leaves, cassava leaves, or bitter leaves. When these are boiled sufficiently, palm oil is added and the water is allowed to boil until it is almost all evaporated. When all of this is completed and ready, six bowls are washed, two large ones and four little ones. The two large ones are used for the rice, one for the men's and boys' rice and the other for the women's and girls' rice. The other bowls are meat and vegetable bowls respectively one of each for the males and one of each for the females. The Gbande word for "bowl" is *kālwī*.

The procedure of eating is identical with that of the meals taken on the farm site. The youngest male serves the oldest male first, and the youngest female serves the oldest female, in separate dishes delineated by sex. Usually the Gbandes do not eat with spoons or *mitáy*. Everyone washes his hands first, one person pours water down from a gourd or *tɛ̄jɛ̄* on everybody else's hands. The men sit around their bowls on one side of the fire in the hut, and the women sit around their bowls on the other side. As a rule, the Gbandes eat in their huts rather than outdoors.

They usually have two basic meals a day, the first one at noon and the other in the evening. These meals must be eaten together by all members of the family and guests during the eight-month period when the farm work is in progress. If any member is absent, they must all wait for him or her before the meal starts, unless it is known that the absent member will not be there for that particular meal. When anyone is not there when the meal is about to begin, one or more members of the family will go to different areas of the village yelling the person's name. If he answers, they yell "*Vāmōbàyɛn!*" ("Come, let's eat rice!"). Although the Gbandes do have a basic meal at noon, the noon meal is relatively light in comparison with the evening meal. Note the term "basic meal." A Gbande may eat bread, potatoes, cassava, plantain, or yams and still consider himself virtually starved for lack of food if he has not had his daily bowl of rice. The Gbandes do, in fact, eat roasted cassava, yams, sweet potatoes, and plantain early in the morning. The word for the verb "to roast" is. *ma.* They do not consider this eating. These vegetables are roasted by burying them under the hot fire. A light fire burns above them for about twenty-five minutes. They are then removed and peeled, after which they are ready for eating. Plantain is roasted by placing it directly into the fire and allowing it to stay there for about ten minutes, then removing it and peeling it before eating.

Hunting and Fishing

Although a small portion of the game killed may be sold in the market to the general public, hunting is done mainly to augment the family food supply or the food supply of the villagers, depending on the type of hunting. If the hunting is organized by the villagers into a communal hunt, the catch is divided among the participants. A portion of the game is put into a special pile which is then given to those who for some reason could not join in the hunt. An area on the outskirts of the village with a two-year's growth of brush is selected for this hunt, so the brush can be beaten down easily. However, this postpones the use of that land for farming since it will take a longer period for that area to completely renew itself. For this reason, communal hunts are rare among the

Gbandes. When they do occur, they are conducted as follows. A circle is made around a large area of low brush. A ring of earth two to three feet wide is cleared around it and kept clean. The circle is about one hundred feet, more or less, in diameter. Each morning the most experienced hunter will go and examine every inch of the cleared ring of earth for tracks of animals that have entered or left the circled brush. This goes on for about a week or more, and a record of incoming and outgoing tracks is kept. When the expert hunters feel that there are more tracks leading into the circle than out of it, they announce to the villagers that the time is ready for the hunt.

Men and boys participate in the hunting. At the beginning of the hunt, about three or four yards of brush are cleared by the men at one end of the circle. Then the young boys start around the other edges of the circle, beating down the brush with sticks as they move towards the cleared area. They do this with loud noises and noisemakers. This frightens the game, causing it to run into the clearing where the hunters are waiting. As the animal jumps out, the men are ready with their cutlasses, spears, or *balay* and sometimes with nets or *bowain* and their bow and arrows or *dagbay*. Very seldom do any of the animals escape. Usually the expert hunters have estimated the number of animals that were in the circled area with some accuracy. This estimate is made with respect to wild hogs and deer only, but the hunt itself is not limited to these animals. Every animal in this area is taken, and the catch may include snails, turtles, porcupines, raccoons, monkeys, ground hogs, opossums, rats, snakes, squirrels, and certain frogs called *gbɛgbɛy*. Other types of animals found there may also be captured; however, this type of communal hunt focuses mainly on such game as wild hogs, deer, and perhaps opossum and raccoon.

The boys are hunters of small game such as birds, rats, squirrels, or opossums. Their weapons include bows and

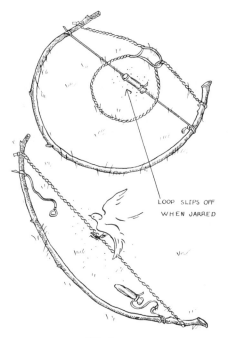

LOOP SLIPS OFF
WHEN JARRED

Bird trap

arrows, slingshots, and traps, all of which they make themselves. Birds and tree squirrels are usually hunted with bow
and arrow, but small birds are also hunted with a special
trap fashioned from a small flexible stick and a twine made
from palm fibers. Two lengths of twine link the curved ends
of a flexible stick about three or four feet long. One length of
twine is taut and tied with a trigger. The other is loose with
a loop formed in the center around the trigger. When a bird
steps on the trigger, the taut twine is opened and the curved
ends of the stick pull the loop tight around the bird's foot.
This type of trap is usually nestled in branches just over the
water, in the clear part of a creek or small body of water
where the birds are known to play. The number of birds
trapped in a day depends upon the number of traps as well

as upon how strategically they are located. The habits of birds are known to the young hunter. He knows the times of day that they usually go to play in the creek, usually morning, noon, and evening; so he usually visits his traps at least three times a day to collect his game and to reset the traps.

Another method of trapping is used for bush rats. This trap is made from a more flexible stick about four feet long and the inner fiber of a vine called *dahay*. The stick is curved to form a complete circle or semicircle. The two interlocking loops that extend from the ends of the stick overlap and form one small circle within the stick. Another taut string tying the two ends of the stick together lies over the overlapping loops with the bait in the center. As the rat bites into the bait the cord holding the ends of the stick is released, thereby

Rat trap

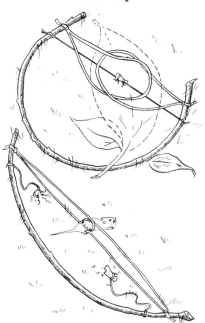

Drop trap

causing the loops to close on the rat's neck. This type of trap
is baited with a bite of the outer covering of the palm nut
called *tuwì*. The trap is hidden by covering it with a broad
leaf. A hunter may have from thirty to forty-five of these
traps. He usually sets them late in the evening in a swampy
area. The traps are distributed by each boy in places where
the hunter thinks rats are likely to pass during the night.
Each hunter will visit his traps early the next morning and
take with him all the traps that had game in them. These
traps are reset in the evening and the process is repeated.

A third method of trapping is designed specifically for
rats and ground squirrels. For want of a better term, I call it
the drop-trap method. Soft, moist, cohesive dirt is packed
neatly upon a flat oval surface of young palm leaves tied to a
stick bent into an oval shape. The end of this oval disk is
then raised until it forms about a 45° angle with the ground
and is attached to the center of an arched stick above it. The

string on the end of the oval disk extends over the top of the arched stick and back through a hole in the disk straight down to the ground. The bait is attached to the string. As the animal bites the bait the string is loosened and the heavy dirt-loaded disk drops down upon its victim.

Most of the hunting activities of the boys take place during the dry season when the rice has been harvested. Each young hunter is held responsible for cleaning his catch. First he burns off the feathers or hair and next cleans out the inside of his catch with a knife. The catch is then strung on long splinters of wood which are suspended over the fire. After the meat is dried, each boy turns over his catch to the oldest woman of the house, whose business is the planning of the family meals.

Adult hunting techniques are extensions of the techniques used by the boys with a few additional techniques. Usually there are two or three very skilled hunters in the village who specialize in catching certain game. They sell some of their meat in the market, giving the entrails to other neighbors, kinsmen, or friends. The men catch most of their game in traps and kill it with their spears at close range. Only the boys regularly make and use bows and arrows to hunt; the men use them only in communal hunts. Perhaps two percent of the men in each village own shotguns acquired through trading. They make their own shot and use it to refill the original cartridges. This is done by laying a soft banana tree branch over sandy ground and punching different sizes of holes in it. As the molten lead is poured through these holes, it congeals instantly in little pellets as it hits the ground. They get this lead by melting down old lead pots that were acquired originally in trade with foreigners. Sometimes they hunt at night with miners' lamps blinding a deer so it is unable to judge its distance from the hunters. The hunters are then free to shoot the deer easily at close range.

Their traps are structured for large game such as deer,

A simple trap

wild hogs, wild cows, hippopotamuses, leopards, water
buffalo, and alligators. Most of the traps are built during the
rest period in the rice season before the rice bursts into
grains. As the land was originally cleared the men took note
of the animal paths they had disturbed. The traps are constructed at points where these paths lead into and out of the
rice fields. Deer and wild hogs are usually attracted to the
wild okra that grows in and around the rice, and in their efforts to nibble the leaves they often trample and damage the
rice. Leopards, in turn, are attracted by the presence of deer
and other game in the area.

There are two types of simpler traps made by using
sticks and piassava palm fibers. In the first type of trap a
hunter selects some small or young trees along an animal
path. He may select two or three and tie their ends together
with piassava fibers, bending them over until their tips touch

the path. At this point a small hole is dug, a noose with a slip knot is tied to the end of the branches, and its loop is laid around the hole. A forked stick is then driven into the bottom of the hole over the trigger which holds the branches in place. As the deer steps into the hole, he releases the trigger; as the branches spring up the loop tightens around his foot and he is held by the trap or suspended helpless, depending on his size and the strength of the branches. The harder the deer fights to escape the tighter the fiber becomes, and the deer is held securely until the hunter arrives.

The second type of trap is made with a firm stick about

Another simple trap

four feet long and piassava fiber formed into a noose with a
slip knot. The stick is driven into the ground next to a deer
or wild cow's path, and the rigid piassava fiber loop is attached to the stick. This holds the loop vertical so that the
quarry's head can enter the loop as he passes. The loop closes
on his neck and as he pulls the stick out of the ground it
catches on the vines. The more the quarry struggles, the
more entangled he becomes, and he may even choke himself
to death. At best he will be unable to leave the area.

Five or six men start early in the morning to construct
the larger traps. They work hurriedly, finishing in half a day
to prevent the quarry from discovering them. The men's
drop-trap functions like the boys' but is a rock trap and is
constructed on a much larger scale. A section of the animal
path about ten feet long is selected, and a fence of sticks
about twenty to twenty-five feet long is built along the sides
of this section. The men next construct a flat platform of
sticks tied side by side, with four logs as the edges of the
platform. A rim of smaller vertical sticks creates an edge

ROCK TRAP

around the platform to hold the rocks. This platform is then suspended in the following manner upon four twenty-five-foot, strong, forked sticks driven into the ground at each corner. A straight stick is inserted into the prongs of each of these sets of heavy forked sticks at each end. A length of piassava cable is tied to the two corners of each end of the platform. These end cables are then looped up and around the sticks inserted into the forked sticks. Two other long sticks with a hook at one end catch the cable with their hooked ends and then the sticks extend inward, flat over the top of the center of the length of the platform, their smooth ends meeting. They provide the pivot upon which the weight is suspended so that they must be held down securely. If not, they would fly up releasing the whole apparatus. The other long cable of paissava fiber that extends over these hooked sticks to hold them down is first tied to one end of a small slender trigger stick suspended across the path midway under the platform. This trigger stick is held securely by two other small forked sticks driven into the ground at the side edges of the path. The cable then extends from one end of the trigger stick upward across the center of the platform over the smooth ends of the hooked sticks, holding them in place, down to the other end of the trigger stick. The platform is then heaped with rocks weighing anywhere from 500 to 1,500 pounds. As the animal steps on the trigger stick and breaks it, the cable is freed, the two hooked sticks fly upward, the cables at each end of the platform are freed, and the whole platform drops, crashing down upon the animal as he is trapped between the two fences. The platform above is so disguised by leaves and tree branches that a tree is marked to warn passers-by.

Another type of large trap is the pit trap. A pit is dug about five feet wide and thirty feet deep in an animal path. The dirt from the pit is taken far away from the pit and (preferably) dumped into a river, because the Gbandes believe that if an animal discovers the dirt he will change his path. Light dry sticks are placed over the pit and they are then covered with dry leaves to make it appear natural. When, for example, a leopard steps on the sticks, the whole thing falls in and he remains trapped until the hunter arrives. This trap is usually designed for big game such as hippopotamuses, water buffalo, leopards, wild cows, or even alligators. Passers-by are also warned of this trap.

The Gbandes have their own method for capturing ground squirrels, opossums, or any burrowing animals. When they discover such an animal hole, they build a small fire of twigs above it. Then they quickly explore the area to find the smoke rising from the other entrance or exit to the animal's home. Two men hold a big bag over this escape hole while one or two others stand over the original hole with large animal horns or elephant tusks. As the men blow on the tips of these horns or tusks into the hole, the animal's tunnel resounds with a thundering noise. The men then grab the frightened animal as it scurries out the other end.

Whenever a leopard is killed, a special war dance has to be performed when it is brought to the village. During the dance women and non-graduates of the Poro school (a Gbande male educational institution) have to be locked indoors. Because of the threat the leopard presents, the killing of this animal represents war and only those qualified to fight war are permitted to witness the ceremony. The leopard skin and teeth belong to the chief or someone else in an honored position. In times past, leopard teeth were costly ornaments that only a few privileged people could afford. Girls of high status used to wear them for necklaces and men of high status attached them to their hats or garments.

The men too are responsible for cleaning their catch. Only deer and monkey are skinned; their hides are used for drums. In the case of deer, the men first cut around each hoof and then slit the skin straight up the inside of the leg. The belly is slit from the neck to the tail and the skin is peeled off the animal slowly with a knife.

Fishing is done by men and women of all ages. In Gbandeland, only the women use nets, however. The net is mounted on a circular ring formed from a flexible stick and is on the order of a butterfly net, only larger. A large ring is used for river fishing and a small one for fishing in creeks and small bodies of water. In either case, the women walk into the water with their nets, dropping them for at least one minute before raising them to see if any fish are caught. They may spend a whole day or several hours dragging the river or creek sporadically in this manner.

The men use poles, line, and homemade hooks or *dōlēnjī* for daytime fishing, but in the night they use only a short line and hook. At night they sit on rocks in the river, holding the short line (about a foot long) between thumb and index finger. As the line jerks, the man pulls up his fish. One man can easily catch a basketful of fish within a short time.

The men also use a type of cylindrical basket which is

Fish trap

constructed in such a way that when a fish, lobster, or crayfish swims into it, he is unable to escape. These baskets are made of woven bamboo or rattan in the shape of a cornucopia and vary in size depending on the type of catch they are designed to hold. The largest basket encloses a smaller one and this smaller one in turn encloses one still smaller. They are identical in shape and are nested in such a way that a fish swimming into the mouth of the largest basket would swim directly into the mouths of the others if he continued in a straight line. However, in whichever basket the fish stops, he is prevented from escaping by a row of short bamboo sticks protruding around the inner edges of each basket's mouth. The closed ends of all the baskets are tied shut so the men can easily untie them and get their catch. There are many forms of these baskets, constructed for different bodies of water and even for different levels of water.

Another method of fishing is to take a movable fence and extend it from the bank of a river out into the water, forming a large loop by bringing the other end back to the

Large fish trap

bank. The men then gradually draw the fence in and the fish are trapped within the loop. There is another method of fishing by which the fish are stupified. The men first collect the bark of a certain tree and crush it with a mortar and pestle. After they put this in the water, the women stir up the fish and distribute the substance by poking sticks down into the water. As the fish are affected they float on their backs stupified, swimming lazily on the surface. The women then just gather them up.

The men also construct in the river large, circular fish traps with a diameter of about fifteen feet. These traps are constructed to last two or more months. They may be built just before the rainy season and may take a month or more to fill with fish before the trap door closes. Tall bamboo poles are tied side by side and stuck into the soft river bottom, forming a circle with an open door where the river current naturally enters the circle and flows through it. The length of the bamboo poles depends on the depth of the water. A trap door of bamboo poles about four feet wide is hoisted above the circle's opening and is held suspended on a pulley. It is attached to a large quantity of fish bait inside the circle. As the fish enter eating away at the bait, the bait eventually becomes lighter than the trap door and the fish are trapped as the door comes slamming down. The men may wait several days to empty the trap after discovering a catch, until the water level is low enough.

Cash Crops

The palm tree is the greatest cash asset in Gbandeland. The red oil made from the outer shell of the palm nuts is sold in the domestic market and also to foreigners. It is valued in foreign markets because of its use in soapmaking. The Gbandes use it for most of their cooking. The palm kernel is the main cash commodity since it is sold almost exclusively to foreign traders. These kernels are valued for their oil content. Some of this oil is used by the Gbandes to make a special cooking oil called *toluwúl>y*.

Palm nuts grow in clusters of a hundred or so. A well-bearing tree usually has five or six of these clusters at the top, each weighing anywhere from fifteen to thirty pounds. Although these trees bear fruit the year round, the Gbandes usually collect the palm nuts on a large scale once a year during the dry season. It is from this that they get a year's supply of cooking oil and the baskets of palm kernels that are sold in the foreign market. The tall trees around sixty to eighty feet high are shimmied up in a manner similar to the way a line man climbs a telephone pole. The men fashion a long cord of three or four whole rattan fibers for this purpose. Peeled rattan fibers are wound around these closely and tightly, and a *dahay* (vine fiber) is wound over this in the same way. These vine fibers grip the tree very well.

A Gbande man stands at the base of the tree. He puts the cord around his back at his waist and around the tree trunk and ties a knot in it. He then leans back and rests his feet on the trunk. As he takes each step up, the cord is inched upward. Some men are quite agile, and a man who can gather many clusters of palm nuts in a short time is esteemed. When he reaches the top he cuts the stem of the cluster with a sharp homemade spear and, moving to the side, lifts the cluster loose, letting it fall to the ground. The boys help carry the clusters; the women gather the loose nuts in baskets and take them to the village.

A whole village may participate in the palm oil process, or two or three families or friends at a time may prepare their oil. There are about four permanent large pits, each ten feet in diameter, lined tightly with flat rocks. They lie at the outskirts of the village and are reserved for this process. The individual palm nuts, about the size of unshelled walnuts, are first cut or plucked off of the clusters, dumped into the pits, and covered with banana leaves. They are allowed to stand two or three days until the shells soften even more and begin to rot. Then everyone stands around the edge of the pit with long poles crushing the nuts. This mashes the fibers of the outer shells which yield the oil. After the nuts are crushed, the pit is filled with water and the men and women stand in the pit scooping out the empty dry fibers. These dry fibers are later used to kindle fires. The kernels, which are covered with a hard inner shell, are next filtered out with a rattan sieve. A large fire is built next to the pit and part of the liquid in the pit is scooped with gourds into a large earthen pot resting on top of the fire. As this liquid boils, the pure palm oil floats on top and is skimmed off. The pot is repeatedly emptied and filled. One of the pits filled with nuts can yield anywhere from one to four barrels of palm oil.

The palm kernels are saved and spread out on the ground to dry for several days. They are then stored in bags in a dry place. Before the men sell them on the foreign market the women crack the hard inner shell of the kernel. Only the perfect whole kernels are sold; those that are damaged or cracked are saved to make the special cooking oil previously mentioned.

If a family is running out of cooking oil, they may process the palm oil on a small scale. The woman may boil the nuts in water and then mash them in a mortar and pestle. She would then separate the fibers and kernels and again boil the liquid and skim off the pure oil.

Aside from its commercial use, the palm tree is one of the most useful plants to the Gbandes and their neighbors. The inner lining of the palm leaf is used for twine and cord. Fishing nets and lines are also made from it. The whole leaves, are used for covering the roof of the temporary hut or gbɛbèy which is constructed during the rice planting. The large parts of the limbs are used for paddles and the outer covering of the limbs furnishes arrows and traps for fish. The older trees which become too tall to climb are cut down and used for planks or boards. The young people use the hard inner

shells of the palm nuts to cover the floors of their huts and to
create mosaics on the wall. (By tradition, only the young unmarried men, who often live together, have time to engage in
this type of activity.) The stems on which the palm nut
clusters grow are used during cooking to kindle the fire.
The ashes from these are later gathered and placed in a
funnel whose sides are lined with leaves. The water that is
poured through these leaf-lined funnels is allowed to evapo-
rate, and its residue is used to make laundry soap and
cooking soda. The young tree buds are eaten.

The social function of the palm tree is, perhaps, even
more important than its economic function. The tree
produces a kind of sap which makes wine. This palm wine is
used to repair social relationships which may have been
damaged. It is used at social gatherings, feasts, and other important events. It is also served to honored guests. Many
palm trees are tried and a certain few are selected to make
the palm wine. If a young boy or young married man finds a
good sap-producing tree it is considered his for life and he
has complete property rights to it. The palm trees selected
for making wine are treated more carefully. In order to climb
the tree repeatedly a boy takes two poles and ties them to
the side of the trunk at a slight angle. He then winds a
peeled rattan fiber around the poles and the trunk, forming
rungs between the poles. Other pairs of poles are tied above
these until the boy can reach the top. The two final poles on
the top have hooks on one end; these are first hooked onto
the branches and then fastened to the trunk. The boy then
scrapes some of the rough scales off the branches so he has a
place to sit. In order to collect the wine he cuts off the end of
the stem on which a palm nut cluster is just beginning to
form. As the stem is cut, a straw is punched into the end of it
and the sap, high in yeast content, oozes out drop by drop
and is caught in a gourd hung underneath. A boy checks his
tree each morning and evening to cut a thin slice off the stem
for a fresh cut, and he empties his gourd at the same time. If

Palm tree ladder

the tree produces even more sap he checks it twice a day. The skillful palm wine maker can make the palm wine sweet, mild, or strong, at will. For sweet wine he washes the gourd thoroughly each time he empties it. For strong wine he merely empties the gourd, leaving a residue of yesterday's wine. The fermentation of this sap is so rapid that the gourd may even have foam on it.

Closely related to the palm tree is the piassava palm. This, again, has great commercial value in the foreign market. The Gbandes cut the piassava leafstalks and bury them in the swamp. After the pulp is softened and the stalks have rotted sufficiently, they then pull them through wooden combs with metal teeth, stripping away the pulp from the tough piassava fibers. These very strong, durable fibers are used by foreigners for ship cables, etc. The Gbandes themselves use the fibers only for their traps. The underpart of the piassava leaf is stripped off for use in weaving hammocks, baskets, and fans. The leaves themselves are used in the dress of the *landáy* (Poro leader) and the dress of others involved in festivities and secret rituals.

The Gbandes also make wine from this tree. In order to do this they must cut part of the tree off. The new growth or very top of the tree is cut off and a great deal of sap oozes out; it is caught in a pot or large gourd. Sap may be collected for one or two months before the tree top dies and becomes useless. As in the palm wine process, a small slice is cut off the tree top and the gourd is emptied twice a day. This produces a large quantity of wine. Palm wine is preferred over piassava wine, although the two taste much alike. The Gbandes consider the palm wine cleaner, since the piassava wine is collected on the ground.

There is a third tree, the kola nut tree, that is very important economically. Every family owns at least fifteen or more of these trees. These large trees bear fruit the year round. The green outer shells of the nuts often camouflage them amongst the leaves. The oval-shaped outer shells range in length from three to six inches. Inside is the cluster of five or six kola nuts, each about the size of an unshelled walnut. They are smooth and round with a thin white covering which can easily be peeled off. The outer shells are soft enough to be cut with a knife. The men climb the trees from time to time with long sticks with a hook on the end, with which the nuts are pulled down. After the nuts are pulled or knocked to the ground, the men walk slowly through the brush feeling with their feet to find the nuts. They gather them into baskets. During the dry season an owner may clear the land beneath the tree for easier gathering. The outer shells are removed, and the nuts in their inner covering are stored in earthenware pots which are buried in the ground. These pots are covered with banana leaves to keep the nuts from drying out.

The men accumulate nuts until there are enough to sell in the domestic markets. When the women take them to market, they first peel off the white inner covering with a small knife or with their fingernails and wash the nuts thoroughly. In the market they are sold in large quantities to the Mandingoes (Malinke people) who, in turn, sell them in foreign markets. Kola nuts are economically valuable since they are one of the ingredients of Coca-Cola. They are also sold in the village to those who are out of them.

These soft nuts are popular with everyone. They have an initially bitter taste which turns sweet as they are chewed. They come in three colors: red, brown, and white. Kola nuts are socially important as a snack offered visitors or guests as a gesture of friendship. Sometimes the children find some fallen kola nuts under the tree. They quickly gather them to nibble on later and bury a handful in the ground under a covering of banana leaves. Men also bury the shelled nuts in small quantities to eat later. The nut in any color will temporarily stain the teeth red when it is eaten. Those who are addicted to the nuts, particularly old men, can be spotted easily by their permanently stained red teeth.

Cotton: Source of Clothing

There are two kinds of cotton from which cloth is made. One kind, by far the most important, is usually cultivated by old men and women who are no longer active in the raising of the other crops, but who, by choice, want to contribute to the material well-being of the family. In this case, they usually grow the cotton in small patches as a garden at the edge of the village directly behind the hut. The caretakers of such patches take pride in their gardens—not in how much the garden yields but in how expertly they maintain it. This keeps the old people busy displaying their talents at farm work. The psychological satisfaction which an owner of such a cotton patch receives far exceeds its material contribution. This type of cotton resembles the cotton grown in the southern United States. This is the type which contributes significantly to the production of "country cloth" or *kolui*.

The second kind of cotton is an unusual type of cotton which is not found in the United States. Each family owns two or three trees. These trees bear cotton once a year. Over the years they grow to an enormous size so that the cotton has to be picked by climbing and using long sticks with hooks to pluck the cotton bolls from the branches. These trees serve two purposes—providing shade for their owners and producing cotton. Cotton from these trees cannot be used by itself to make cloth as is the case with the first type. It must be mixed with the other cotton. This mixture produces the finest native Liberian cloth. However, the price of the finished product is determined not by the quality of cotton used but by the design of the material.

Spinning thread out of the fiber is strictly women's work. The cotton bolls are first picked and collected. Each boll is placed on a smooth, lightweight, wooden block about two feet square. The seeds are gradually pressed out of the fibers as a smooth, eighteen-inch, iron rod is rolled tightly and slowly over each boll. The seeds are saved for next year's crop. Then the bolls are pulled and stretched on a bow string

Spinning cotton fibers

until the fibers are spread out evenly. These are then given
to another woman who winds them together on a slender
two-foot stick. These fibers wound on sticks resemble cotton
candy. Next the women spin these fibers into thread. This is
done with a hand spindle shaped like a child's top at the
bottom with a stick extending upward through it. As the
pointed heavy base of the spindle is inserted into a shell disk,
the end of the ball of cotton fibers is tied to the top of the
stick. As the women spin this spindle, the fibers are spun in a
circular manner. The women smooth and guide the strand
by running their fingers up and down as the fibers thin and
twist into thread. They work on one arm's length of fiber at a
time until the thread is even and fine. After one section is
spun, it is wrapped around the spindle stick and a new section is begun. This goes on until all of the cotton fibers are
used up.

There are two methods the Gbandes use in making a

design in the finished material. The first is dyeing the thread and weaving the design into the fabric. The second is dyeing the design into the fabric after it is woven. These dyeing techniques and the intricate patterns woven in clothing material are discussed thoroughly in Chapter 10 "Gbande Art," subsection "Dyeing." If the threads have been dyed to be woven into a pattern, or if the material is to be dyed later as an entire piece, the next step in the process of making cloth is the weaving. This is strictly a man's affair. Most of the men have learned this technique as young men. There are a few professional weavers who may be called in from another village for a special project, such as a wedding garment that must be finished quickly. In such a case, a professional can weave in one day what may take another man a week. If the people for whom he does the work are not relatives, he is paid for his services by help with his farm work. Spinning thread, dyeing, and weaving material are all activities of the dry season when the farm work is slack. Clothing is not replaced often because the heavy woven fabric is very durable and lasts a long time. The Gbandes use this woven fabric for all of their needs including their daily dress and their sleeping cloth.

Before the weaving is even begun, the amount of each color of thread needed in the woven design is calculated. The material is woven in very long, narrow strips. The length of the strip of material depends on the thread available at that time. A Gbande man may decide he wants fifteen warp threads of red, ten of white, six of brown, and so forth, to create stripes in the material lengthwise. There are standard designs which are woven repeatedly and they are referred to by specific titles. The weaver begins measuring the warp threads by tying the end of the first color of thread lowest on a peg driven into the ground; he then proceeds to unroll the spool. Because of the length of the fabric strip to be woven he may extend his thread on pegs around two or three huts until he reaches the last peg. At the first peg he

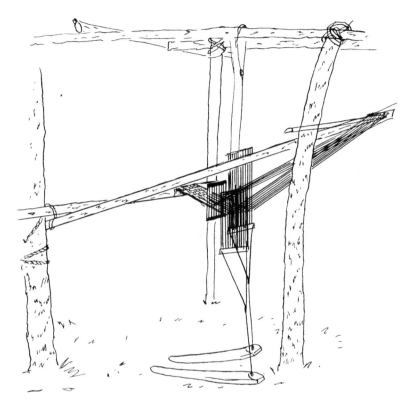

Loom and weaving

again carefully ties the second thread next to the first. Meanwhile other men have been giving him advice on what pattern to weave and have been helping him with this procedure. After this peg is completely filled with the warp threads in a striped pattern, he is ready to weave the woof thread (one color, usually white) into these.

There are two or three looms in each village. Each family has its own heavy wooden comb and shuttle which con-

tains the spool of woof thread. The harness of the loom is suspended horizontally about four feet from the ground by four
poles, one at each corner. The set of warp threads enters the
loom harness and slopes downward to the weaver as he sits
on a piece of wood. As the warp threads extend out of the
loom a certain length they are held in place on the ground
under a weight. As the weaver progresses he keeps pulling
the weight until he reaches it, and then he moves it back.

The set of cords which separates the warp threads into
two sets (every other thread) is controlled by two foot
pedals. As set A of the warp threads is up and set B down,
the shuttle with the spool of woof thread is tossed between
them with one hand, while the other hand sharply pulls the
heavy wooden comb down upon the woof thread. As the
weaver reverses the pedals, set A of the warp threads de-
scends through set B and the shuttle is passed through again.
The small spool within the shuttle makes a clicking noise as
it slides along hitting the ends of the shuttle's reel. A weaver
may develop his own clicking rhythm as the shuttle sails
back and forth. Weaving requires good coordination between these hand and foot movements. The finished cloth is
reeled onto a large spool in the man's lap. As this fills, the
cloth strip is wound onto another spool on the ground, but
the strip is never cut.

After this the men take the long strip of finished material and measure and cut pieces the correct length for a garment. This is done by one man's holding the end of the material on the ground with his toes. The material is then
stretched the correct length to another man who holds it
with his toes. This goes back and forth until they get the
number of pieces they want. Then the long strip is cut. The
men then skillfully sew the strips together to make a large
square piece for the garment. They are responsible for the
sewing of all of the garments, those worn by men or women.
The women, however, do the mending. The blacksmith
makes small iron needles for this but in recent years

umbrella spokes have been filed down and fashioned into needles. The men then take the square piece of sewn material to one of the men in the village who is skilled in cutting out the neck hole of the garment and appropriately decorating it.

Another cloth is woven in white strips. It is sewn together by the men and then a design is dyed into it by the women. This material is used strictly for women's apparel. Some of either kind of cloth is then sold in both the domestic and foreign markets but most of it is used by the villagers themselves. It may be sold as striped woven strips, striped woven strips sewn together, pieces of solid white woven material, or pieces already dyed in a design.

The average man's everyday dress is simple and allows for free movement. The pants consist of a waistband (single width of woven material) with a strip of wider cloth attached front and back that passes between the legs. This waistband is tied on the side. The shirt is made of one rectangular piece of material. The neckhole is cut in the center. As the length of material extends over the man's chest and back, the sides of the garment form large armholes that are open except for a small side seam at the bottom of the garment. This loose shirt extends to the man's knees. A Gbande man has one or two sets of this everyday dress.

Each man eventually has one big ceremonial gown to wear on special occasions. It is fashioned in the same manner but is made of a wider and longer panel of material. This wider panel flows over the shoulders to the wrist, forming a wide loose sleeve. There are no side seams. This gown is ankle length. The cut-out neckhole is the same and has an embroidered pocket below it. This is made so it is accessible to the left hand. Most Gbandes carry weapons in the right hand so the left hand is considered free or harmless. If a Gbande man had his right hand in his pocket, he might be thought to be concealing a weapon.

The chief wears a short everyday shirt like the one

described first but he always wears a long gown over it. He is very often given presents of apparel.

Sometimes in the morning a man will merely wrap himself in the piece of cloth he sleeps on. One corner of the material is thrown over his left shoulder and the other corner is thrown over this. The drape is similar to that of a Roman robe. The wearer can move about easily without its falling off. He may eat in the morning and move about the village attired in this way. However, if he is going hunting or going out of the village, he changes into his everyday attire.

The men have two hats, one for everyday and one to wear with their dress gown. These are made of one strip of matching material with a circular crown. When they aren't being worn they are kept folded in the neck pocket of the gown. Very few Gbandes wear anything on their feet. Some men have homemade leather sandals which they wear occasionally. The men generally do not have any other adornment such as jewelry or skin decorations. They cut their hair short and many of the older men have clean-shaven heads. Young men and boys wear the same general attire.

The women also use the woven material for skirts or over-garments. They wear pants of this fabric that are much like regular western women's underwear. Over these pants they wrap a small kilt-length piece of material around their waists, secured with many strands of beads. The overgarment is a large, rectangular piece of material wrapped just over their breasts and under their arms, extending to their ankles. Each morning they immediately dress in this. They have usually five or six changes of daily dress.

If a woman is doing hard or strenuous work or needs more freedom of movement, she removes this outer garment. For special occasions or for going to market the women have blouses fashioned out of the dyed material. These blouses, which have a simple scooped neckline and short sleeves, are worn with a piece of the woven material wrapped round as a long skirt. The women wear kerchiefs of a lightweight mate-

Women's clothing

rial daily, but their best and most brightly printed kerchiefs are saved for festivities or going to market. These are purchased in the foreign market, and when a man or boy has done some trading, it is a source of pride to bring home a pretty kerchief to his wife or mother. One of a woman's status symbols is the amount and variety of her kerchiefs.

Daily every woman wears jewelry made by the village goldsmith or silversmith. Pierced earrings, necklaces, bracelets, and anklets are common as are the strands of beads around the waist. A woman saves her more exquisite jewelry for special occasions. Long hair is the rule for women, and they wear it plaited or parted in the center and fashioned into a roll on each side of their heads.

The young women sometimes have a small design of cicatrization (scar tissue) above their breasts or on their backs or stomachs. Daily they wear the kilt-length skirts with strands of jewelry crisscrossing their breasts. After a girl graduates from Sande training (training at a female educational institution) she covers her breasts. Nursing mothers and old women are usually bare-breasted.

Trade and Commerce

The Gbandes rely very much on domestic trade and commerce. Domestic trading is largely a woman's job. However, there are a few commercial activities which are reserved for men only. Among these activities, to name one, is the trading of palm kernels once or twice a year. Most of this trading is done in the city of Pendembu, a border city located in Sierra Leone. It usually takes the men four to six days to make the round trip. These kernels are sold there to middlemen who in turn sell them in large quantities to foreigners. The men carry the kernels on their backs or heads in burlap bags each weighing about a hundred pounds. The money received from this trade is to be used for head and hut taxes and to buy a few extra things for the house.

By far the most important trading activity is that conducted by the women. There are two domestic market places in Gbandeland designed for the women to use in carrying out their trading activities. The first is centrally located in the city of Gbololahum, a religious (Christian) center, and the second is located on the outskirts of Kololahum, a political center. The market in Gbololahum meets only on Fridays, whereas the one at Kololahum meets daily. These domestic markets provide mostly foodstuffs, but other items can also be found. Foodstuffs include rice, cassava, bananas, plantain bananas, yams, kola nuts, palm oil, nut oil, palm wine, dry meats, and fish. In the case of dry meats, Gbande law requires that the seller be able to identify the different kinds of meat she is selling. She must keep a small piece of each kind of meat with the hair still remaining in order to guarantee its identity. This rule of identification also holds true for fish. The fish must be intact—head, scales, and all. These identifications are absolutely necessary because of the many taboos against eating certain animals or fish.

Both markets are open grassy areas where the women, dressed up, come to sell and trade their goods. The women choose areas at random, spread out their mats or brush the area clean, and lay out their goods in baskets or other containers. Meat and fish are usually hung up or displayed on wooden scaffolds. Other items of commercial interest in these markets include chickens, sheep and goats, cotton, thread, country cloth, leather work of all kinds, gold rings of different kinds, baskets, pots or other cooking utensils, slippers, handbags, and mats. Almost anything that is of local significance can be bought in these market places. Because of their market activities, the Gbandes are among those indigenous peoples of Liberia who are quite independent and self-sufficient. They need Western money only to pay taxes to the Liberian government or to buy a few Western articles.

The medium of exchange in these domestic markets is a slender iron rod eight to twelve inches long. It has two

Iron money

pointed hooks at one end and a rather flat tail at the other.
One iron, *koluŷīla* as the Gbandes call it, is equivalent to one
cent; twenty such irons constitute a unit in the same way that
one hundred cents make up a dollar. Interestingly, a unit is
referred to as *gboloŷīla,* which means "one salt." One may
speculate that a bar of salt might have been the unit of
exchange, as was the case in the Congo area before the introduction of iron [5, p. 86]. But the idea may have been
borrowed from another area of West Africa. At any rate, the
prices of commodities are measured against *gboloŷīla,*
gbolofɛ̄le, gbolosāwa, gbolopū, etc., or "one unit," "two units,"
"three units," "ten units," etc. Ten units would be two
hundred irons, because twenty irons constitute one unit.
With these irons, or multiples of them, one could buy anything, even slaves.

Important Domestic Animals in Gbandeland

The Gbandes have many domesticated animals which live with them in the village. Such animals as cows, sheep, goats, dogs, cats, ducks, and chickens play an important role in Gbande life. There are even a few people who own horses and hogs. However, the most important domesticated animals to the Gbandes are dogs, chickens, and cats.

Every household must have a dog or two, especially households that have infants. The dog is as important to a Gbande mother of young children as diaper service is to the mother of young children in a middle class American family. The dog takes care of all the wastes from the child, such as feces and vomit. It cleans the child very gently of waste in any form. Once the child does anything that needs cleaning, the dog—the ever ready and willing worker—is called as one would call a maid to come and perform her duty. The generic name for "dog" is *kēke*, and when the dogs hear the call, they run in that direction. However, only the dog of a particular household will go in and perform its duty. Otherwise, there would be a dog fight. It is amazing to note that very few dog fights take place. These animals tend to respect the territory of other dogs, although I know of no special training given to them in this regard.

Dogs also help clean up human waste found around the edge of the village, left there during the night by grown children or even adults. In the old days, there were no provisions in any Gbande village for carrying away human wastes. This important function was performed by one of two agents. The creek or river might serve as a toilet. Usually the men used the part downstream and the women the part upstream, with a considerable distance between them. Men were not permitted in the women's area nor were women permitted in the men's. But the problem, was that the creek or river was always a considerable distance from the village. This meant that it was inaccessible at night or in rainy weather. Therefore the edge of the village served as an alternate toilet site. There the dogs served as sanitary agents par excellence.

Although dogs are eaten by some Gbandes, they are not raised for eating. Dogs are primarily domesticated animals, performing the functions already mentioned. Dogs are not too well fed, only with bones and a minimum of other foods. Dogs are loved and considered members of their respective households but they are not considered pets in the Western sense. They are valued for the services they perform. It is an unthinkable act for anyone to kill a household dog intentionally, since the traditional Gbande village could scarcely exist without dogs. Moreover, dogs protect the children of their household from other dogs as well as intruders, whether other animals or humans.

The chicken is as important in Gbande culture as the dog, but for different reasons. Honored guests are offered chicken; it is considered a choice meat. The importance of an honored guest is expressed by the quantity and quality of chickens killed in his behalf, especially if he brings his servants and wives with him. This custom is possible because chickens are plentiful and most Gbande families possess many of them. Although there are goats, sheep, hogs, and cows, not all Gbandes own them.

Chickens are also slaughtered frequently on the graves of ancestors. Since ancestors occupy honored positions in the village, they are being offered the best when chickens are killed on their graves. (See the chapter on religion for a complete discussion of the ancestors' spirits.) The offering of chicken to the ancestors' spirits takes place after dreams or at any important undertaking of the family or a member of the family. There are also monthly offerings and in a time of crisis, such as sickness or other difficulty, chickens are offered on the ancestors' graves.

Another area in which chickens play an important role is in the Gbande use of "medicines." Perhaps an explanation of the concept of "medicines" would be appropriate at this point. Medicines are physical objects made from a mixture of clay and other materials. They may be inherited or obtained from the *sowì* or doctor. The medicines are generally the province of men, but women can have their own medicines. There are different kinds of medicines which are supposed to perform different functions. What the medicines have in common is that they are all "offered" chickens. Usually, there is a special closet or room in the house where these medicines are kept. Such closets are always kept closed and they can be looked into only by the owners of the medicines or persons having similar medicines. Uninitiated boys or members of the opposite sex are prohibited from viewing them. The medicines are considered protectors of the family and the home. They are very often consulted before any significant task is undertaken. For each consultation they must be offered chicken. The chicken is killed and the blood rubbed on the medicine. The consent or refusal of the medicine to grant the request of its owner is demonstrated by the position in which the chicken dies. The medicine is usually asked to let the chicken die in a particular position if it is willing for its owner to undertake a given task. Such a position may be on its belly or back. Regardless of the outcome, the medicine has performed its duty and is rewarded with chicken blood. Such chickens are eaten only by the owner of the medicine and other initiated members of the Poro or Sande school, those of the same sex as the owner. The chicken also plays a dominant role in community feasts. Therefore, a household without chickens is unknown among the Gbande people.

The cat is an important animal to the Gbande, but at the same time it is the most neglected among all the domesticated animals. It is neither loved nor fed. Most households have a cat, but cats are seldom seen around the house.

The important function of the cat is to protect the rice from rats. Since the rice is kept in the attic, most of the cat's time is spent there. Cats are not trained to obey in this manner, but since they are not fed they have to obtain their meals in the best way possible. Once rats are in the attic there is no other way to get rid of them than to have a cat catch them or drive them away, because no amount of trapping could do the job. The Gbandes have many other animals but they are much less important than the dog, chicken, and cat.

Ownership of Property and Building of Huts

Ownership of property among the Gbandes may be grouped into three categories: communal, familial, and individual. Communally, the land belongs to all Gbandes within Gbande territory without regard to lineage or clan. However, the land is sectioned by village, and once a person becomes a member of a given village he has to work within the land of that particular village. This is because there are well delineated, well understood boundaries separating one village and its land from another, as described at the beginning of this chapter. When one is a village member he is expected to share the communal responsibilities of the village. This does not mean that he cannot leave one village to join another (although this is seldom done). What it means is that one must declare membership in a given village in order to gain recognition of claims for land for farming and other activities. After one does this, there are no restrictions on participating in the general common affairs of the community, except for those affairs considered the prerogatives of special individuals. Without this declared membership in a village, one is considered a stranger.

Villages usually contain 150 or more huts. They are quite permanent, and new villages are seldom originated. However, if there happen to be two prosperous, important men in one village, each with a number of industrious sons, one of the men may decide to start a new village. He will then take his extended family, his wives, his sons, and their

wives and children with him. This new village is usually
built a two-day's walking journey from the main village,
whose villagers help clear the land and build the huts. Later,
this new village may attract a few others as reports come
back about how good the land is or how easy the unwary
animals are to trap. But the family who leaves to build the
new village has many close ties to the old village. Their dead
are usually buried there and they return for ceremonies or
festivities. For this reason a smaller village usually takes
many years to grow and sometimes it may even be abandoned. Only in extremely rare case of an epidemic or similar
catastrophe may an established village be abandoned.

Gbande villages are laid out or structured without a
particular design. There are no streets, in the true sense of
the word. There are usually two to four roads leading in or
out of a village. Families own lots in the village. Huts are
built on these lots, and sometimes the dead are buried on
them, unless the family wants to bury its dead in the public
burying ground often located in the center of the village or
immediately outside it. Sometimes domesticated animals,
such as cows, sheep, and goats, are expected to sleep on the
family lot. The area around the hut is raked clean of all grass
or shrubs, and these lots are kept meticulously neat. The
Gbandes frown upon anyone with grass around his hut. They
say such a person is just making a den for snakes. Each family is responsible for keeping its lot in good condition.

Huts are built in a random fashion in terms of style and
location. The exception is that the hut of the male head of
the extended family is constructed close to the hut in which
all the female members of the family and their children live.
Other adult married male members of the family build their
huts wherever they can find a suitable space. The family
head has first choice, followed by males next in line by age.
Adolescent boys who are close friends often join in building
their own hut; otherwise, they continue to sleep in the huts
of their married male adult relatives. The number of adoles-

Hut building

cent boys in a hut is usually four to six and is never more
than eight. There are a number of such huts in every Gbande
village. As these boys mature and get married or go to live
with someone else's wife,° the membership of such a hut
decreases. When the last member of the group moves away,
the hut is immediately reoccupied by the younger siblings of
the original occupants and their friends, who are now adolescents.

By and large, most of the huts are permanent and the
thatched roofs are replaced on the average of every eight or
ten years. Some new huts are built approximately every four

°Extramarital arrangements are discussed in Chapter 4 "Family-
Kinship Groupings," subsection "Regulation of Sexual Behavior."

years as the Poro graduates marry. When a new hut is built
or thatch is replaced, almost everyone in the village has a
part in it and all work together. Most of the huts are round
but there are a few rectangular huts. The rectangular huts
are fairly new to Gbandeland and are built for paramount
chiefs and other priviledged individuals, such as government
officials. There is little or no distinction between the hut of a
tribal chief, a village chief, a village headman, or a com-
moner. They are built of similar materials and in a similar
fashion.

The men use eleven-foot poles, each driven firmly two
to three feet into the ground, to form a circle of poles
twenty-five to thirty feet in diameter. (The larger female hut
may be more than sixty feet in diameter.) Beginning at the
base of the poles, one heavy rattan fiber or thin wooden stick
is tied to the outside of each pole in the circle. Another fiber
is tied to the inside of onto each pole in the circle at the same
time. These fibers are attached to each pole with a shorter
piece of rattan fiber. After the first fibers are in place, two
other fibers, inside and outside of the circle, are tied four or
five inches higher than the first. This is continued until the
fibers form a lattice.

The base for the conical-shaped roof is made with poles
tied together at the top forming a peak and extending to the
upper edges around the hut. The building process for the
roof is as follows. Two strong crossbeams are first extended
and tied over the top of the hut structure, crisscrossing each
other in the center. Other poles are added to form the attic
floor. A large stick with a fork at the bottom is placed over
the place where the two main crossbeams meet directly in
the center. It is tied firmly so it will remain vertical. A rattan
fiber is tied around the ends of four roof poles. These poles
are arranged like the ribs of an umbrella; they are suspended
from the vertical roof-support pole in the center. The roof
poles are then spaced and tied to the top edges of the
circular hut wall. Then the other roof poles are added. These

Roof-making

are also latticed with fibers to support the thatch.

A certain type of smooth grass called *tuhuwe* is used for the thatch roof. This grass grows in a few rocky areas in Gbandeland.* The men cut the blades of grass, pile them, and let them stand at least three days to dry. The blades are then laid side by side in a row, their root ends even. The blades are then tied in small bunches to a long vine fiber with another fiber knotting each one to form a long strand resembling fringe. These strands of thatch are then rolled up and handed to the men on ladders to be unrolled and tied in successive overlapping layers around the roof, beginning at the bottom. The strand for the bottom-most edge of the roof

*Bush cows graze on this grass. During the dry season these patches of grass sometimes catch fire. The Gbandes believe the fires are started when a bush cow scrapes its hooves on the rocks. These fires, however, do not engulf the thick moist forest.

also contains some stiff waxy leaves about ten inches long that form an eave to keep the rain from running down the clay walls of the hut. The blades of grass used for the roof pack together when they become moist and keep the rain out quite effectively.

The hut is now ready for the walls to be daubed with clay. Early in the morning, on lowland close to the river, the men dig down four feet to uncover an area of moist clay five by ten feet. The children bring buckets and pots of water to pour on the clay while six to ten men jump around waist-deep in the clay, stomping it to make it soft and sloppy. Moist clay from another area is added and the men mix it carefully with their feet until they get the desired consistency. Then the children hurry with armloads of clay to the hut site. Some men also carry the clay on litters to the site. One man stands outside the hut and another inside pitching handfuls of the clay at the same area, packing it tight and smoothing it. They later build fires in the hut and let the clay dry for a week.

Next an outer white clay is smoothed over the hut for the same reasons a frame house is painted. This is redone approximately every two years. This clay is found close to the riverbed and is already soft and smooth. The women sometimes mix it with cow manure to make it dry with a hard surface. This latter practice is common mostly in the larger villages where there are more cows. Some of the adolescents make decorations on the walls of their huts with this clay.

Each hut has two doors, the front door and a smaller back door. Several months before the hut is built, the doors are shaped from a very large tree root and cut to a certain size. Sometimes heavy weights are laid on the shaped roof so it will lie flat. The door openings in the hut are structured when the hut is built, to fit the doors. The cut door is rectangular with two tabs sticking out, one at the upper left corner and one at the lower left corner. These tabs are inserted like pegs into holes in a piece of wood at the top and bottom left-hand corners of the door opening. The door then can swing open and shut.

The floor of the hut is smoothed and any clods of earth are pounded with paddles. Sometimes someone sleeps on the floor on a mat, and sometimes the old women like to sleep next to the fire.

The beds in most Gbande homes are made of clay and are built right next to the wall. These beds are usually rectangles of solid packed clay about six feet long and two and a half feet high. Sizes may vary to accomodate one, two, or three people. On the average there are one or two beds in a married adult male's hut and six or more beds in the joint females' hut. There are also beds made out of sticks. For these, a general platform is built with wooden slats. A mat is laid over these slats and loose dry grass and soft palm leaves are laid over this and covered with another mat. Some Gbandes use big flour sacks or burlap bags gotten in trading and stuff them with this grass. Mothers sleep with their infant children, but children who are weaned sleep together in a separate bed.

The fireplace is located in the center of the hut. The smoke rises, and as it filters through the thatched roof, it helps to keep the supplies stored in the attic dry. This fireplace is the center of activity for the whole family. For example, it is the kitchen where all the food for the family is prepared. Water to take baths is heated here. Here children play, women gossip, stories are told, and plans are made for family affairs.

The attic is entered by climbing a notched tree limb attached to its opening in the ceiling. The opening is usually near the wall's edge but not right next to it. In one corner of the hut sits the water pot from which everybody drinks. All of the household utensils are kept around the water pot. There are usually a few chairs made especially for the older women of the hut. These chairs are really stools made out of wood. Other occupants either sit on the floor or squat down.

In the adult married male hut or the adolescents' hut there is not the luxury of water pots or chairs. These huts serve only one purpose—a sleeping place. Men and boys eat and drink in the big female hut. Farms are also owned by the extended family. As mentioned before, once a family cultivates a section of land, it becomes the property of that family until the crops are harvested. In such farm areas, adjacent families carry on much borrowing as well as mutual aid. Each farm usually has a separate entrance. At the immediate entrance to the farm, medicines, as described earlier, are very often buried to ensure good crops and to protect the farmer, his family, and their belongings against witches and bad spirits. These medicines are seldom used against animals, pests, or other forces such as drought or storms.

Ownership of farms is always given in the plural possessive case—*ne gbolia* that is, "our farm," and never "my farm." Land, villages, domesticated animals, farm houses, banana and orange orchards, kola trees, and some household utensils, among other things, are also referred to in the plural possessive. Even children fall into this category of common ownership by the local group. There are, however, many items which are owned by individuals.

Among the items owned by individuals are medicines, work tools, clothing, gardens, household utensils such as spoons, musical instruments, money, combs, traps, guns, knives, ornaments, and jewels. Although many items such as those listed are individually owned, they can be borrowed or used freely whenever requested of the owner, except, perhaps, the medicines. The art of lending serves at least two purposes. In the first place, it enhances the status of the lender; secondly, it strengthens the social relationship between the lender and the borrower. It is true that the desire to accumulate personal items cannot be underestimated, but neither can the desire to lend. It is through lending that reciprocal obligatory relationships are strengthened, thereby reinforcing cohesion and the plurality of communal ownership. To put it another way, when one lends to a neighbor, one is investing in that neighbor. Therefore you wish him well, including his family, in order that he may be able to pay that which he borrowed. Moreover, lending is a form of insurance in that when one becomes a lender to someone else, he can always go to that person to borrow from him.

A type of circle is in operation here, in which one is a lender at one time but becomes a borrower at another time. In this type of culture it is not too difficult to see why no one has a monopoly on wealth, for there is more virtue in lending without interest than there is in accumulating. It is sharing with others that determines one's social status, and hence the more frequently one shares, the higher is his social status.

Chapter 4
Family-Kinship
Groupings

IN MOST SOCIETIES the family begins with marriage, although the form may vary from culture to culture. Likewise, the functions of the family vary from culture to culture, that is, certain functional aspects are stressed by one culture while different ones are stressed by other cultures. Therefore, a discussion of the form which Gbande marriage takes is in order.

Marriage

The most frequent method of getting a wife in Gbandeland is by an arrangement made between two boys who are close friends. Such arrangements are usually made during their adolescent years, or the arrangement may be made by parents for their children. Much less frequent is the marriage initiated by the parties themselves.

The arranged marriage contract between two adolescent boys who are close friends is made in anticipation of extending their friendship to involve their offspring; when this happens they will arrange to have their children marry. Once it is decided who will be the father of the bride, the father of the groom starts behaving like a son-in-law toward the prospective father of the bride. He continues this behavior until the pledge is fulfilled, at which time his son, the groom, assumes these obligations and responsibilities. The pattern of this contractual arrangement is rigid with few exceptions. One of the exceptions occurs when the prospective father-in-law has no daughter or when his youngest daughter is older than the prospective son-in-law. Another exception occurs when the father of the prospective son-in-law has no son. If any of these conditions exist, the kinsmen of the defaulting party make the appropriate substitution in his behalf. Among this people, marriage is as much a group concern as it is an individual's. Therefore, such a substitution would be made only when it became apparent that the combination agreed upon would not be possible. At any rate, the contract must be honored.

The children of such a contract are told at a very early age the nature of the friendship between their parents, in great detail, and they are told that they are going to be husband and wife when they grow up. They are encouraged to play together as often as possible. This makes possible frequent visits between the children as well as between their parents. It is believed that such visits will help to increase the sentiment of love between them in later life.

A second kind of marriage is that arranged by parents when their children are already grown. This usually takes place between two chiefs or two doctors (sowì). Such a marriage is a sign of a treaty between the parties involved. It is less frequent among "commoners."

The last kind of marriage is that of romantic love in which the young people fall in love with one another. In this case the boy will first talk with his sister to find out whether the girl really loves him; if she does, then the boy will talk to his mother about his intentions. The mother, in turn, will talk to her husband or the boy's father on his behalf. If the father agrees, then a tracing of the girl's generations will be made in order to make sure that there are no kinship connections between them. When it is established that their marriage will violate no incest taboo, the father with a few of his male relatives will pay a visit to the girl's father who immediately sees to it that the visitors are given food and perhaps palm wine. Then the girl's father inquires about the nature of their visit. (Let me interject here that Gbande custom demands that a visitor be fed before any business is transacted. This is why visitors are given food and drink immediately before they are asked about the object of their visit.) The oldest of the visitors then announces that they wish very much to become his children. At this point, the girl's name, as well as that of the boy's, enters the conversation. The visitors say *"jaw>lèy,"* translated as "cold water." Then *towolòy* and *tɛhenày* (kola nuts and a rooster) are given to the girl's father. The father will then say, *"Tokol>mbu bɛlɛn̂ggīwu hūtɛ,"* translated literally as "My hand is under but let me hang my head," meaning "Your words are well spoken, but let me have a conference with the other relatives of my kinship group." Another time is then arranged for a return visit.

The girl's father will now summon and inform all the leading elders of his kin group, that is, those that can be reached, both male and female. This later meeting serves two purposes. The first is to review the generational background of the boy. This review is necessary as a means of double checking any kinship connection between the families. The second purpose is to find out from the girl whether or not she loves the boy. Of course, this is a formality since the girl's answer has already been made known privately to the boy. Nevertheless, she is asked whether she loves the boy. *"Ilūn̂gg> lɛn̂gga n̂ggiɛ̄?"* means, "Do you love him?" The usual response from the girl goes as follows: *"Sīn> yāndɛ,"* that is, "Whatever you say" or "The decision is entirely yours." The elders then tentatively decide to accept the offers or gifts from the boy's family—tentatively because the boy will be on probation until the consummation of the marriage. During this period, if he is found wanting by his prospective in-laws, the whole arrangement may be stopped there and then.

When the boy's elders come for the second visit, the

girl's father and his elders again feed their guests after which the visitors present more gifts and the elders of the girl's father says something like this: "*Hi lōkō lōma*," that is, "Our hands are on your request." This time, there are many hands and the gifts have not only touched the hands but are now under the hands. This means that the request is granted. If the request is not granted, reasons are given to the satisfaction of the boy's elders and that will end the matter. But if the decision is favorable, the boy and his family are now obligated to perform any kind of service asked of them by the girl's relatives. I might add that all these kinds of marriage are usually negotiated before the girl reaches the age of marriage. The arrangements are well advanced before the girl or the boy goes through the formal traditional education which is an absolute prerequisite for Gbande marriage. It is only after graduation from their respective schools (Poro and Sande) that young people become eligible to marry.

The ritual of a Gbande wedding ceremony is basically the same throughout Gbandeland but the festivities which usually accompany it vary with the social position of the bride and groom (particularly the groom). The ritual of the wedding ceremony is performed by the fathers of the bride and groom in the presence of their respective kinsmen and friends as well as important personalities who are invited. The wedding site is chosen and prepared by the bride's kinsmen several days before the wedding. The wedding is held in the front yard of either the bride's grandfather's house or her father's house. Her family is responsible for providing the firewood, palm oil, dishes, and cooking utensils; for setting up the seating arrangements for the guests; and for arranging for a place to hold the wedding dance. When the time comes, her family cooks and serves the food for the feast. While the bride's relatives are making these preparations, the groom's kinsmen and friends assemble themselves in the groom's home two or three days before the wedding, bringing together their contributions to the bridewealth. As a rule, the Gbandes do not have a set amount for bridewealth but expect the groom and his kinsmen to be generous. Since such generosity is a measure of family status, and since marriage unites families as well as individuals, the quantity and/or quality of the bridewealth necessarily reflects family pride. In times past, a wedding between the children of two chiefs called for the groom's family to give many slaves to the bride's family in addition to iron money (the traditional money of the Gbandes), cows, goats, sheep, and so on. Similarly, the bride's family sent along a few slaves to serve her in her new home. (There were three types of slaves: war captives, those who had been pawned or sold, and those who had voluntarily given themselves in servitude to the chiefs.) Assistance from kinsmen and friends in raising the bridewealth is a necessary right and obligation because of the reciprocal nature of these duties. Although this help is considered a right and obligation on their part, it is performed entirely on a voluntary basis. The grand festivities, which usually last for at least three days and may exceed this limit, are held the day before, the day of the wedding, and the day after the wedding. These festivities are reserved only for a marriage between the children of two chiefs or other persons of similar social status. One of the ways in which chiefs display their wealth is by providing food and a good time for everyone who visits the village during the wedding festival. Those who cannot afford these elaborate festivities are obliged to provide a feast on the wedding day for the families and friends of the bride and groom. The expense of this feast is shared by their kinsmen but the preparation of the feast is done by the bride's family.

On the day of the wedding the bride and groom are adorned in the best new attire that their relatives can afford. The bride is dressed in a three-piece outfit consisting of a headpiece, a blouse or chest piece, and a *lapā* (a piece of cloth wrapped around the waist). These are usually made from the same material, delicately designed according to the taste of the bride's family. Either homemade or imported material may be used to make the outfit. Brightly colored material with a design has priority over solid colored material, with the exception of silk. They feel that solid colored materials are dull and should not be used on an important occasion such as a wedding. In addition to this three-piece dress, the bride is adorned with gold necklaces, earrings, and bracelets. She also wears anklets, armlets, and waistbands which are made of either leather or beads. These are also designed artistically by professional bead or leather craftsmen. The quantity and quality of these adornments are related to the social position of the bride and groom.

The groom is also attired in an elaborate and exquisitely designed cap and gown. His trousers need not be made of the same material but they must be in good taste. The groom does not wear any jewelry. His social status is measured by the type of material used as well as its quality and design. As a rule, Gbande men do not adorn themselves with jewelry of any kind, except armlets or armbands made of leather which hold talismans. The talismans are believed to protect the wearer from danger. Jewels are designed only for women, and for this reason the groom's garment is even more exquisitely made than the bride's.

In performing the ritual of the wedding ceremony a circle is formed by the wedding guests. The immediate family of the bride and groom constitute the inner circle; the other relatives, honored guests, and other spectators make up the outer layer of the circle. The bride is made to sit down on a stool placed on a mat covered with white country cloth. She sits facing east and her father stands close by her at her right side or to the north of her and places a piece of iron money upon her head with the front of the iron money projecting directly over her face. The groom is made to stand directly in front of her, facing her and consequently facing west. He places his right hand upon the iron money on her head. The groom's father stands at the left of the bride or south of her. The fathers, like the groom, place their hands upon the iron money. The bride's father is the first to speak, saying, "*Domāñggi ihiti tilūñgga ñggi aga ni lōahon kɛɛ kōlawez hambāñgga*," meaning, "May the relationship between these two and between us be as strong and good as this iron money." The groom and his father reply, saying, "*Sɛtandeñggā egano kɛɛ gafoɛn ñgga tɛlua gelev>l>ñggala hawɛn*," meaning, "May this request be granted by our ancestors in the name of Gelewolongala (God), the Maker of all things." Then the guests and spectators respond, saying, "*Sīña ta gehɛn ti dolē tulahōn iwa*," meaning, "May the couple be blessed with good health and with many children." This is followed by each of the bride's relatives and friends giving her advice. She is required by custom to listen to each piece of advice and answer, *Kɛgɛ siāndɛ*," or "I will do as you want me to." Then comes the wedding dinner. The menu consists of rice, chicken, dry meats, and fish cooked with palm oil. Palm wine is served to the men but the women drink water.

Most Gbande weddings take place during the first half of the dry season when the farm work has just ended and food is abundant. The actual wedding ceremony starts early in the morning and lasts till high noon. The rest of the day and evening is reserved for eating and merrymaking.

When the festivities are over, the groom and his family take the bride to their village. There a modest welcoming ceremony is performed. The bride is prepared by the groom's mother and the other women of his village. They examine her to ascertain her virginity, and they provide her with the proper food, such as rice and meat cooked with palm oil. Then they dress her in the proper clothing, such as black and white attire that has never been worn before. They arrange her hair in one of the traditional styles—many small plaits or six small plaits.

The couple's bed has been made up with white sheets. Early the next morning the mother of the groom and some

leading women of her village go to the newlyweds' bedroom.
The couple is asked to leave the room and the women examine the bed sheets very carefully for blood or specks of blood.
If some blood stains are found, there is shouting, singing,
and rejoicing by both the groom's and the bride's family
because she has been found clearly to be a virgin. But if no
blood is found the groom's mother finds out from her son if
anything happened between them. If he says no, then there
is still hope that she is a virgin. If he says yes, the bride is
considered no good, because she has not only deceived her
husband but disgraced her parents and all her kinsmen. It is
a grievous offense for which she is ostracized by her husband
and kinsmen. This is a calamity that no Gbande bride wants
to face. Usually, but not always, the bride has to tell who
took her virginity. In times past, such persons were punished
by death.

Polygyny

The form of Gbande marriage is polygyny. However, not
many Gbande marriages are polygynous. On the other hand,
it is the desire of every Gbande young man who has any
claim of high birth to wish for two or more wives. And every
Gbande young lady of high social standing wishes to marry a
man who has a number of wives. This is because the number
of wives is indicative of high social status. Most Gbandes
have no more than one or two wives except for chiefs who
may have thirty to fifty or more wives. In the olden days, the
number of wives a chief had was directly related to the size
of his rice farm. The Gbandes say, "*Gbey nda ña hā poi ti ta
gɛ̄ na, na l> si ɛn ndō poi ti ta lī na,*" that is, "Where there are
young ladies, there will the young men go." For this reason,
a chief who has many wives will also have many young men
in his service. Such young men are supposed to keep their
love affairs with the chief's wives a secret as a sign of respect
for him, although he is very much aware of their activities.

There are one or two wives who are absolutely reserved for the chief. One of these two wives is the first wife, who is usually the head wife. She is supposed to be closer to the chief than any other person; therefore, she knows more about the chief's private affairs than anyone. It is believed that the chief seldom makes important decisions without consulting her. She is the backbone of the chief and the link between the chief and his other wives, as well as between him and his other wives' parents. She is also the main channel for any outsiders who wish to become the chief's in-laws and for the chief's prospective wives and their parents. She is the judge advocate for all the other wives; her decisions, in most cases, are not questioned. There are, nevertheless, a few cases which have to be referred to the chief for final decisions. She is, therefore, the trustee of the chief's affairs and she needs to confer constantly with the chief, which makes her an important person in the chiefdom.

The only other wife who is normally reserved for the chief has similar responsibilities but in different ways. Her status, unlike that of the first and/or head wife, does not depend upon her age or rank in order of marriage, although these two criteria are the standards which command respect and obedience. As will be shown later, the oldest girl of the family gets married before the younger sisters. This, of course, is in keeping with the rule of seniority which is supreme in Gbandeland. This second special wife does not meet any of these criteria; she is usually one of the youngest. She may be the twentieth or the fiftieth wife, but her status is equal in some ways to that of the first or head wife. Her position is similar to that of the first wife because in the first place she was requested, or rather, her parents were asked for her hand for the chief in the same way in which the first wife was acquired. Most of the other wives are offered to the chief either by their parents or by other wives. They are not sought by the chief as the first wife and the one now under discussion.

This wife has the privilege of high honor and respect bestowed on her by the chief upon the advice of his indigenous doctors or diviners, the *sowois*. She is a secret wife of the chief who has been selected by the ancestral spirits to give youth and strength to the chief in all his activities. She is, therefore, the choice of the senior members of Gbandeland, the ancestral spirits and because of the beliefs involved in this choice she is expected to live up to this high standard in her honored position. She is not the wife of the chief alone but also of the ancestral spirits; thus, every member of Gbandeland expects her to maintain her position. These two wives, therefore, are the only ones who are reserved for the chief with respect to sexual intercourse and do not enjoy the sexual freedom of the other wives with the young men in the chief's service.

Regulation of Sexual Behavior

Sexual behavior in Gbandeland is far from promiscuous; it is well regulated and institutionalized. The relationships described for chiefs hold true for anyone who has more than two wives. The nature of sexual freedoms and restrictions can be discussed under three headings. In the first place, virginity is required of girls and to a great extent is an absolute criterion of their marriageability. In times past, a girl found not to be a virgin at the time of her marriage was ostracized by her husband and his family, her own family, the community, and her peer group. She was ostracized because of violation of the rule requiring deference or respect to her parents and of the rules originating in the rites and vows of the Sande school. Any violation of this school's rules is considered disregard for fellow Sande members. The fear arising from the idea of violating the restrictions placed on sexual intercourse restricts a girl's behavior; otherwise Gbande girls would be freer in their sexual behavior.

In most cases, Gbande women are relatively free to have

extramarital sexual relations with other men. Such relationships serve a double purpose: first of all, for a married woman to have another man fall in love with her and to have sexual intercourse with him enhances her prestige, for it shows that she is desired not only by her husband but by other men as well. It would disturb a woman as well as her husband if no other man loved her but her husband. Such extramarital relations also give assurance to the husband that what he has is good because other men desire it. For the young wife, this gives her popularity not only among the men but also among her co-wives and other girls in the community. Extramarital sexual relations are also important in an economic sense. If a married girl has an extramarital sexual relation, she is obligated to reveal the name of her partner to her husband at any time he requests it. The Gbandes refer to such a proceeding as "*ñahày dāwōñggā,*" which is to say, "The woman has called my name." When a woman calls a young man's name, her husband summons such a man immediately for questioning; if he answers in the affirmative, which is usually the case, he is then asked to repair the damage he has inflicted upon the husband and his wife by paying the sum of money appropriate to the status of the particular wife involved. Such a payment may run from two to five hundred dollars or perhaps much lower. Moreover, the amount may be considerably lower if the man involved is a relative. In such a case, the same man's name may be called repeatedly. Finally the husband may let such a young man live with his wife; however, she is still his wife, and her children by the other man still belong to the husband.

Perhaps there are many reasons for marriage among the Gbandes, but one reason, often expressed as the main purpose of marriage, is to have children for the perpetuation of the family—and ultimately the Gbande people. The quest for children, among other things, may indeed be one of the chief reasons for the practice of a polygynic system of marriage. A

marriage without children is a calamity which cannot be en-
dured. In order to avoid this calamity, a second wife is necessary; if one can afford more, three or four wives provide a
greater insurance against childless marriages. Children are
desired because the Gbandes firmly believe that every child
that is born to a family is not merely a newborn individual
but the reincarnation of one of the ancestors who has come
to perpetuate the family. For this reason, infants are very
often referred to by the grandparents, if their spouse is
deceased, as either *nihīengi* or *niyáhay* (depending on the sex
of the child or the speaker), meaning "my husband" or "my
wife." The mother-child relationship is so close that when a
child cries, it cries with the word *ndē ndè*, which is "mother
mother," and never with *kɛkɛ́*, or "father." If a new family
moves to a village where a child has recently been born, it
will be difficult for the new family to find out the real name
of the mother or the father of the infant. The real names of
the parents are now reserved for close friends. This is
because children give status, and those who have the
children must be respected. Hence, not having children
means low status, or at least the lack of high status. The life-
blood of a Gbande village is the number of children it has. A
man who has many children is considered a wealthy man.
Therefore, the aspiration of every Gbande family is not so
much to accumulate material wealth but to be blessed with
many children. This is well expressed by the Gbandes as
follows: "*Nui ā ndoolé dahéeñggi ēhà.*" Literally, this means:
"One who has many children, his name will never die."

Preferential Marriage

The fear of extinction of the family's name is a calamity
which no Gbande faces with equanimity. For this reason
both levirate and sororate marriages are permitted. These
will be discussed a little later.

Gbande marriage is exogamous marriage par excellence,

because both parallel and cross-cousin marriage is prohibited. There is no word for cousin in the Gbande language. All cousins are referred to as brothers or sisters. Therefore marriage with them is prohibited. This complete or almost complete exogamy makes possible the widest network of kinship relations. The network is maintained by a permanent arrangement between families in which one is always a donor and the other always a recipient. This practice calls for both levirate and sororate marriages, with some restrictions upon the former. A brief illustration of these two concepts follows.

Levirate in the sense intended here should not be confused with polyandry; a complete levirate can take place only when a man's brother dies. (Complete levirate goes beyond the mere mating with one's brother's wife.) Mating with the wife of an oldest brother occurs frequently. In this case, the wife is obligated to reveal the name of the younger brother to her husband whenever her husband requests it. When confronted by his older brother, the younger brother is expected to do two things. First, he invites a few of the family elders to go with him to his brother and plead for him. Second, during the course of the elders' reasoning with his brother, the younger brother usually advances to his brother, prostrates himself before him, gently puts his hands on the brother's feet, and says, "*Kɛgɛ ȳī vɛlɛni, belēn̄ggi i w > w > hò,*" which means, "My father, permit me to demonstrate my humility as abject submission to you. Let me be your footstool." Of course, this is a period of great emotional display. Usually the older brother is expected to forgive his younger brother in the presence of the elders. The matter usually ends with a gift of chickens which are killed and eaten by all parties.

The reverse situation is neither prescribed nor proscribed; that is, the older brother does not normally mate with the wife of his younger brother though this may happen occasionally. However, an older brother is not only permitted but even expected to marry the wife or wives of his deceased younger brother. One of the reasons for the lack of reciprocity between older and younger brothers in this matter lies in the fact that older brothers are sometimes referred to as "father" or "kɛkɛ́," and therefore they are respected as fathers. By Gbande custom a father does not apologize to his children for anything at any time. He is always right in whatever he does with regard to his children. For these reasons, older brothers do not mate with wives of their younger brothers. If this happens, then the whole system of senile deference, upon which Gbande culture is dependent, would crumble. The term senile deference refers to the respect for and submission to seniors by juniors. Levirate marriage occurs only after the death of a brother. It does not matter whether the deceased brother is older or younger. His widows are obliged to marry one of his brothers, in many instances by the widows' consent. The selection is sometimes made by the widows without regard to senior or junior brother so long as they stay within the family.

If a widow decides to marry someone outside her late husband's family, she automatically forfeits the right to her children, and the right to claim any property which she might have helped accumulate, and any other claims. Moreover, her parents or relatives and/or the man who wants to marry her has to refund the bridewealth to the relatives of the deceased husband. The bridewealth includes services by her deceased husband or the husband's relatives done for the wife's parents or relatives as part of their obligatory duties to the wife. Because of these complications, marriage outside the deceased husband's family is discouraged although not proscribed.

The oldest male of the family is also allowed to marry his deceased father's wives, with the exception of his mother and aunts. The father's wives have the alternative of marrying anyone else inside the husband's family.

The practice of sororate marriage in Gbandeland is distinctly different from that of levirate. As a rule, the oldest sister must marry first; her husband is then permitted to marry as many of his wife's younger sisters or cousins as she will allow. If a man marries the younger sister first, the older sisters are considered mothers-in-law because younger sisters refer to their older sisters as "mother." In contrast, a woman is not permitted to marry her husband's brother while her husband is still living. Thus sororate marriage, at least among the Gbandes, does not require that one party be widowed, as is the case with the levirate. If a man desires to marry his wife's sisters, he must start with the oldest of the sisters or forfeit the right to marry the others. Here again, the rule of senile deference is the reason or one of the reasons why the oldest must be the first to marry.

Once a man is married to the senior sister his chances of marrying the younger sisters are greatly enhanced. This practice is not as exotic as it may appear. For example, this was the reason Jacob, the Biblical character who was in love with Rachel, found himself mated with Leah, the oldest daughter of his maternal uncle, Laban. It is written that Jacob had to work another seven years in order to marry Rachel (Genesis 29:26). This type of marriage may be considered sororal polygyny par excellence, whereas the levirate may be considered a delayed polyandry, since a woman may be married to two or more brothers only if she has been widowed. This practice is not exotic either. A similar one is recorded in the Bible in a case in which seven brothers in succession marry the same woman, each husband dying in turn (Luke 20:29-31).

Potential wives are the wives of one's relatives, senior or junior. Such wives are treated as and referred to as "*yahāīn ti*" or "our wives." However, this does not mean mutual sexual privileges except in those levirate cases mentioned previously. What this means is that each wife is treated as a real member of all of her husband's kin-group family. She has the right to request material favors or any other help from any of her husband's family, and members of the husband's kin group are obligated to protect her and take up for her against any other family or individual in the community.

The concept of ideal wives includes all the children of one's in-laws—those that are already born and the generations yet unborn. This concept is based upon the feeling that once one becomes linked with a family it is good to stay a member of that family, rather than obligate oneself to many families. In this respect, the families that are involved may have a mutual contract, one being the donor and the other the recipient. However, it does not follow that such ideal wives will indeed become real wives.

Real wives are those wives who have been betrothed. In such a marriage, the age of the husband and the wife or wives cannot be taken into consideration, since wives are the wives not only of the husband but also of all the husband's family. Therefore, a one-year-old girl, for example, can be betrothed to a forty- or fifty-year-old man. Implicit here is the idea that sexuality is far less important in marriage than having a wife who has the potential of perpetuating and increasing the family.

This kind of cultural arrangement leaves little or no room for widows, because once a woman becomes married into a family she remains a wife of that family. It is the right and obligation of the deceased kinsman's male relatives to see to it that one of them, by order of seniority, marries her. Such a wife is treated with the greatest of respect and courtesy in deference to her late husband. Likewise, there is no concept for "old maid" in the Gbande language, for no woman remains unmarried; regardless of how she may look, she is a potential wife for the family known to be in-laws to her family. A beautiful woman is one who is fat and bears many children. A fat woman enhances the status of her husband because, in the first place, the fatness of one's wife is an indication of material prosperity. Secondly, a fat woman is assumed to bear big, strong, healthy children. This does not mean that slim women do not get married; the difference is that such women have to be satisfied with a position of second or third wife. However, such wives can raise their status by having many children.

The institution of the family is designed to furnish integration and stability in Gbande society. As implied throughout this chapter, Gbande society is delineated into a type of moity, or rather a superficial moity in which the rules of endogamy and exogamy are enforced. By this arrangement, one family is always the donor, whereas the other is always the recipient. Hence, Gbande society is a reciprocal obligatory society. Because of the reciprocal pattern, the alternatives for selecting a wife or husband are limited. This fact, more than anything else, may be responsible for the non-existence of old maids in Gbande society. In the past, Gbande society was highly endogamous; exceptions are cited in Chapter 2 "The Gbandes and Their Neighbors."

The Extended Family

Households are polygynous among the Gbandes and are based upon the extended family. In such a household the wives of the family's grandfather and of his sons, grandsons, and nephews all live in a large single house or hut; each of the husbands lives in a separate house or hut. The oldest male, in this case the grandfather, is the head of such a household and has express authority over and responsibility for the actions of members of his household. As mentioned elsewhere, the household is also an economic as well as a social unit. In such a household, joking relations are well established, particularly between males and females. However, this relationship is somewhat restricted between grandparents and grandchildren because of the rule of seniority; that is, the grandparents and grandchildren are considered to be of adjacent generations in contrast to parents and children, who are considered to be of alternate generations. The grandchildren are thought of as the grandparent's parents who have been reincarnated. Therefore, as children, they occupy the same position as the grandparents, but a little higher than their grandparents because they are supposed to be their seniors. However, the older a child becomes the more he takes on his own identity and the further he becomes removed from the position of seniority. When he becomes an adult, he occupies a position of less respect or honor.

In Gbandeland a father derives his greatest satisfaction from others of his community, particularly from those who are his juniors. This does not mean that he does not enjoy respect from his own family, but since he has to defer to both his parents and younger children, he cannot at the same time demand respect from them at that age.

Descent is patrilineal and primogenital, but since property is owned by members of the household, the position of the head of the household is one of guidance rather than exclusive rights. He can neither dispose of nor use such property for personal gain. He has as much right as any other member to own personal belongings, but whatever is owned by the family must be treated as communal family property (although leaders usually initiate any activities affecting the property). Therefore, the rule of descent among the Gbandes is patrilineal.

The patterns of residence for the Gbandes as a group are by no means simple. A pair of newlyweds usually moves into the residence of the husband's family, that is, the village of the husband's family. This is traditional patrilocal residence. However, if this residence is considered in terms of households, the pattern of residence becomes very complex, if not confusing. For example, such residence is unilineal since, by and large, Gbande newlyweds have little or no choice as to residence. However, neither the husband nor the husband's parents share the same household. The term household as used in this context refers to the family members who are living under the same roof. In this case all women of a family usually live in the same household; that is, the mother-in-law and daughters-in-law share one house, while each adult male member of such a family lives in a separate house built immediately before he got married. It would not be wrong to refer to this type of male housing arrangement as neolocal. Each wife spends the night in her husband's house, leaving the children with the older women of this female unilineal household who are no longer interested in sex. But if any of the males or all of them have more than one wife, such wives usually take turns sleeping in the husband's house. In this case each wife usually spends three nights sleeping with her husband, while the others sleep in the female unilineal house, except when her visit is disturbed by physiological inconvenience, such as menstruation. In this event either the head wife or the wife next in line will take her place, depending on the husband's desire. Moreover, one could very well argue that the Gbande form of residence is unilocal, because the wife or wives are always members of the husband's parents' village and household but the reverse is never true—that is, the husband is never a member of the wife's parents' village.

The status of grandparent is one that is almost always sought after. People who occupy such status, by Gbande tradition, are expected to set the pattern of behavior not only for their family but also for the community and indeed for the entire Gbande society. Those who have gained the status of grandparents are indeed grandparents throughout Gbandeland and respected accordingly. They are the model for Gbande behavior.

The relationship between grandfather and grandmother would indicate that the grandfather is the indisputable leader of his family. He is honored and respected by all and his decisions are usually final. However, in reality, there are very few decisions which he makes without consulting his first wife, the head wife. At times, an important decision may involve the whole family, both adult males and females. The grandfather's wife or wives are his lieutenants who are charged with the responsibility of seeing that rules are learned correctly and obeyed by the members of their family. The wives are always, at least most of the time, available to their grandchildren, their children, and their husbands, in that order. Their decisions and recommendations to the grandfather about their children, especially grandchildren, are usually accepted. This chain of influence was well learned by missionaries in Gbandeland. These missionaries usually appeal directly to the maternal grandmother for her grandchildren. Although this is a patrilineal society, children when they are young are the responsibility of their mother and hence their mother's mother, rather than their father's mother. This does not mean that the paternal grandmother has nothing to do with her grandchildren. It simply means that she is less involved with her grandchildren than is the maternal grandmother.

The relationship between a man and the mothers of his children is one of sentiment, caution, and respect, much more so than between a man and a wife or wives without children. The wives who are bearers of children are the direct veins between a man and his ancestors. Without such wives, it would be impossible to perpetuate the family. For this reason, the husband has a great sentimental attachment to them. The husband takes great care not to offend them for fear the child may sense such an offence, for the sensing of this offence by the child might make it return to the ancestor's spirit world. The husband's cautiousness and respect is even greater for wives who are pregnant or who have young children, because this is the period in which life is uncertain for both the mother and child. These considerations are much less important for the young wife or wives who are not in such a condition.

Status and Role of Women

Contrary to popular belief, Gbande women are no more relegated to an inferior position than are other women of the world. Such judgments are no more than mere opinion usually reflecting a cultural bias. Obviously opinions attempting to define the best social status for women or to prescribe the essential ingredients for their happiness are conjectural and can hardly be scientific. Throughout the world, differences in the status of women are relative, and naturally most investigators consider the social status of their women to be superior to that of women in the culture being studied. In truth, no culture seems to have evolved a social status for women which satisfies both sexes. Among the Gbandes, the women appear to enjoy a complementary relationship with the men. Overtly the Gbande male appears to enjoy a dominant role; covertly the female may dominate. This apparent paradox should be easily understood by Western man.

The relationships between co-wives can be understood only against the background of the family as well as the household structure. At the outset it must be made clear that any distinction between family and household structure is an abstract one and hence purely academic; nevertheless, it will both facilitate and clarify any explanation of the Gbande social system. The understanding of this distinction contributes to an understanding of the reasons for the stability and reduction of tension among co-wives.

In the first place, co-wives are selected for the most part by rule of seniority, the oldest daughter marrying first. In Gbande society those who would occupy the position of cousin are considered brothers or sisters with respect to sex. Therefore when the oldest daughter gets married first, she keeps her seniority position, which has priority and is the very essence of Gbande society. If a man has such women as wives in a polygynous family and household, he is firming the cornerstone upon which Gbande society is built. This cornerstone is the respect for seniority. Because of the deference which juniors are expected to give seniors there is little or no outward manifestation of jealousy between co-wives; that is, there tends to be an absence of competition for the husband's love. This is by no means a denial of the existence of petty jealousy between co-wives from different families or between co-wives for the welfare of their respective children. Notwithstanding, such jealousy is kept well within bounds so that the mechanism of integration is always the central focus for everyone.

One point calling for elaboration, however, is that contrary to popular belief, Gbande women are emphatically not subordinate to their husbands, although it may appear so to the outside casual observer. What is really happening is the allocation of role by sex. Gbande women let their men play the public role, and this public role is what is observed by the outside casual observer. I might add that this phenomenon of delegating public roles to men holds true for most cultures to some degree.

Gbande wives have many roles but the most significant of these roles is the childbearing role. The fulfillment of this role is among the ultimate aims of every Gbande wife as well as every Gbande husband. It gives meaning to the union between a man and a woman and between them and their kin. It is so important that a woman's prestige and social status in the community are probational rather than completely accepted until she has her first child. Her prestige, social status, or esteem in the community is especially enhanced if the first child is a boy. In this case, as mentioned elsewhere, both mother and father take the name of the first child, instead of the other way around. The number of children a woman has is directly related to her prestige within her own family and community.

The second most important role which a wife has to play entails her responsibility for the welfare of her children.

Her responsibility for her child begins with birth. If the first child is a boy, she will abstain from sexual intercourse and breast-feed him for four years. She will also refrain from eating certain foods, from saying certain words, from seeing certain things, from walking certain places after sundown, from dressing herself or the child too well, and from certain other acts. The list of restrictions to which a Gbande mother must submit is indeed long. The same sort of restrictions hold if a girl is born, the difference being the number of years for which the mother observes the restrictions. For example, the restrictions for a daughter are observed for three years, whereas for a son they last for four years. During this period the mother is held to blame for the most part for almost anything that happens to the child. However, if it is known that she is doing everything possible but that her child still meets with unusual difficulties or even death, her ill luck is attributed to witches. (The Gbande word for witch is *kɛlɛ̃ŋgi*.) For this reason, mothers with young children are in most cases extremely careful in their behavior and relationships with others, even with animals and objects.

The third important role which a wife plays entails her responsibilities to her husband. Gbande women are trained to exercise self-control in matters concerning their husbands in the presence of others, especially if these others are outsiders or strangers. They are trained not to condemn their husbands except under extreme provocation resulting from the husband's actions. Wives are expected to make suggestions to their husbands, and some of these suggestions may indeed be a direct and sometimes bitter criticism of them for actions completed or anticipated. More often, a husband's public actions are by and large influenced and controlled by private opinions and suggestions. Usually a husband does not make major decisions without consulting his wife or wives, as mentioned earlier, because any mistakes resulting from his action are blamed not only on him but on the family as a whole. Therefore, since the wife or wives are partly in

partnership with their husbands in all affairs of living, they
are expected to take definite stands on major issues. However, they do so in private. Their opinions are taken quite
seriously, as indicated by the expression "*Nuisī kelegele n̂ggo
āl> a w>ħl> n̂ggi ñáhày wan*," which means, "He who is
wise is one who listens to his wives." Finally, when a girl assumes the status of a married woman she also assumes the
status of an adult with corresponding responsibilities to her
family and the community in which she lives. She is expected
to behave as an adult and participate in all affairs designated
for adults. However, at the same time she is not condemned
if she makes a mistake in her newly acquired role. Rather she
is helped and encouraged to keep trying. It is believed that
every new role carries responsibilities which require
learning through practice. The psychological implications of
the understanding given junior members of the adult community cannot be overstated. It is because of this that the
junior members are able to assume their new roles with ease.
These new responsibilities include the new wife's relations
with the children of her husband or co-wives. She is expected to be a mother to all such children and to treat them
as her own. Mistreatment of a child, especially a child of
one's household, is an act which is unthinkable. But any co-
wife has the full right to reprimand any child of the household in the same manner in which she reprimands her own
child. The children are expected and required to respect and
obey all their father's wives, and all the wives are called
mothers by the children. This leads us to consideration of
kinship terminology.

Chapter 5
Kinship Terminology

THE IMPORTANCE OF the role of kinship relationships among the Gbandes, as among most indigenous Africans, cannot be overemphasized. Kinship ties are the foundation upon which other social relationships are structured. They are the building blocks of economic, educational, political, religious, and other similar institutions. Unlike the domestic unit in Western society the domestic unit of this people frequently consists of more than one nuclear family; the family members cooperate in farming and in raising and distributing the bridewealth that permits young people to marry, thereby uniting not just individuals but families. Moreover, kinship groups cooperate in religious ceremonies; in providing education (traditional as well as modern) for their members; and in enforcing the social controls which keep individuals from straying away from the path of customary virtue. Kinship groups constitute the foundation of political organization and participation. In short, all of these activities are based on the assumption that the important kinship members, however they may be defined, live and work in the same area, more or less. This structural relationship results in a strong sense of kinship obligation and dependence. One shares with his relatives and one grows strong and safe through having many close family or kinship ties that are actively functioning. This kind of kinship structure is geared to a single, homogeneous, compound family group. One submits to family or kinship discipline because it pays off and because there is little or no alternative. Gbande society is composed of units of kinship groups which approximate Emile Durkheim's concept of mechanical solidarity in that their society has few specializations of function; there is a single coherent, homogeneous, and sacred cultural tradition which tells everybody how to behave [11, p. 109]. Strong public opinion based on face-to-face interaction brings deviants back into line. This kind of social solidarity is based upon custom, custom which is embedded within and dictated by the exigence of kinship ties. On the whole, Gbande society has fewer kinship terms than, for example, Western society. This lack of terms actually broadens the network of kinship obligations. For the Gbandes, kinship terms imply rights and obligations. These rights and obligations are related to a person's age and his line of connection in the kinship system —that is, whether he is older or younger than the speaker or whether he belongs to the father's or the mother's line of descent. There are a number of overlapping kinship terms whose meanings cannot be understood without an understanding of this kinship structure. Like almost everything else, the relationships between kinsmen fall into various categories and must be identified by titles or names. But these terms, which make perfectly good sense in their proper language and culture, are sometimes amazingly difficult to translate. In fact, kinship terms are probably among the most difficult of all words to translate from one language to another. As we shall see, this is especially true for Gbande kinship terms. The fact that there are scores of ways of grouping kinsmen and many different principles of categorization has been known for a very long time; this knowledge has not eliminated the difficulty. Although Gbande kinship terminology is associated with institutions or social groups, it is much more closely associated with social roles. In short, Gbande society has terms for the categories into which they classify those kinsmen they recognize as kinsmen. Their terminology system shows wide variation. There is always, in folk evaluation or face-to-face evaluation, a relationship between kinship terms and an ideal mode of behavior. This ideal mode of behavior gives meaning to the content of kinship terminology. A discussion of a few selected Gbande terms will illuminate the enormous complexity and difficulty of translating kinship terms from one language into another. Our discussion will be limited to the following kinship concepts: father, mother, brother, sister, uncle, aunt, nephew, niece, cousin, mother-in-law, father-in-law, sister-in-law, and brother-in-law.°

Father

The term "father" or *kɛkɛ́* as used by the Gbandes has a much broader application than the English term. It refers to the biological father but is not limited to defining him alone. It includes all of the biological father's male relatives, that is, his brothers (both older and younger) as well as his male cousins. On the other hand, the term may also refer to a social father whose relationship is nominal who need not be connected with the biological father in any way. The term "social father" refers to the man who pays the bridewealth (described in Chapter 4 "Family-Kinship Groupings," subsection "Marriage"). He is the legal husband of the bride; and since a married woman cannot have illegitimate children, her children are the children of the man who is recognized as the one who paid the bridewealth, although the real or biological father may be known. Among the Gbandes, as among most indigenous Africans in sub-Saharan

°The Gbandes do not have specific word equivalents for our terms brother, sister, cousin, nephew, niece, mother-in-law, father-in-law, and sister-in-law. These terms are used here for illustrative purposes.

Africa, chiefs (who usually have many wives and
consequently many children) are social fathers to most of
their children.

Moreover, the term "father" is equally applicable to
one's senior male siblings. For example, one's older brothers
and male cousins are addressed kɛkɛ́ on all formal occasions.
As mentioned earlier, the right to inherit or marry the
widows of one's deceased father is reserved for the oldest of
the sons. Custom demands that he marry his father's widows
with the exception of his biological mother and her sisters
and cousins. If the deceased man died without a son old
enough to marry his widows, any one of his male relatives
old enough to marry them is eligible and is encouraged to do
so. Hence a man's oldest brother or his father's male relatives
are the potential social fathers of his children.

Mother

Similarly, a child formally addresses his mother's sisters and
female cousins as "mother" or ndē ndé. Consequently the
term mother is not limited to the biological mother. Moreover, a child will call all of his father's wives "mother." As
mentioned in Chapter 3, all of a man's wives function as
social mothers to all of his children, including both the real
and the social children of their husband. This relationship is
one of the hallmarks of the integration and harmony in a
polygynous household consisting of women with diverse
social backgrounds. Each woman is bound by custom to
regard every child of the household as her own. This type of
behavior justifies the title of mother for each of them. In like
manner, a woman's sisters or female cousins will regard her
children as their own and vice versa. This latter relationship
between sisters or female cousins and their children is embedded in the very fabric of the kinship relationship and en-
dures longer than the relationship between a man's children
and their social mothers in the household. The relationship

between children and their social mothers, although very functional, may weaken at the death of the common father.

I have used the terms "real mother" and "biological mother" synonymously here, and I have arbitrarily adopted the terms "real father" and "biological father" for similar use. The concepts "social mother" and "social father" are more complex and difficult to explain. For example, the concept "social mother" refers to three distinct groups of persons. One's mother's sisters constitute the first group. The members of this group are ranked close to the biological mother, and indeed their rank is given recognition in the way mentioned before. Sisters share reciprocal rights and obligations for each other's children in all areas of socialization. The Gbande society and community expect them to perform the tasks of a real mother for their sister's children, and the children are expected to obey them accordingly. The second group of social mothers is constituted by one's older sisters. They are called "mother" out of deference for seniority. Their responsibilities to their younger siblings are numerous but relatively unimportant. They help generally to take care of their younger brothers and sisters. These older sisters are addressed as "mother" on formal occasions or when they are addressed in the presence of strangers. This latter point is an important one to keep in mind. A researcher who is ignorant of the various contexts in which the concept is used will not probe enough to ascertain its real meaning. The lack of such probing is a critical point affecting most cross-cultural investigations. The third group of social mothers is made up of one's mother's co-wives or father's other wives. In this group, those who have children tend to share a reciprocal socializing responsibility for their children as mentioned earlier. They tend to exercise love and nominal responsibility for all of the children of their common husband while he is alive and while they are living with him.

In most cases the death of the common husband and father leads to the dispersal of one compound family and subsequent formation of another. When a family is dispersed in this way, the nominal obligatory responsibility that held between co-wives and between their children also decreases. The fact that in such a family the mother is called by the name of her first-born, rather than the child's taking the father's softens the drifting away of family members.

Social Fathers

The concept of social father is much more intriguing than that of "social mother." Categorically, all of one's father's brothers are social fathers. The fact that all of the father's brothers are potential husbands to one's mother has been mentioned in Chapter 3. Similarly, one's older brothers are addressed as father. As stated before, a woman may marry any of her husband's children except her own and her sisters' children. They are all potential husbands to her in case of her own husband's death. Among this people the role of the social father might indeed have more influence on the children than that of the biological father. (Much of this was discussed in Chapter 3 but for purposes of clarity it is repeated here.) The point of interest here is the intricacy surrounding the concept "father." The man who pays the bridewealth is the father of the children. If a married man dies without children, it is the right and obligational responsibility of his brothers to have children by his widows in his name. It is not unusual at all for a Gbande to say that his father died five or ten years before he was born. In this case the dead man was the one who paid the bridewealth; therefore he, rather than the biological father, is the legal and social father of his widow's children.

Siblings

There are no words for "sister" and "brother" in Gbande kinship terminology. Instead there are terms for "older siblings" and "younger siblings" which are used without sex distinction. For example, the term *ndĩa* refers to older siblings whereas the term *ndēgē* refers to younger siblings. It is of interest to make clear at this point that the Gbande have no term for "cousin" either. Cousins fit into the same general category as *ndĩa* and *ndēgē* with the following qualifications. A mother's sister's children and father's brother's children constitute a closer type of kinship relation. Members of this group are also referred to as *ndĩa* and *ndēgē*. These are comparable to parallel cousins. They are considered members of the in-group kinsmen. The second group is composed of one's mother's brother's and one's father's sister's children. The members of this second group are referred to in the plural as *nĩ ndĩa* and *nĩ ndēgē*, which mean "our older siblings" and "our younger siblings" respectively. These approximate cross-cousins. They are the out-group kinsmen because they belong to a different lineage.

Aunt and Uncle

This brings us to the discussion of the concept of "aunt" and "uncle." It must be apparent by now that "aunt" or *tēna* refers to the father's sister and while the "uncle" or *kēɛn* refers to the mother's brother. "*Jāagbɛ*" is the term the Gbande use to refer to their nephews and nieces. As is the case with titles *ndĩa* and *ndege*, there is no gender or sex distinction between female and male *jāagbɛ*. Only one's mother's brother's children and father's sister's children can have the distinction of using the term *jāagbɛ* for their mother's brother or father's sister, since one's mother's sisters and one's father's brothers are called "mother" or "father" respectively. *Kēɛn* (the mother's brothers) are supposed to give the head of all animals they kill to their *jāagbɛ* (nephews and nieces). This is purely custom. With the exception of the grandparents, *kēɛn* and *tēna* are known to spoil or greatly indulge their

brother's and sister's children. To some degree they corre-
spond to those who have a joking relationship with these sets
of children. They are expected to give expensive gifts and to
be overtly emotionally involved in all matters concerning
these children. One can always depend upon an aunt and
uncle for moral and emotional support. They are supposed to
be able to keep a secret, and therefore one can talk freely
with them. Those *tēna* and *kɛɛn* who who are older than one's
parents tend to exert great influence in matters concerning
their *jāagbɛ*.

The Gbande have no term for "sister-in-law." A man's
sister-in-law is considered his mother-in-law if she is older
than his wife. But if she is younger than his wife, she is either
a real or a potential wife. The mother-in-law and father-in-
law are called "mother" and "father" respectively. This
leaves only one set of a wife's relatives—her brothers—unac-
counted for. They are referred to as *dēmēna*. The term is
used for either a real or a potential brother-in-law.

Chapter 6
Growing Up
in Gbandeland

THE PROBLEM OF caring for and molding the newborn individual into a social being is a universal problem which no society can afford to ignore. Without it, no society would perpetuate itself for very long. The interaction between the individual and his society in a cultural milieu makes the molding process of the individual possible. Just exactly how this is done is still a moot question. The answer is perhaps as mysterious as the process, and the quest for it is a common meeting ground of all the sciences dealing with the problem of why man is human. It is, therefore, in examining the nature of the problem of enculturation or socialization that biology, psychology, psychiatry, sociology, and anthropology, to name a few sciences, come together. The common interest, among other things, is that they are all concerned in the subtle alchemy by which the human animal is translated into a human social being. While this is the case with human societies in general, individual societies manage the task according to criteria unique to themselves.

The question, then, with which this chapter is concerned deals with the process by which the individual born into Gbande society becomes a Gbande. The basic answer to this vital question must be sought in the process of enculturation and/or socialization. This process can be demonstrated best by arbitrarily categorizing the periods of growth as follows: ages 0–5, the period of infancy and early childhood; ages 6–13, the period of childhood and early adolescence; ages 14–18, the period of adolescence and young adulthood.

Infancy

The task of socializing the child during the period of infancy and early childhood, as designated in this work, is in the hands of the mother and the other female members of the joint household, as well as the grandmothers if they live in the same village with the child. These are the individuals who are responsible for the social well-being of the child. They are the weavers of the child's moral fabric as well as inculcators of etiquette. Tradition demands that the child's social behavior be not only a replica of that of his family, as perceived by this group, but also of Gbande standards of proper behavior. This is the group charged with the responsibility of cultivating the child during the most formative years of his life, that is, the first five years. It is this training that will enable him to measure up to the expectations of his village and Gbande society at large.

During this period, the child is taught not only how to eat but what to eat. He is also taught toilet training and a general pattern of cleanliness that entails taking a bath twice a day. Children are breast-fed, male children for four years and female children for three years. The major reasons for the prolonged breast-feeding are the belief that the mother's milk is the best food for the child and the fact that it is always available. Since the mother is the chief source of the child's food supply, she must strictly observe taboos concerning what she can and cannot eat or do during the entire period of breast-feeding. She must abstain not only from certain foods but also from sex, because it is believed that sexual intercourse will contaminate the mother's body, which will affect the child's health. This belief is based upon the fact that the child not only feeds on the mother's breast but spends most of its time during this period of infancy with the mother, including sleeping with her. It is believed that the child's main food supply, the mother's breast-milk, will dry up if she engages in sexual intercourse. This abstention also constitutes a birth control method for the Gbandes since another child cannot possibly be conceived for at least three or four years.

In most cases, but by no means all, the mother is blamed for almost anything negative that happens to the child during the period of breast-feeding. For example, any feeble-mindedness, congenital disease, or even slowness in learning to walk may all, more or less, be attributed to the mother's failure to keep the required taboos. However, in some cases, the child's troubles or difficulties are attributed to witchcraft. Nevertheless, because of the fear that she might be blamed for any undesirable things that happen to her child, every mother is careful not to violate any of the rules which are supposed to be in the best interests of her child's health.

At about the age of two or three weeks the infant is given his first solid food, which consists of rice mashed to a nearly liquid pulp. Rice is the staple foodstuff among the Gbandes. (A Gbande is quick to point out that he has not eaten anything all day, however much other food he might have consumed, if he has not had his rice.) The love of rice is a behavior which the child is taught from infancy. The rice is cooked as usual for household use, but the crust or burnt part at the bottom of the pot is carefully mashed with the hands until most of the grains disappear. This is forced into the child's mouth by a special method the mother uses. First she puts a little of the mashed rice in the palm of her hand. As she puts her cupped hand with the rice close to the baby's mouth, with her thumb over the baby's nostrils, the baby gasps for air and crys. The mashed rice is pushed in, and

down it goes. This is repeated over and over until the mother
thumps the child's stomach and decides it is tight and full.
This process is repeated at least three times a day. The child
is bathed before his first feeding and bathed again immediately after his last feeding. The mother's milk and the
mashed rice are the only food given to the child until he is
able to eat other things by himself as a supplement to rice.
When the child is weaned and old enough to eat regular
rice, he or she must eat with people of the appropriate sex,
that is, the boys with the men and the girls with the women.
It is a custom among the Gbandes that members of the family must eat their main meals together if they are known to
be in the village at mealtime. There are usually two meal-
times, noon and evening. The morning meal or breakfast is
an individual affair. An individual may want to eat cassava
or plantain or some other foodstuff. These foods are usually
roasted over the fire or baked in the hot ashes.

With regard to toilet training, the infant urinates or
defecates whenever and wherever he wants to, pretty much
as infants everywhere do. Since the children are naked, as
soon as the child urinates or defecates, the ever-ready
mother's best friend, the family dog, is there to clean up immediately. (This role of the dog in Gbande society was discussed in Chapter 3.) If a baby should urinate or defecate on
a childless woman, it is a good omen interpreted as meaning
that she will soon be pregnant. When the child is about four
or five years old, he is taught not to defecate publicly but to
go behind the house in the banana bushes which constitute
the outer edges of the village. He is taught not to spit or
cough while others are eating. He is not permitted to blow
his nose or clear his throat at mealtime. He is not to chew
with his mouth open, neither is he permitted to pull anything out of his mouth publicly while eating. He can do these
things only by excusing himself to go to a place where he can
neither be seen nor heard by those at the meal. This is a criti-

cal period of socialization. The child becomes the concern not only of his kin but also of his village.

Preadolescence

For a child of six to thirteen, the whole village acts as the socializing agent, helping the child in every way possible to obtain the desired and acceptable ends as proscribed by Gbande society. The child is taught to refer to his primary group (the members of his household) with kinship terms, such as "mother," "father," "grandmother," "grandfather," and "younger and older siblings."* The child refers to the members of his community or village as "my people." They in turn refer to him as "our child." This kind of joint effort by both the secondary group (community) and primary group (family) in the enculturation or socialization process is absolutely imperative, because any misconduct by an adolescent is a reflection on the village as well as on the family. To guard against this catastrophic event, the village or community members play a guiding role to supplement the efforts of the child's immediate relatives. Since the child represents not only himself or his family but also his entire community, child-rearing in Gbandeland is a very serious undertaking which requires the effort of the whole community. The Gbandes in their wisdom believe that a newborn individual is really nobody. He must be molded into somebody, and what better "somebody" than a Gbande? Hence, the making of the new organism into a Gbande is a task which must be performed by the family-kinship group and community members alike. Since, to them, the Gbande way of behavior

---

*The latter terms are used in place of the terms "brother" and "sister" or "cousin" because the Gbandes use positional terms ("younger" or "older") in designating siblings, instead of using sex designations.

is the only right way, the child must be trained by all to know this way. The whole Gbande society is either directly or indirectly involved in this process of making adult Gbandes out of growing children.

The period of early adolescence (6–13 years of age) is perhaps the most critical period in the process of growth. It is during this period that the child learns to discriminate by sex. He is taught to associate more with people of his own age and sex group. He learns to work with adults of his sex, thereby learning to do the appropriate prescribed tasks of that sex. He also learns to play and to work with the opposite sex. The emphasis in enculturation of the early adolescent is on group sentiment and togetherness, which is, in my view, the major theme in Gbande society. During this period of the child's life, every adult member of his community is a teacher and/or referee. This is the period of intensive informal training. The games played by children are designed for instruction. Such games are replicas of adult work. Every play activity represents division of labor by sex and requires cooperative competition among the participants. These play activities are watched with interest by the adults. Adults do not interfere, but they are expected to give advice whenever requested by the children. Every adult is expected to know the game and give the right advice. This is not hard to understand, since children's games are, by tradition, standardized—that is, most games children play were once games played by their elders. Children's games are designed to provide both fun and learning; the game must be played correctly. For example, if the game is for each male child to tell a funny story in the second and third persons, the storyteller. must use gestures and body movements as well as sound effects to represent each character's personality and to set one role apart from another as well as from his own role. Since everybody knows the story, the storyteller dare not leave out any detail however minute it may be. If he does, he must begin the story all over. As for the girls, they play games related to household quarrels or motherly duties.

This period of the child's life is considered the most advantageous for basic training that will result in proper orientation to the Gbande way of life. It is believed that this immediate preadolescent period is one of curiosity and experimentation, one in which the child is susceptible and amenable to whatever course of training is provided for him. The training for occupational specialization within sex groups comes later in the child's life. In most cases, such occupational specialized training is given during the time of formal training in the Sande or Poro institutions of higher learning. This is also the period in which boys' and girls' activities become differentiated. For the boys, cooperative competition becomes the order of every game they play. The idea of cooperative competition is crucial, because the level of ability in cooperative play is the sole criterion by which their peers rank them.

Adolescent Males

Among adolescent males, different forms of play or games help to develop the skills or techniques required of all Gbande males. For example, degrees of skill in use of the bow and arrow, spear, sword, and slingshot, as well as in ability to tell a story artistically and to debate effectively are taken as indices for ranking each adolescent. Therefore these play activities may be considered self-regulating socialization devices par excellence. However, the single most important game which the adolescents themselves use for ranking each other is *dapī*, Gbande for "wrestling." The term "wrestling" as used here refers to the display of physical skills in competition with an opponent of equal size. A victory in such a competition is one of the criteria for gaining a high social status in the male adolescent social group. Every village has its own rank order of wrestlers, the leader of which must excel in both wrestling and the other activities indicated above.

Each age group within this age bracket has its own rank

order, based on performance in these activities. The leadership of any age group in this age bracket may change several
times during this period. There are two ways by which a
change of leadership may come about. First, one may
become a new leader of one's age group by out-maneuvering
the old leader in wrestling and in a significant number of the
other activities. Second, one may become a leader by out-
classing someone who, although he himself is not the recognized leader of one's age group, has already defeated the
recognized leader. This second case usually involves a boy
who is visiting from another village. New boys are unranked
and must enter into wrestling competition and the other activities with their age groups. (Such competition was very
common in the recent past, that is, in the 1930's and 1940's.)
If someone from another village defeats one's leader, and if
one is then able to defeat the stranger, one wins the leadership. Wrestling is so much an integral part of adolescent culture in Gbandeland that every boy knows the rules. For example, fist fighting is not permitted, and no attempt is ever
consciously made to injure an opponent. There is nothing
more impudent than trying to hurt an opponent. The object
of this physical combat is the display of physical prowess and
skills rather than injury of an opponent. As a matter of fact, a
deliberate attempt to hurt an opponent usually results in dis-
qualification from the competition and ridicule, because such
a tactic is "un-Gbande."

Whenever a boy visits or moves to another village, he
became unranked and therefore on probation until he proves
himself in wrestling and in play competition. When he has
been in the new village for about a week, he is invited to the
edge of the village by his age group; there he is introduced
to the other boys by the leader of the group, who is usually a
little older than the rest. Each boy then introduces himself
by giving his name and rank. The leader then repeats each
boy's name and rank to the visitor or stranger, completing
the challenge. The visitor then selects an opponent to start

the competition, usually someone with a low rank. If he is able to outmaneuver this opponent and throw him down four times, he is declared the winner of that match. He then wrestles an opponent with higher rank. The process is repeated until he is defeated. At that point, his rank is fixed. From then on, he is accepted and can then become a full-fledged member of the group with all the rights, privileges, and obligations of any other member. This is the first approximation of ranking, but it is by far the most important of the competition. It usually takes about two or three weeks to complete the ranking of the new member. The ranking must be completed before the new boy is allowed to participate in inter-sexual activities. Such participation means that he is accepted not only by the boys of his age group but also by the girls; it indicates his full acceptance by all members of the adolescent community. Once the age group accepts him, the new boy is introduced to the parents or adult members of the community. By now his social integration is well advanced; he is no longer a stranger but one of the in-group.

If a new boy is afraid or reluctant to accept the challenge, he must be persuaded by being taunted or ridiculed. The leader may take a leaf or stick, take off his pants, clean his backside with the leaf or stick, and throw it into the face of the visiting boy. If this technique fails to incite the visitor to action, the leader employs what is considered the most humiliating insult—spitting into the palm of his hand and rubbing the spit on the new boy's face. He follows this up by taking a handful of dirt and throwing it bit by bit into the face of the visitor, at the same time calling him by a feminine name. If this method does not incite him, he is taken a little farther into the woods. There the leader asks him to stand aside by himself. The leader draws a line with a stick across the path or the only road which leads to the village and dares the visitor to cross it and follow the boys. The boys usually move a few yards away, leaving the visitor behind the line, and eat fruits such as bananas, oranges, and pineapples. During this period, the visitor is constantly invited to come and join the party. At the same time, he is ridiculed by the youngest boy in the group who now challenges him and boasts that he, the little one, can beat him with the little finger of his left hand, or that he can beat him with his hands tied to a tree. To be insulted by a younger person is one of the worst things that could happen to anyone in Gbande society. Finally, if this method does not work, the new boy is simply ostracized from the group until such time as he has enough courage to accept the challenge.

Adolescent Females

The situation described above is for a visiting boy, who has to prove himself through wrestling and all the other activities designed for ranking before he is accepted by his peers. This does not apply to a visiting girl. A visiting girl is at first neither fully accepted nor fully rejected by her age group. Nevertheless, she is greatly admired by them if she can teach them new things, such as songs and dances from her village. She becomes fully and easily accepted later if she is clever enough to learn the songs and dances of her hostesses. If she is a smart girl, she usually becomes the topic of the adolescents' conversation. The other girls usually discuss her with their brothers and among themselves. A smart visiting girl is a popular girl. She is often praised by other girls in front of their brothers, and she also receives many invitations to the homes of girls whose brothers want to meet her and take a closer look at her. If she is slow and dull, she is tolerated but not completely accepted by the other girls. The girls' lack of complete acceptance of the visiting girl is expressed in their refusal to invite her to their homes. However, skill in singing and dancing are not the only criteria by which girls are rated, especially by the boys, whose ratings count most. A girl may have many other qualities which, indeed, make her attractive to boys. Therefore, any quality or look a girl may have could be an asset to her. In short, the boys have to prove their masculinity but the girls never have to prove their feminity. As a matter of fact, any definition of a beautiful girl among the Gbandes is an elusive one, since the definition of a beautiful girl may mean many things: an attractive girl, a smart girl, a talented girl, a quiet girl, a girl with a good disposition, or even a homely girl, among others! When all these characteristics are put together, very few girls, if any, will fail to be designated as beautiful in Gbandeland. This may be among the reasons why no girl remains unmarried among this people.

Adolescence

The third and final age group, the adolescent age group, 14 to 18 years of age, experiences the end of the active informal socialization and the beginning of the formal enculturation. This is the transitional period. The adult members of the community are satisfied with the informal training which they have so carefully given the adolescent members, who now stand at the threshold of becoming adults. This is the period of reviewing and acting out things already learned. The community relies heavily upon the good nature of the members of this group and their willingness to help whenever help is needed. They are said to be honest and dependable at all times. They are now truly ready to embark upon the most rigorous training, in the formal institutions of training—the Sande and Poro schools. These schools consummate the transformation of the individual from child to adult. During this period, the adolescents are old enough to travel out of Gbandeland to the neighboring territory, but they must do it in the company of other adult Gbandes. Any adult Gbande at all will suffice. These adults become the guiding and socializing agents, acting in place of the kinship group and/or the community.

Implicit then in the enculturation or socialization

processes are three focal points. Initially the child's needs
and socialization involve his mother, other female members
of the household, and his female grandparents. Secondly
there are the neighbors and community or the village of
which the child is a member. They join this primary group as
soon as the child begins to interact with others. They now assume as active a part and as strong an interest in the training
of the child as they would with their own child. The third
and final focus is the point where the whole of Gbande society becomes the Gbande community because all Gbandes
become involved in socializing the child. These three focal
points express vividly the basic theme which runs through
Gbande society—the theme of the reciprocal rights and
obligations of all its members, young and old, beginning
with the members of the household. The child is loved by everyone in his household. In turn, he is taught to love everyone in his household. He is taught to refer to possession of
his house in the plural, that is, "our house" and never "my
house." Accordingly, he relates himself to each member of
the household by the appropriate kinship terms discussed
earlier in this chapter. These kinship terms are easily transferred to any member of the child's village when away from
home or any Gbande when away from Gbandeland. Those
who use and accept these kinship terms are expected to play
the appropriate roles. For example, if one calls another
"uncle," one is expected to treat this person as his uncle, and
the supposed "uncle" is expected to treat the "nephew" as his
nephew. Likewise, if one calls another "mother," that individual must be treated as one's mother, and she is expected
to treat the "child" as her child. In this way, every Gbande
becomes related to all other Gbandes when they are outside
Gbandeland, whether or not they know each other. This
type of communal sentiment is derived from the child-
rearing process used by the Gbande people.

   The pluralism and togetherness that permeate these
Gbande child-rearing practices stem from the principle of

reciprocity, which is the essence of the Gbande way of life. An important aspect of this principle of reciprocity is the keen spirit of cooperative competition which is encouraged in children. Since competition is designed to help the child improve his skills at whatever task is to be performed, Gbande society is a society of *cooperative* competition rather than cut-throat competition. Each family is in direct cooperation as well as competition with all other families. Each strives to be the ideal family by Gbande standards. For example, each family wants to have the best reputation in the community. Each family wants to be the family with the best farm, the one best equipped to help others at any time, and the one that observes fully all rules of Gbandeland. This idea of quality is instilled in the child by the example of every adult member and older sibling of the family. The making of a child into an adult Gbande is a major and tedious job that requires the conscientious effort of every adult in the community. When the child is old enough to begin doing useful work, his training takes on a new dimension. The adults now watch the child with interest in order to discover his potentialities and his likes and dislikes. The child is not scolded for making mistakes. Instead, the adults correct him through examples, over and over again, to make certain that he understands the explanation and examples. However, if the child does not comprehend the explanation, and still makes the same mistake, he is encouraged very gently to do something else. By the process of elimination and substitution, the child will finally find something congenial. Hence, every Gbande child is good for something.

Social Control

The Gbandes seldom use punishment as a major device of socialization, although it is used whenever necessary. Such a punishment is usually in the form of a spanking or the threat of a spanking. This can be done by any Gbande adult,

especially an adult of the child's community. Frequent
rewards instead of punishment are more important factors in
child-rearing. Children are loudly praised for good behavior
and for things well done. Their performance may be relatively clumsy even by Gbande standards, but if it is the best
that the child can do, he is loudly praised. The child also receives other tangible rewards. For example, when he is
learning to walk, he is given two sets of small bells which are
strung together and tied around his ankles. As he walks, the
bells jingle to the rhythm of his steps. It is believed that the
jingle of these bells acts as a reward, encouraging the child
to walk quickly and to increase his agility. Other rewards
include a child's own tools and things of that nature. The
emphasis is always the training of the child to become not
only a human being but also a Gbande, which, for them, is
the highest virtue.

Gbande society is not immune from conflict despite this
method of socialization and enculturation. For example,
adults do wrestle, but their wrestling is quite different in
some respects from that of adolescents. It is different in that
it may or may not be play. If it is play, it is not for the purpose of ranking, because such ranking has already been done
at graduation from the Poro school. Nevertheless, adult
wrestling is similar to adolescent wrestling in at least one
respect—that at no time will one opponent consciously attempt to injure the other. The wrestlers do not use knives,
guns, sticks, stones, or any other objects that might cause injury to an opponent. For the Gbandes, adult wrestling essentially involves strength and the technique or skill of
maneuverability. Once an opponent is down, he is held
down by sheer strength until he becomes exhausted and
gives up or somebody separates the two. There is never any
fist fighting or kicking. With the exception of a fight which
ends up in court, fights end quarrels on the spot. Once the
combatants agree to shake hands in Gbande fashion, that is,

glancing their thumbs off each other's middle fingers, the matter is finished.

In most cases, however, adult wrestling is serious, and often it results in family conflicts. If such conflicts reach the family level, the male elders of the community take it upon themselves to investigate the matter. This investigation is aimed at ascertaining who is guilty rather than who has won. Once this is established, the matter can be settled by the male elders. However, if a younger person fights an older person, no matter how right the younger person may be, it is he who has to apologize to the older person. If the older person happens to be a kinsman, the younger person has to prostrate himself before him, put his hands on the foot of the older man, and say, "Ÿī *velene kày,*" which is to say, "I apologize or I beg you." The younger person then offers chicken and red and white kola nuts to the older man as an indication of his being truly sorry and asking forgiveness for his folly. At this point, the elders of the community immediately join in chorus with the younger person in pleading with the older one to grant forgiveness. This proceeding is only a formality because there is no record in the memory of any living person in Gbande country of any such request's being refused. Once forgiveness is granted, the matter is closed forever, and the younger man vows never to repeat this type of misconduct.

However, even with the Gbandes' emphasis upon solidarity and avoidance of hostility, one type of injury may lead to real fighting with intent to hurt the opponent. This is the injury suffered by a Gbande when an equal abuses or calls his parent or parents names. This is a very serious matter. Every Gbande boy is prepared to die in defense of his parents' good name, because he is expected by his peers (the dead as well as the living members of his society) to offer such a defense at any cost. For this reason, every care is exercised to avoid maligning anyone's parent, regardless of how

serious disagreement may be. (In contrast, personal abuse is
not a good enough reason for anyone to engage seriously in
fighting; the assumption here is, "Why fight when you can
abuse back?")

Fighting in any form is reserved for men and boys. It is,
indeed, considered deplorable for women and girls to engage
in fighting of any kind. If there is an occasion for women or
girls to fight, or one on which they must fight, the one who
feels she is right simply puts her hands on her head and crys
out the name of her mother. If the dispute is with another
woman or girl, the matter is settled quickly by the woman's
elders. This does not apply to a dispute between a husband
and wife. Women may, indeed, have a verbal battle, but
never a physical one. With regard to a dispute or fight between a man and his spouse, such a fight is not usually
fought in the daytime or out-of-doors. It must be done in as
much secrecy as possible, because it is strictly a family affair.

On the whole, socialization in Gbande society
emphasizes non-hostility; there is little or no respect for a
person with ill will toward another. For the Gbande, a happy
community is one in which its members exercise understanding and tolerance. From this standpoint, wealth, which
is an important criterion for a happy community in the Western world, is not a standard for happiness in Gbandeland.
Human understanding and getting along with one's fellow
man are among the basic ingredients which make up happiness and, hence, a happy community, because a happy people inevitably produces a happy community.

Therefore, fighting is minimized and wealth is shared,
because it is through the minimization of disputes and
sharing of wealth by common consent that one is truly able
to exercise an empathic sensitivity—that is, to assume the
feelings of others. In this situation fighting, in itself, is obviously meaningless; so is wealth, unless it can evoke a mutual understanding in some way. Wealth may or may not

bring about integration. Reciprocity, for the Gbande, is the very vortex of a community—a value stemming from, perhaps, the total wisdom of Gbande society.

Chapter 7
Educational Institutions

IT IS AN accepted fact in anthropological and sociological circles that human beings are born with various potentials for learning, and that no one is born fully adapted to life in any particular culture. Understanding how people learn their culture and become adapted to its demands is a major concern of anthropology and sociology. The inquiry has two aspects. At the obvious level, individuals must learn the skills necessary for making a living and adopt the normative behaviors necessary for carrying on the social life of their group. At the less obvious level, all cultures encourage and reward certain types of personalities while at the same time discouraging and punishing other types. The essence of education, then, is the teaching of the youth to discriminate desirable and accepted behavior from behavior that is undesirable and rejected by Gbande standards.

To most Western peoples, "education" has come to mean the activities that go on in the formal institutions of their society, known as "schools," supplemented perhaps by readings and lectures that are less formally organized. To the social scientist, especially to the sociologist and the anthropologist, "education" is a much broader process which includes all learning mechanisms. Whether or not it is formalized, it results in the acquisition of culture by the individual, the formation of his personality, and the process of his socialization (his learning to accommodate himself to life as a member of a society).

In all societies, then, education is a continuous process which begins at birth and progresses with greater or lesser intensity throughout the entire life of the individual. By virtue of this process, the individual learns the ways of his culture and comes to participate more or less fully in it. He also acquires a personality, which is a complex pattern of rational faculties, perceptions, ideas, habits, and conditioned emotional responses. Personality is derived partly from certain genetically controlled capacities or predispositions, partly from the many statuses and roles the individual assumes during a lifetime, and partly from the training given to him in a particular culture. Concurrently the individual becomes socialized. He learns to accommodate himself to living with others in his society and to integrate his own desires and ideals with the systems of values common to his group.

Informal Education

Among the Gbandes, informal education is the responsibility mainly of the family and relatives and secondarily of the community at large. Informally, a child learns at a very early age to do those things expected of his sex. As he grows older he becomes competent in such activities and is encouraged by other members of his sex in the community. The child is not ridiculed for making mistakes, rather, each mistake is considered a stepping stone to future excellence. In addition, mistakes form the bases for appraising the child's ability to perform different tasks, providing cues to lack of aptitudes or areas heeding attention. It is through this informal education that the ground work is laid for the most rigorous training. The rigorous training, by virtue of its intricacy, is an institution of formal education.

Each sex receives this formal education separately and at a different age. The male institution is sometimes called

Sale, but more often *Porogee* or *Poro*; the female component is sometimes called *Graga Bush*, or *Bundoe*, but more often *Sande* (sometimes spelled with a "y" in place of the "e"). Without a doubt, these schools are examples of formal education par excellence and are formally recognized as such within the communities. The ostensible object of these schools is to turn immature boys and girls into full-fledged members of the adult community. Their aim is to convert the raw individual into a responsible tribal member, or more accurately, to give him a new name at graduation and to indicate his new status. His new name entitles him to procreation and all the responsibilities of adulthood and parenthood. The schools require the individual to change his behavior and attitudes from those of one stage in life to those of another. At each stage more is expected of him and his responsibilities increase.

Formal Education

The Poro and Sande schools have been referred to erroneously as secret societies by many investigators. These schools are often described by these investigators as institutions that impose sanctions on behavior in nearly every sphere of life. However, the initiatory aspect of these educational institutions seems to be the one considered by these non-members and is often emphasized by investigators who have worked in societies with similar institutions. The idea that Poro and Sande members are expected to bear hardships without complaint and the idea that they must grow accustomed to hardships are both honest interpretative errors made by outside observers with different cultural vantage points. (A better term would be "outside analyzers" because non-members, especially outsiders, are limited in actually observing these schools in their proper site.) The hardships which, these investigators assert, Poro students are expected to endure include: sleeping at night on beds made of sticks; being covered with cloths which have been soaked in water; and remaining outdoors if it rains. The first part of the statement is true; the students do sleep on beds made of sticks. But this is also true of the majority of the Gbande people with the exception of a few among those living on the coast who can afford other beds. Therefore, it is not unusual at all to find such beds among Poro students. The other supposed hardships—"being covered with cloths which have been soaked in water" and "remaining outdoors if it rains"— are both non-existent. No doubt, these errors stem from exaggerations by the informant that remained unchecked by these investigators. I myself am a Mende and a graduate of a similar Poro school, and I did not experience the hardships described above; nor did I see or hear of anyone who did. There are no more hardships for those in training than they may expect to find in real life. Almost everything that is done in training is done with the hope of duplicating real life situations.

Initiation

Among the initiatory rituals, the following are pertinent and common to all Poro schools. At the initial visit to the school site the students are usually blindfolded, except for those who matriculate at night. The purpose of the blindfold is to give the Poro school professors a chance to dress in their appropriate regalia, because it is absolutely forbidden for an incoming student to meet and see them without their appropriate apparel. With their proper attire they are considered transformed into someone superhuman and, therefore, impartial in their reception and treatment of the students, particularly new students. When the blindfolds are removed, the students find themselves surrounded by creatures (the professors in their attire) they have never seen before. The only recognizable living person besides themselves is the person who removed their blindfolds. Close by are two or

more of their acquaintances who are smeared with blood and
appear to be dead. The blood, of course, is animal rather
than human. The students are told to be calm but to take a
good look at everything around them. After this episode,
when it appears that they have seen enough, they are again
blindfolded and made to walk short distances on three different paths, holding each other by the hand. First, they are
made to walk a relatively smooth and straight path; then, a
rough, crooked, swampy path; and finally, they are led to
walk a smooth and a rough path up and down hills back to
the point they started from. The blindfolds are removed.
They are then given food and water and allowed some time
for rest. After resting they are told to repeat the process on
the double, but this time without the blindfolds. When this is
done and they are all back, they are told to take a bath in the
river, helping to wash each other's backs. When this is done,
they are brought into the center of the camp where, for the
first time, they are allowed to meet the other students who
have preceded them. These other students form a ring
around the initiates. They are then introduced to each other
one by one, after which they are all introduced to the Poro
professors, who are now dressed from the waist down. Each
of the professors makes a brief welcoming speech. Then the
elders present also make some brief remarks, telling the newcomers of their new responsibilities, of the meaning of what
they have seen and gone through, and of the fact that this is
just the beginning of what they are expected to see and go
through. They are assigned to living quarters. Then the boys
are left alone to talk. The excitement and joy of meeting old
friends and kinsmen are so intense that the boys usually
spend the whole night outdoors if the weather permits. The
"upperclassmen" (for want of a better term), or those
students who have recently been initiated, serve as hosts to
the new arrivals. The hosts are always anxious to entertain
their guests by telling them what they have been through
and how much they have already learned. The guests are

equally anxious to know what awaits them. When the limited store of experiences of the hosts are exhausted, and the storytellers begin to repeat themselves, the boys turn to singing. Most of the songs are not new to them, but this is the first time most of the newcomers have sung them, because only now are they free to do so openly; most of the songs are sung only by graduates and/or by those who are in school like themselves. These songs are sources of great sentiment and excitement for all members, representing a force that binds them to each other and the obligations which each one has to the other and to all graduates of Poro and Sande schools. These songs express their allegiance to the Poro school, Gbandeland, and the continent of Africa. The boys usually stay up all that night. They are joined by early visitors and by the advanced students who did not stay up with them during the night. They then sing a sentimental song, at which time they all hold hands and form a big circle. After this they have their first meal with the other students. When the meal is over, the boys are assigned to different work units. The number of units depends upon the size of the enrollment. Usually, there are no more than twenty persons to a unit. The Poro leaders believe this number to be an adequate one for effective work. Each unit is in constant competition with all other units.

Significance of Initiation

The activities described above are among the most important rituals in the initiation ceremony; therefore, each of them carries a special meaning. The first blindfold symbolizes a newborn individual who has arrived into the world helpless and sightless. The single person with whom the initiates find themselves and who removes their blindfolds symbolizes the interdependent nature of human beings; that is, he symbolizes the fact that regardless of their strength, humans can never be self-sufficient but must always depend

upon other human beings. The appearance of the Poro
professors in their full regalia symbolizes the beauty of Poro
membership and instills in the initiates the proper respect
and obedience to authorities and elders. Their acquaintances
who lay smeared with blood and who appeared to be dead
signify that blood is the supreme sacrifice and that they are
now dead to immaturity and born to maturity—that they are
now dead to stupidity in order that they may become wise.
They have traveled from childhood to manhood. They are
asked to look around them and to observe everything
symbolizing the fact that humans learn a great deal by
careful observation. The second blindfolding symbolizes the
fact that the world is basically an enigma and that no one
has a monopoly on understanding nature. Hence, humans
are to a certain extent in partial darkness as to what nature
will or will not do. The different kinds of paths the initiates
were told to walk blindfolded, holding hands, indicate that
in life one must expect moments of happiness and joy as well
as moments of bitterness and sorrow, that one can also experience a mixture or combination of all of them. The holding
of hands again signifies the interdependency of human
beings. The repetition of the walk later without blindfolds,
without holding hands, and on the double represents the
shortness of the life and daylight in which one can do useful
work. It also symbolizes the fact that the success of the
whole depends upon the contribution of each part; that is,
each member is expected to fulfill his obligations fully, for it
is in so doing that life takes on meaning. Finally, the coming
together of all members including the professors and the
placing of the initiates in the center mean that all members
have reciprocal obligations; the initiates now from the heart
of the school and the older members form the outer layer of
the school, protecting the new members.

For anyone to conceive of these or any other activities
of the Poro school as punishments or tests of endurance is to
misunderstand the functions of this school. These activities

are not meaningless games but a real preparation for the career of life upon which the society depends. As can be seen, the initiation component of the whole training occupies very little of the total time spent in the Poro school. The loyalty that develops among the members is a natural outcome of the constant association they have with each other under various circumstances, a relationship in which no member gives orders to another.

The initiation is repeated as each new group comes in because the students do not all enter the same day, week, or month. Newcomers have to be initiated just as new college freshmen have to be initiated. There is always excitement in participating in an initiation. It is the great moment that everybody looks forward to, because it brings about the rededication and reassurance of one's belonging to the group.

The Poro school is a conservative institution like any other school in that it is resistant to change, especially radical change or change emanating from an external force, such as Western ideology. Young men are often pulled away from Western schools for the purpose of receiving the traditional Poro school training. This may mean an interruption in Western school training of from one to four years for many Gbande boys. I personally know several young men who were taken out of government and missionary schools in order to receive their Poro school training and who later became employed by Firestone or some other foreign company as headmen, never re-entering those Western schools for further education. It is, therefore, misleading to emphasize only the initiatory functions of these societies. The term "secret society" should be reserved for such societies as the Leopard Society, Crocodile Society, or Snake Society whose members are not known by their communities. If anyone is suspected of being a member of such a society, he is usually asked to leave the community at once; if he fails to leave when requested, he is expelled. Members of secret societies are considered malevolent and therefore un-

desirable. These are the societies which are believed to have
a special type of initiation for new members. The members
and activities of these societies are not known except at the
level of speculation. They are never accepted or approved of
by the larger community in which they exist. The attributes
of these societies are the essence of secrecy. The term "secret
societies," if it is to convey any meaning at all, must be used
solely to describe these or similar societies and nothing else.

Both Poro and Sande are total formal educational institutions because of their compulsory nature among the
Gbande. Traditional Gbande society demands that every
boy and girl enroll in these schools. Consequently, the only
secrecy about these schools is in terms of the opposite sex.
Whatever goes on in the male school is supposed to be
withheld from females, as well as from those males who are
too young to attend. Likewise, the activities in the female
school are supposed to be withheld from males and from
younger females. These schools and their teachings are also
concealed from foreigners or strangers, male or female. One
of the characteristics of these schools is that nobody fails or
drops out.

Though the initiatory role of these schools takes only
one to two weeks at the most, the schools are conducted for
four years for the boys and three years for the girls. The initiation together with the training act as unifying forces in
these schools. (In contrast, the circumcision rite, which lasts
as long or longer than the initiations, does not produce any
new permanent social bonds.) In order to facilitate the
schooling, the school for each sex is held separately and at alternate periods; the Poro school is held four years, then the
following three years the Sande is held. Anyone who is of
age but who (for some reason such as being a newcomer to
Gbandeland, or being away from Gbandeland when his or
her sex was in training) has not attended these schools is considered *gbōlōwā*, which means "stupid."

In my description of the training given to the Poro men

and Sande women I shall focus mainly upon the former, since I am a graduate of the Poro school. With regard to the latter, the Sande, my knowledge is somewhat limited, since men are not permitted to know its teachings or operation. Nevertheless, I shall attempt to give as brief and accurate account of the Sande as is possible.

Poro

Generally the approximate ages of the Poro students at the time of matriculation range from eighteen to twenty-two, meaning that the approximate ages of the graduates range from twenty-two to twenty-six. However, in an extreme case of need, the entrance age required might be lowered considerably. I was twelve years old when I went into the Poro school and stayed there less than a year. This was because only eight months were left before graduation time and the next Poro school session was three to four years away. Since my parents were influential, they saw to it that I attended this particular session. (Besides, they wanted me to continue my Western schooling without a long interruption.)

There are three ways by which one matriculates into the Poro school. The first method of matriculation is simply enrollment by volunteers—those likely candidates who are twenty or older and have quietly realized the inevitability of such training. The second method is enrollment by a hesitant or reluctant inductee who is persuaded to join by having relatives and friends who are Poro members accompany him into the school. The third method of matriculation takes care of those boys who are frightened and will not go. Their matriculation, for lack of a better word, may be described as kidnapping. They are usually lured to an appropriate site by their male relatives or friends; there they are easily kidnapped. This was the method by which I myself was inducted into the school.

Each Gbande village has a permanent site for the Poro

and Sande school. It is believed that Gbande ancestors
selected these sites in the remote past. They are always well
preserved and are clearly marked off by all the paraphernalia which symbolize and identify them, in order to avoid
any mistake. These symbols of identification are designed for
members, potential members, and non-members as well.
Whether or not school is in session, the sites are reserved for
members and members only. No other persons are allowed to
go to these sites at any time. The violation of this rule (that
is, trespassing on the Poro site) is supposed to result in disappearance of the trespasser. But since even the very old
Gbandes cannot recall any such violation in their lifetimes,
the exact nature of the penalty is unknown. All that is known
is that an infraction of a Poro or Sande rule could carry a stiff
penalty, including the disappearance of the offender.

During the first year of the school the students are cared
for by their respective communities. After the first year the
school becomes self-supporting or relatively self-supporting,
except for things that cannot be obtained from the land. For
the first three years the students are kept in absolute
seclusion from the outside world, out of sight of the opposite
sex as well as of those who have not yet been enrolled in the
school. During these years both students and teachers are
under a rigorous and strenuous training schedule.

The subjects taught are diversified and require many
specialists to teach them. I shall mention some of the
required general subjects taught everybody, or those which
everybody is expected to know, and I shall also comment
briefly on the specific subjects. The first general subject is
history, beginning with the genealogy of each student, the
history of the Gbande people and their immediate neighbors,
and the history of the region of Africa of which they are a
part. Students are also taught the history of the continent of
Africa and the history of other lands—the lands of strangers.
The next general subject, classification of plants and animals,
is divided into study of those that are harmful and non-

harmful, those that are edible and non-edible, and those that can be used for emergency healing and those that cannot. Thirdly, students learn the planting seasons of the various types of crops and where they should be planted for maximum yield. Fourthly, students study the habitats of plants and animals and their breeding seasons. They are also expected to learn the positions of the sun, moon, and stars, for this is important in the planning of activities, and the different seasons of the year together with the activities suitable in each season. Socially, they learn how to get a wife or wives and what their subsequent responsibilities are; respect for old people and for women; tolerance for strangers, small children, and weak people; the art of sharing and caring for others, irrespective of who the other person is; loyalty to classmates and fellow graduates, male or female, to the community of which each becomes a member, to the rules of Gbandeland, and to the elders of the Porogee and Sandegee schools; and finally, the rights of the individual as expressed in the context of reciprocal relationships between seniors and juniors—obedience to one's senior and respect for the rights of one's juniors. These, among other things, are the general areas covered. Every student is expected to know this information. He may be tested orally by any of the Poro teachers on any subject at any time. The ability to perform well on these and other tests gives each young man his class ranking at the time of graduation.

Now we will examine the specific subjects taught during the three years of intensive training. First, each student is carefully observed from day to day by the experts so that they can discover his interests, talents, and potentialities. Once hidden abilities are discovered, a teacher (or teachers) specializing in that particular area directs the training of the student in the specialized area. Thus, every student is exposed to both general and specialized training. Sometimes training extends far beyond the four years required for graduation. For this reason, some of the young men may become

apprentices and remain so for many years after their graduation. The special skills are those needed by students
becoming herbalists, blacksmiths, specially skilled hunters,
and those persons who are given the responsibility of diag-
nosing different types of sicknesses. Some of these skills may
require as many as eight or more years of training before the
student achieves competency.

Landáy

During the three-year period of intensive training, the
young men are supposed to have been swallowed by one of
the super leaders of the Porogee called landáy. There are
many super leaders connected with the Porogee, and some
may be seen by anyone, including females and non-
members. There are also others who may be seen only by
graduates or by those who are in training. Each of these
super Poro leaders has a specific name. Besides landáy there
are ñágbày, lāneboge, and others. The generic
name for all of them is gafùi, which really means ñgali waláy
or "Big Things." (The term gafùi has been greatly confused
with the word gaf>wēn, because it has been defined as the
"Poro spirit." Actually the word gaf>wēn means "spirit" in
general and has nothing to do with the Poro school. Such
confusion is understandable. The pronunciation difference
between the two terms seems so slim that without a knowledge of the Gbande language it tends to disappear, and the
two terms become one and the same.)
    Now, let us return to the idea of the young men's being
swallowed by the landáy. The socio-psychological implications of this idea cannot be overstated. It serves as an agent
of social control because young boys are often told that if
they do not behave well, gafùi or ñgali walāy will swallow
them up. The ability of the landáy and those who are the
conductors of the school to swallow misbehaving boys is
regarded as both real and symbolic. It is real in the mind of

every Gbande boy to the extent that the future of each boy seems to hinge on what happens when he is "swallowed" by the *landáy*. Its symbolic meaning is crucial in understanding the deep religious meaning of this school. Symbolically, it means that the young men are now dead to all things childish and are born fully matured. At the end of the three years, the Poro students can be seen by anyone, women as well as non-members. However, they are not allowed to go into the village without escorts. They are escorted by the young men who were graduated in the previous class. The escorts serve as interpreters for the students when talking with their female relatives, friends, and other non-members. Interpreters are necessary not because of a difference in language or difficulty in communication, but because the students are not yet purged; hence they are forbidden by Poro rule from communicating with such persons without interpreters. Immediately prior to their appearance before non-members, their heads are shaved clean and their whole bodies from their heads down are heavily coated with pure white clay. The white clay represents the feces from the bowel of *landáy* who swallowed them during the time of their enrollment. Each student carries a white staff as a symbol of his status.

Graduation

On the day of graduation the students are rushed into a river very early in the morning. They are washed hurriedly by the Poro elders and are rushed out of the water by their big brothers who were their interpreters. Rushing in and out of the water is an absolute necessity because of the belief that the last person out of the water will be plagued with ill luck for the rest of his life. Moreover, it is believed that the *landáy* will also try to capture the slow ones, and if he succeeds, that will be the end of that student. I, myself, was helped by several big brothers; otherwise, I would not have made it. After

the washing the boys are conducted to a special hut where
the male leaders of Gbandeland and their male relatives
greet them. This is the moment of great family pride, and all
the elements of family rivalry are demonstrated at this time.
First, each family tries to buy the best and most expensive
suit for its graduate or graduates. Second, each tries to
present the most costly gift to its graduates. And third, each
tries to contribute conspicuously to the public feast which
terminates the school session, in order to gain public praise
and recognition. The feast lasts about two weeks, at the end
of which each graduate is given a new name in addition to
the general positional names given to the first and last
persons entering the school.

The new name of each graduate symbolizes his new
status, which means that he can now participate freely in important affairs of the community and is entitled to honor and
respect in any society that has this type of educational institution. His passport is a column of several marks running
from the back of his neck to the middle of his back and
branching out in a pair of columns under each arm. These
marks represent the imprints of the *landáy*'s teeth and were
supposed to have been made at the time the student was
swallowed. Since the *landáy* symbolizes death and rebirth,
those he has swallowed are new men, endowed with a mature sense of their responsibilities in their respective communities and Gbande society at large.

Classmates are identified by a common name irrespective of age or size. This common name is $s\bar{a}v>l>$, which
means "reciprocal obligation to one another." This obligation
extends to the families of the classmates at all times, even if
the fulfillment of such obligation means death. This type of
obligation extends also to all graduates of the Poro school, as
well as to those of the Sande school to a lesser degree. The
importance of these educational institutions cannot be overemphasized. They define and control the rules of social interaction in almost everything. One who has not been

Landáy

educated in either institution is considered a stupid person, for which the Gbande term is *bōlōwā mòin*. A stupid individual is a lonely person. He cannot get a marriage partner for himself; he cannot hold a political office; he cannot participate in any decision-making process; and he is not allowed to mingle freely with those who are graduates of these institutions. The restrictions imposed upon a *bōlōwā mòin* far exceed those enumerated above. What is important here is the functional role of these institutions which permeates all aspects of the Gbandes' way of life.

For example, any disputes between chiefs or two different groups are settled by Poro order. Both the announcement of the death of an important person and the burial of such a person are assumed by Poro leaders. The Porogee is the most integrative as well as the most conservative institution in Gbande society. For instance, it integrates all male graduates and to some extent integrates them with the Sande graduates. It encourages those who are not yet educated to become educated members of the society. This encouragement to the uneducated is based upon the firm belief that education is the essence of our human qualities, guiding our responses in both the familiar and the unfamiliar. Without education, a man is not much better off than the lower animals. The education received in these schools is so important that no one fails. All who enter are expected to graduate together because there is no dropping-out or re-entering. All members are considered men of unity. They can eat foods which are taboo to non-members or forbidden to members of the opposite sex. They share secrets and decide issues of community interest. Anyone who is not a graduate of these schools is not considered a human. One's status of manhood is reached only after the completion of Poro training. The Poro school is indeed the highest arbiter in Gbandeland. The Poro leaders are respected by kings, chiefs, and commoners alike. They are consulted on important matters and in such cases their decision is final. Without the Porogee, the life of Gbande males would be much less than what it is. This is no less true for the Lomas and Mendes and is true for the Gissies and Belles to a lesser extent. (These people are neighbors of the Gbandes.)

Circumcision

One other common error investigators make is to consider circumcision a crucial part of Poro school training; this emphasis is misplaced. Circumcision rites take place between the ages of six and ten years, which is several years before the boys are ready for the Poro school. Since there is no special site designated for circumcision, it can take place anywhere around the village. The circumcised boy may be visited by family and friends, both male and female, on the very evening of his circumcision. Although circumcision is a family affair, community members may contribute something; such contributions are much less than those given to the Poro school. The day of the actual circumcision is the only free field day for the initiates and their assistants. (More will be said about the free field day in following paragraphs.)

Boys are usually circumcised during November or December. As may be recalled, these are the months of the Harmattan, a cold, dusty, bitter wind. The circumcision is performed at about 5:00 or 6:00 A.M. by a specialist and his assistants. Because the specialist performs the operation with a straight razor and because stitches are not used, he is followed by his assistants who carry pieces of special freshly-cut sticks which ooze a yellowish kind of fluid. This fluid is dropped directly into the wound and causes the blood to coagulate almost at once. After the operation the boys are to remain perfectly quiet for about two to three hours in order to complete the coagulation and perhaps to ease the pain since no anesthesia has been used.

The free field day begins immediately after the operation. This is the day on which all the boys who have been circumcised previously but have not yet been educated in the
Poro school rush into the village singing the following song:
"Ya ya gbōlō lē n͡gga kē n͡gg>i waya n͡galī a gba lē." The term
gbōlō has no English equivalent, but the other part of the
phrase means "the razor has come down." While they are
singing they are allowed to catch chickens, cut bananas, pick
oranges, or get anything edible. Of course, even though the
initiates because of their wounds do not actively participate
in the fun, they are still the special honored guests and the
objects of the fun. After this free field day the initiates have
to be cared for by their families and friends. The boys
usually live on the outskirts of the village during the day, but
they spend the night together in any house large enough to
hold them. At the end of the first week they are taken to a
creek very early in the morning, about 4:30 or 5:00 A.M., and
they are told to sit down in the cold water and remain for at
least one to two hours. This is necessary in order to soften
the dead tissues around the wound. If there is no bad infection when their wounds are dressed, the initiates are now
free to move about and to engage in play and other activities. The boys are still required to live together until after
the second dressing of their wounds is removed, when they
are free to go home. If anyone's wound is not quite healed he
can make special visits to the surgeon for special attention
until his wound is healed. Let me point out that uncircum-
cised persons usually are not enrolled in the Poro school. If
such a person requests enrollment he is immediately circumcised and is not permitted to participate in any activity until
his wounds are healed. Obviously, these individuals often fall
behind in their assignments, causing their classmates to ridicule them. For this reason parents, especially fathers, want
their boys circumcised before they reach the age of entering
the Poro school.

Sande

The Sande, a formal school for girls, is open to all girls between the ages of twelve to fifteen. The first two of the three
years of training are spent in absolute seclusion from non-
member females and (as a rule) from all men except the
blacksmith, who is usually freed from such restrictions
because his role is vital to both Poro and Sande institutions.
(Members of both schools depend on the blacksmith to
provide the tools required for their various tasks.) The first
two years are said to be years of intensive training in all affairs designated for women. For example, they are taught
how to care for a husband and children and how to fulfill
their community responsibilities. They learn the rules
governing the relationships between co-wives, children,
in-laws, and potential husbands, and they learn the relationships between the graduates of the Poro and Sande
schools and between graduates and non-members of the
schools. They are said to be trained in all the rules concerning pregnancy. At the end of the two-year period of
seclusion the girls are free to be seen by their male relatives,
friends, and any non-members. As with the Poro men, the
Sande girls must be escorted by graduates who serve as interpreters for them during these encounters. The young
women are said to undergo a rigid type of initiation which is
culminated by clitoridectomy of each girl. Gbande men speculate that each student is responsible for preserving a portion of her clitoris after it has been cut off. After she dries it,
it is pulverized into powdery dust and kept securely until
graduation and marriage. When she gets married, a very
special secret ceremony takes place in which a bit of the
girl's flesh is mixed with ritual food which is unknowingly
eaten by her husband. This is supposed to cement the relationship between husband and wife by making them one
flesh and one blood. The unity of flesh and blood is believed

to be a prerequisite for prolificness, and the criterion of a successful marriage is the number of children. The ceremony also indicates that the girl was a virgin at the time of her marriage, a state desired for every bride by her parents and in-laws.

Although the above description is the one commonly given by men of Poro education, we cannot be certain at this time about our knowledge of the Sande school. The authenticity of the above description cannot be checked because of the sensitivity of the informants. It will have to remain a speculation, because it is taboo for anyone to ask a Sande graduate about any aspects of the Sande training or initiation. This is also true for the Poro school. This taboo is as old as Gbande society. We must wait until more is known about these institutions before any positive statements can be ventured.

No girl is eligible to marry until she has graduated from the Sande school. She is not permitted to participate in community affairs or to engage in a woman's activities until she is a graduate. As among the young men, the first and last of the young women enrolled are given positional names. The name given to the first girl enrolled is *gbanā*. It means "strong" or "hard." Symbolically, the word refers to the nature of the new social relationships between classmates and all previous graduates of the Poro and Sande schools and the relationship between their communities, including those that are neighbors or strangers. (The word "strong" or "hard" when used in connection with a social relationship by the Gbandes refers to a relationship which is faultless and sure and which is, or should be, understood by every Gbande.) The last person enrolled is given the name $k\bar{>}po$, meaning "war path," which is supposed to illustrate that knowledge is not inherited biologically or genetically but is achieved and therefore must be obtained through perseverance. The greatest enemy to be conquered is the self. If one is able to win over oneself, understanding and winning over others is only a matter of time. The name also implies the fruits of such a victory: respect for others and their property, love for children regardless of their relation, respect for one's husband, love for co-wives and old people, and so on. The student must attempt to achieve these goals. All other members of the school are also given new names which are said to be based upon other criteria.

In short, the purpose and significance of the Poro and Sande schools as educational institutions are the glorification and reaffirmation of traditional ways of life. These institutions are the most genuine and most conservative elements in the societies in which they exist. Their roles in present-day Gbande society are nothing less than a nativistic movement par excellence. This is because most Gbandes, especially the older ones, find no assurance of the preservation of human dignity in any other institution except the Poro and Sande schools. Therefore, they are anxious to maintain these traditional institutions, which are the very essence of the Gbande way of life. One does not become an adult simply by accumulation of years but by being trained in the Poro and Sande schools. Therefore, it is not advisable to allow those who are not so trained to participate in any serious affairs of life, whether the matter concerns only themselves or the community as a whole. If there is any single element which unifies the Gbandes and their neighbors, it is their joint membership in the Poro and Sande schools. This membership, which includes all graduates of these schools, entitles persons to call each other brother and sister and to have reciprocal obligations to each other. All disputes of major significance are settled by either Poro or Sande rules. Work that requires community effort or help required from neighbors during times of distress is regulated through the training received in these schools.

Western Education

Western formal education is not new among the Gbandes. As was pointed out before, the Holy Cross Mission of

Liberia, one of the best and oldest missionary schools in
this part of the Liberian hinterland, was built in Gbandeland by the Anglican Episcopal Church. This mission school
in Gbololahum was by far the most adequate institution of Western education in this area of Liberia. The only
other such institution was the one set up by the Liberian
government at Kololahum, one of the biggest towns in
Gbandeland, which is also the government headquarters of
the Western province and the residence of the Kololahum
District Commissioner. The history of the school is complex;
it was not an institution within itself but a part of the administrative mechanism of the national government for
reasons other than educational. At the end of two years the
whole school system faded away into oblivion. Many reasons
could be suggested for the failure of the school at that time. I
use the word "suggested" since there are usually no satisfac-
tory official records which could be used to confirm reasons
why government projects succeed or fail. Therefore, the
reasons suggested here are only strong educated guesses, but
they are probably close to the truth.

Before World War II there was little or no interest in
Western education, especially for the people of the hinterlands. Such interest when it existed was merely a glorified
novelty. In those days, the people of the hinterland were
somewhat subordinate to the government employees. Chiefs
were compelled to send their children to the government's
new school, and their failure to furnish enough students
often engendered heavy fines or sometimes dismissal from
their position. During that period there were few trained ed-
ucators or teachers available. In most cases, a teaching position was obtained through one's connection with people in
the government rather than through academic merit or excellence. The appointment of a teacher at Kololahum was
therefore made on the basis of his close relationship with the
District Commissioner or others in the echelons of the national government. Few of the teachers (or perhaps it is cor-

rect to say none of the teachers) in this school could have
had more than fifth or sixth grade educations.
The lack of facilities and materials also contributed to
the dissolution of the Kololahum school. The students
usually attended classes for one or two hours in the morning,
doing anything their teacher might think of: physical exercise, rudimentary addition, spelling, and so on. There was
neither a curriculum nor a required set of books. The teachers often did not know what they needed and were usually
uninterested in the school. They were more interested in the
prestige of being schoolmaster than in being a good teacher.
This was a school without chairs, benches, blackboards,
paper, or pencils. There were often no more than two sets of
old books, one set for the first grade and the other for the
second. Such books, soon either torn or lost, were not
replaced. Finally, the inadequate preparation of the teachers, coupled with their lack of interest in the school or in education in general, made it difficult for the school to survive
or grow. The school was nothing more than the old saying,
"When the blind lead the blind they will sooner or later fall
into the pit." So the school of Kololahum did end in obscurity; its eventual death was only a question of time.
Both the missionary and government schools among the
Gbandes excluded girls from their educational program.
Western school was thought to be for boys only. Although
the missionaries knew better, no attempt was made to
change this incorrect image of Western education. The
Western type of education was considered a waste of time
and a fulfillment of obligation to the government, like any
other obligation such as paying hut tax or head tax, rather
than something beneficial to the individual. For this reason
the boys sent to school were those who were considered lazy
or who were unable to contribute to the farm work or other
domestic work. In other words, it was not the best individual
who went to school but the one who was considered less
promising by traditional standards. Women were forbidden

simply because their place was in the home caring for their children and husband. Since Western education had no special goal in Gbande society, there was no need to send girls to school. This was the view held by the Gbandes. Of course, it has some justification from their point of view, because they were more or less ignorant of the place of Western education or its function. What is difficult to understand is why the government and the missionaries failed to encourage them to send girls to these schools. Throughout the continent of Africa there was a relative reluctance to educate women in general. Only since the Second World War have African girls seriously begun attending Western schools. Now, there are numerous Gbande girls who are interested in Western education for the purpose of getting a job.

Chapter 8
Communications

It is a known fact that society exists only in concerted action and that if men, who are capable of independent action, are to act together as a unit, each must somehow be able to anticipate what his associates are doing or are likely to do. Without some appreciation of such interaction to create effective and meaningful cooperation between its members, the existence of any society would be difficult if not impossible. How, then, can such appreciation be achieved? Direct mind-reading is apparently impossible and cannot be the answer. Man must settle for the best available substitute, which he set out to create. This substitute consists of the external gestures which are symbolic and are indications of inner experiences. When, and only when, these external gestures acquire common symbolic meanings for the interacting group do we have what is called "communication." Through communication, men interact by making inferences on the basis of these gestures.

In spite of the numerous possibilities for error through wrong inferences, concerted action rests solely upon the process of symbolic communication, without which cooperation of the kind that characterizes human society is virtually impossible. For this reason, communication is the touchstone of any society. Consensus is established through reciprocal role-taking, and role-taking is possible only in the context of meaningful communicative social interaction. The product of this type of communication is not merely the modification of the listener's attitude or behavior but also the establishment of some measure of consensus. "Consensus," as used here, is the sharing of perspectives by those cooperating in joint social action. It is an on-going process, a sharing that is built up, sustained, and further developed through a continuing interchange of meaningful gestures. The communicative process is not a single instance of stimulation and response like the reaction to a scream of terror, but a sequence of exchanges within a defined larger context. Consensus is rarely complete even for the purposes of a relatively simple enterprise. It is always partial, and there are invariably areas of uncertainty. It is the uncertainties that occasion most of the social interchanges between people who find themselves in a social situation. The uncertainties are successively minimized or eliminated with each gesture, enabling each person or participant to contribute his share and to enjoy greater confidence in the responses of others.

In most situations, then, communication is a continuous process. Men who are acting together try to develop and maintain mutual orientations in order better to coordinate their respective efforts, and the interplay must continue until the task is accomplished. The concept of "communication" as used here refers to that interaction and interchange of gestures through which consensus is developed, sustained, or broken. For this reason, the social behavior of human beings the world over consists of acquired responses to the meaningful responses of others. In other words, human interaction is a symbolic communicative interaction which involves a mutual exchange of meanings. The essential feature of this symbolic communication is that one person infers from the behavior of another (whether speech, gestures, or posture) what idea or feeling the other person is trying to convey. He then reacts not so much to the behavior as such but to the inferred idea or feeling. The other person then reacts to his response in terms of this idea or feels the meaning behind it.

Such a pattern of meaningful symbolic communicative

social interaction and exchange is, indeed, the essence of the Gbande society. Since the Gbande society is non-literate, its members must depend exclusively upon memory to impart their culture to the younger members of their society. The elders and the village historians are the Gbande library, encyclopedia, and dictionary. They are responsible for imparting knowledge of all kinds to the youth. They begin the memory training of the child as soon as he or she begins to talk. The training is intensified as the child grows older and culminates with the training in the Poro and Sande schools. The training starts with memorization of the child's own family tree, going back at least five or more generations. This is followed by memorization of important historical events. Memorization with great exactitude is regarded as the single most important device in communicating, as well as in mastering some areas of knowledge the Gbandes deem necessary such as folktales and folklore.

Gbande Society

Before continuing this discussion, I should mention that Gbande society is not only a non-literate society but also a small, early homogenous, and almost face-to-face-interacting society; its members have to depend upon the explicit meanings of the symbols used in their communication system. Ordinarily, we think of communication in linguistic terms. We are concerned primarily with phenomes, words, and sentences, among other things, and put less emphasis on the wide variety of acts that may serve as effective media of communication. Therefore, I submit that language is primarily a vocal actualization of the tendency to see realities symbolically, that it is precisely this quality which renders language a fit instrument for communication, and that it is in the actual give and take of social intercourse that language has been complicated and refined into the form in which it is known today. Besides the very general function which language fulfills in the spheres of thought, com-

munication, and expression, which are implicit in its very nature, there are a number of social derivatives of language
which are of particular interest to students of society. Language is a great force for socialization, probably the greatest
that exists. This statement refers not only to the obvious fact
that significant social intercourse is hardly possible without
language, but also to the fact that the mere existence of a
common language is a peculiarly potent symbol of the social
solidarity of those who speak it. The psychological significance of this goes far beyond the association of particular
languages with nationalities, political entities, or small local
groups.

The function of language in the acquisition and transmission of culture is obviously as important to the Gbandes
as it is to other human groups. This function is as important
in complex cultures as in cultures on the level of the Gbande
society. A great deal of the cultural stock of Gbande society
is presented to new members in a more or less well-defined
linguistic form. For example, proverbs, medicine formulae,
standardized prayers, folk tales, standard speeches, songs,
genealogies, and the history of important events in
Gbandeland and/or elsewhere in Africa are a few of the more
obvious cultural entities preserved through language. The
Western ideal is of pragmatic education, which aims to
minimize the influence of standardized lore and get the individual to educate himself through as direct a contact as possible with the realities of his environment. This ideal is certainly not realized among the Gbandes, who are often as
word-bound as the humanistic tradition itself. Thus, those
who are endowed with strong lungs and a good quality of
voice do not go without social rewards.

Village Crier

For example, a man who is endowed with strong lungs and a
good voice, by Gbande standards, is elected by the elders of

his village to a position of extreme importance and responsibility, that of the village crier. The village crier has the subtle responsibility to alert the members of his village at all times about all up-coming important events. He is the mouthpiece of the village elders and leaders and the ears of the village masses. As a rule, the Gbandes are not time-bound and time-conscious as Westerners are, except when it is absolutely imperative; in this case, the meaning of the activities of the village crier become clear. The pitch of his voice and the number of times he cries as well as the rate of speed with which he goes around the village are somehow related to the urgency of the matter he is announcing. For example, if the pitch of his voice is very high and if he runs fast around the village four times, this signifies that he is summoning all eligible men to meet at once in the designated village meeting place. If he goes once around the village very slowly and calls in a loud low-pitched voice, he is summoning only the elders and leaders of the village to meet. If his voice is of medium pitch—a pitch between the two described above—and if he goes around the village more than once but not more than three times, this suggests that all eligible men should be in readiness for a meeting or for action of some sort in the near future. The important role played by the village crier among these peoples cannot be over-emphasized. He is the watchman of his village, who guards the village against any surprise event. He is the radio, television, telegram, newspaper, and open letter to the villagers.

Horn

The horn as a means of mass communication is irreplaceable in Gbandeland because it is both easier to carry and easier to learn to play than, for example, the drum. Moreover, the horn does not require any maintenance, or not as much maintenance as the drum, because it has no strings or leather as does the drum. Because of its simplicity and its ever-readiness, the horn is widely used as an instrument of dissemination of news throughout Gbandeland. The horn is used to warn the Gbande people about an approaching stranger or any unusual phenomenon. It is also used to summon eligible men to a designated place for work or for any other activity requiring communal participation. It may be an activity requiring an immediate decision after public debate and discussion. The horn is also used to announce the arrival and/or departure of important individuals. The horns that are popular for these purposes are those of the elk and wild or bush cow; sometimes the tusk of the elephant is used for the same purpose. Any adult Gbande male can blow a horn. The only horn which is blown by a special individual is the one which announces the arrival and departure of an elite individual. The other horns can be blown by any adult male who is designated by his village leader to perform this task.

Drums

Another medium of mass communication among the Gbandes is the drum. Contrary to popular opinion, the drum is not as important a medium of mass communication as the horn among this people. In the first place, drumming requires far more complex skills than blowing a horn. Furthermore, drums are used more for entertainments of various kinds than for communication of news. One of the main differences between the use of horn and drum as communicative instruments is the fact that the horn is used almost exclusively to convey immediate news of importance to the community or to certain members of the community, whereas the communicative role of the drum is primarily restricted to religious festivities and other merry-making activities. It is also used to accompany chiefs and other important individuals. The functions of the drum described here do fall

Drum

within the legitimate realm of mass communication, but they are obviously of a different order. Let me hasten to point out that the use of the drum to send messages from village to village was already a lost art at the time of my observation. Any Gbande younger than forty would be unable to understand or to remember messages conveyed by drums between

villages. As a musical instrument, the drum does communicate with and indeed stimulate a large body of Gbandes
at one time. Besides accompanying chiefs, it may be used by
workers, as are other musical instruments. Its biggest and
perhaps most clear-cut function is to stimulate interaction. It
tends to have a catalytic as well as cathartic effect upon the
participants. In this case, the drum is an instrument of communication in a very general sense. Nonetheless, the time
has long passed when the drum was used for intra-village
and intra-tribal (ethnic) communication.

The popular *taaniñggi*, commonly known as the "talking
drum," does not really talk any more than does any other
drum or musical instrument. I can only speculate on the
reason for such a designation by Western people. In the first
place, this type of drum is sufficiently small to be manipulated in the armpit. The manipulation is made possible by
numerous strings which hold the monkey skin forming the
two drumheads. The player controls the tones by tightening
and relaxing the strings in his armpit and at the same time
beating the drum with a specially prepared drumstick. This
act produces a rapid change of tones, which gave rise to the
idea of talking by those who know less or nothing about this
drum or about African languages. The change of tone is not
and does not represent a language in itself even for the
Gbandes. Rather it demonstrates the talent of the artist, or
drummer. There is no school to train *taaniñggi* players, and
yet there are a few Gbande males who have acquired the
proficiency of *taaniñggi* players. Such persons must rely
upon their native ability and inner urge to be a *taaniñggi*
player, disciplining themselves to long hours of practice. One
of the reasons for anyone's wanting to be a *taaniñggi* player
is that the *taaniñggi* is the most used and most prestigious
drum in Gbandeland. Its player must also be a vocalist. The
taaniñggi may be played singly or in a pair. It may be played
for entertainment or to accompany important individuals, as
is the case with the horn. The horn is not a substitute for the

taaniñggi when it accompanies a leading figure, because the horn is limited to the announcement of arrival and departure of such individuals. On the other hand, the *taaniñggi* is played at both these times, as well as morning and evening and at other times, to provide entertainment for such leading figures and their guests. Certainly, one cannot deny that these functions make *taaniñggi* drumming a form of mass communication. The *taaniñggi* is versatile in its uses and meanings because it is varied in its tones. But the horn is even more versatile in its uses and meanings because a player can vary its tone or pitch more. Hence, as a medium of communication, the horn is much more important than the drum, because it may relate to the whole community or to a specific group or groups within the community.

Gbɛkày

An instrument which is perhaps less important than the horn and the drum as a communicative apparatus is the *gbɛkày*, a stringed instrument somewhat resembling a guitar in function. It is used by both adult men and adolescent boys in solving riddles of different levels of complexity. Its function is the communication and keeping alive of ancient myths and legends. It teaches the young men the art of deductive reasoning and helps adult men improve their reasoning. This form of communication, combining teaching and entertainment, is usually a nighttime activity. There are basically three tones or pitches made by the player of this instrument. For example, there are tones indicating to the panelists or those attempting to solve the riddle that they are on the right course. There are other tones indicating that the panelists are completely off course, and finally, there are also tones for "yes" responses. (This kind of communication reminds me of the television game "What's My Line.") The experts tell the riddle to the player of the *gbɛkày* in private. When they gather together, the young men begin the questions by identifying broad categories such as: animals; men-women (to them men and women are not animals); vegetables; or minerals. Once the general category is established, the young men take turns asking questions. As long as one is on the right course he will continue to ask until he gets a "no" answer; then the next in line takes it up, and so on until the riddle is solved. If the player is not sure how to answer a double-barreled or doubtful question, he confers with the experts—the adults. The opinion of the experts is not subject to dispute. This kind of communication bridges the past, present, and future in such a way that there could be no generation gap between old and young in the traditional Gbande society. The riddle and the response given by the *gbɛkày* are virtually the same throughout Gbandeland, so that when one learns the solution of a given riddle in one village, one can have little or no difficulty in solving the same riddle in another village. In this sense, it is a device of mass communication to a given audience among this people.

Other Instruments for Communication

Let us now turn to communicative devices other than musical instruments. These do not have sounds in themselves; rather they are symbolic elements of mass communication. They are: the elephant tail, horse tail, and cow tail. They are listed here in the order of their importance. All three are used to transmit information from leader to leader or from an elite individual to subordinate leaders. However, the information they disseminate varies in intensity, from the elephant's tail for the most intense to the cow's tail for the least. They are like telegrams or special delivery letters in Western countries. Each village has in readiness a number of fast runners who are responsible for keeping themselves in good shape and ready to go at any time. The message is whispered in the ears of each runner four times; he repeats it four times and immediately takes the symbol of the message and runs as fast as he can to the next village, straight to the chief's house, where he is met by the runner of that village. He repeats the message to the new runner in the presence of the chief four times. The new runner likewise repeats it four times and takes it to the next village. This continues until the message gets to its destination, where its content is disclosed to the masses. This must be done by the chief to whom it was sent before the other chiefs or leaders tell it to their people.

The fastest runner is not always the best messenger. The best messenger is one who is both fast and mature and who is capable of reporting news accurately. The best messengers are used in carrying messages symbolized by the elephant tail, which is the symbol of the most important message. The elephant tail symbolizes the enormity of the matter or problem, which requires diligent deliberation, perhaps for several days or weeks, before a decision can be reached. The decision arising from an elephant-tail message may be made by the whole Gbande society or leaders and be implemented by them, or it may be made by a region or regions, but it is never made by the villages alone.

In similar manner, the horse tail, next in the order of importance, is received and carried from village to village and from hand to hand until it reaches its destination. At this point, the recipient promptly announces the reason or the content of the message to his people. Then other village chiefs or leaders proclaim the news to their people. Messages associated with or symbolized by the horse tail are conveyed by the fastest runners, but they need not be as mature as those associated with the elephant tails. The horse tail symbolizes a matter of great urgency which requires an immediate response. It is a matter which must be decided at the village level instead of the regional level. Although the decision takes place at the village level, the sum of the village decisions expresses the opinion of the Gbande people, and implementation may affect the whole society. Young men or adolescents are expected to play a significant role in making village decisions. Besides these functions, the elephant and horse tails are sometimes carried by elite individuals as symbols of their respective social positions. In this case, these symbols have two meanings. They represent the scope of their carrier's influence and the length of time that their carrier has occupied his social position. They may also be related to the age of their carrier. Old age is an honored position.

The cow tail's symbolic function as a medium of mass communication is similar to that of the elephant and horse tails. However, it is less exciting because it suggests a warning based upon a speculation and may or may not require any action. It alerts the Gbandes to an eventuality. As the Gbandes say, "To be alerted is better than to be taken by surprise." For this reason, the cow tail is an important element of mass communication for the Gbandes. Besides the general communicative function described above, the cow tail is used as an integral part of the tallest Poro Being as he dances. This dancer is called the *lánib>géy*. I am not sure what the significance of the cow tail's use by the *lánib>géy* is, except that it keeps his hand occupied as he dances. Cow tails are sometimes used by dancers who skillfully and gracefully manipulate them as they dance, apparently to give their movements an added dimension of grace. From this point of view, the cow tail is a sign of social status like the elephant and horse tails, but to a much lesser extent.

What is of prime importance is that, although there are elements of similarity and difference between these media of communication, the message which each conveys is unmistakeably clear to every Gbande adult and adolescent. Without the use of these instruments as media of mass communication, it would be difficult to alert the Gbande people to impending events that merit their attention. One cannot sufficiently emphasize the importance of these communicative devices in Gbandeland and how much the planning of daily routines is dependent upon them. In the absence of the telephone, these instruments serve as the means of summoning the people from far and near in the shortest possible time to meet at a designated place. The relay method of carrying important messages is also used in carrying letters from Monrovia and other points of dissemination to outposts of government employees and missionaries. The letter is covered neatly with specially treated leaves to keep it from getting wet or smeared. It is carried by placing it in the split of a slender stick about two feet long. Once it is wedged deep in the split end of this stick, it is tied securely in place with a homemade twine. Once this is done, it is carried from village to village by the village runners as described before. The letter is considered as important as the elephant tail because of the distance it has to cover to get to its destination. Such a letter is addressed to an individual, as letters usually are, but for the Gbandes the post or destination is more important than the person to whom it is addressed. This is why it can be covered up and yet get to its destination. Its destination is spoken four times to each new carrier, who repeats it each time in the presence of the chief or headman. Even if the letter was not covered, the carriers would not be able to read the name of the owner.

By way of conjecture, let me propose that important forms of communication also emanate from animals and plants. People in Western countries (those who can afford it) generally go to bed late and get up with the alarm clock. Among the Gbandes, people go to bed when it is too dark to do anything, particularly when the moon is not shining, and get up with the chickens, especially the rooster. The roosters are the faithful and dependable timekeepers—far better than alarm clocks in Gbandeland. It has been observed that each rooster crows at three o'clock every morning for a given number of times for about fifteen minutes, then stops. At about five o'clock in the morning the roosters start crowing again and continue to do so until daylight. They crow again at noon and at five o'clock in the evening, each time for

about fifteen minutes. Activities in Gbandeland are as much
regulated by these roosters as life in Western countries is
regulated by clocks. When to get up, when to eat, and when
to go off work depend, to some extent, upon the voices of the
ever-ready faithful timekeepers, the roosters. Very often if
people want to undertake an early trip, they arrange to leave
at either the first crowing or the second crowing of the
rooster, which is equivalent approximately to 3:30 or 5:30 A.M.

There is also a species of wild bird which the Gbandes
call the *tutùy*. I do not know the Western name for this bird.
I found a number of adult Gbandes, both male and female,
who claimed to understand this bird. I was taught to in-
terpret a few calls. Meanings are attached to the frequency
and pitch, as well as the number of times the bird calls. A
certain pitch and frequency and number of times indicate
that it will rain soon, that hostile or friendly strangers are
coming, or that it is wise or unwise to undertake certain en-
deavors. The Gbande pays attention to the rooster and to
this species of bird in regulating his behavior. From this
point of view, I feel they constitute a legitimate component
of the Gbande communicative system. But it is not at all
difficult to err in interpretation of the rooster or the *tutùy*
message, even if one is a Gbande. For example, a rooster
awakened suddenly may mistake moonlight for daylight and
crow prematurely. This happens frequently, according to the
Gbandes. Likewise, since the message of the *tutùy* depends
upon the pitch, frequency, and number of times it calls, if it
does not repeat the full call a listener may easily miscount
the number of times it called or miss the pitch level. The
errors are entirely the fault of the interpreter, not the bird.
For this reason, the meanings of this form of mass communication, although accepted by this people, can only be
conjectural.

There is one form of mass communication which is used
only by members of the Poro school when the school is in
session. This form of communication is a loud cry uttered by

either the initiates and/or their chaperon to warn all unini-
tiates and females to get out of their path as quickly as possible and to hide themselves and their faces from the initiates. This is the cry of death; that is, "Death! Death!" is the
meaning of the cry "*Sāysày*." A similar but not identical cry
is uttered by the initiates and/or chaperons of the Sande
school for a similar reason—that is, to warn uninitiated girls
and all males away from their path. This form of communication is understood by every Gbande. Its symbolic
meaning is intrinsic to the Gbande social control system.

The Gbandes also have universal "No Trespassing"
symbols as well as symbols indicating intention to own land
or property for a year. If a man wishes to restrict a new path
he has made, which more often than not leads to something
of interest to him, he simply pulls up stalks of a certain type
of tropical grass of the sugar cane family and places them at
the entrance of the new path. No one will knowingly jump
over them, particularly not women or uninitiated men. The
pathmaker alone has the right to jump over them. Every
adult, initiated, Gbande male is eligible to use them. This
grass is a universal symbol of restriction and is so recognized
and respected by every Gbande. If one is invited by the man
who set up the restriction, the man has to remove the stalks,
let his visitor in, and replace the stalks. He repeats this
procedure to let his visitor out.

Another symbolic communication of this nature is the
placing of a bunch of leaves in a specially designed stick
which is split at the top end to hold the leaves. The stick
with the leaves is then placed in a clearing where it is visible
to anyone who passes by. This is a sign of intention to own a
piece of land temporarily for a farm site for that year. (For
further details, see Chapter 3 "The Gbande Mode of Making
a Living," subsection "Subsistence Crops.")

Some other media of mass communication, designed for
specific groups, are not discussed here. I am referring to
those symbols of communication whose meanings are known

only to Poro and Sande members and those that are known
only to Poro and Sande leaders. There are also means of
communication open only to doctors (called medicine men).
I omit them simply because they are extremely limited and
restricted to a small segment of the Gbande people.

Chapter 9
The Gbande Religion

RELIGION IS VERY important and pervasive among the Gbandes, and unless a person understands it thoroughly, he will find it difficult, if not impossible, to understand Gbande society. I must hasten to point out at the onset that it is a bit misleading to consider the Gbande religion a typical religious institution, since it is a practicing one which permeates the whole of Gbande life. By its very nature, it cannot be separated from the daily routine of life. The Gbande religion involves ultimate values for this people because it is intertwined in the fabric of their lives. There is neither an established day of worship nor a hut in which to worship. The Gbandes do not have a paid religious functionary per se, nor can any village or any separate group be considered a typical community of worshippers. The entire Gbandeland constitutes the religious community and all the Gbandes are the worshippers. Nonetheless, a discussion of any religion, whether or not it has any of the above attributes, must rightly begin with the deities, the supernaturals, or the gods.

The Gbandes, recognize at least four types of deities in the hierarchical structure of their society. First, there is God, the creator, who is supreme and who is the giver of all things, good and bad. Second, there are the ancestor spirits. These spirits are the intermediaries between the living and the supreme God. The Gbandes believe that the living can never communicate with the supreme God because they are too sinful to associate directly with perfection, the essence of God. The ancestors, who have been purged by the penalty of death, are now in a position to intercede on behalf of the living members of their kin group. They are always in the presence of the living members of their families to mete out punishments and rewards to them. The ancestor spirits are always just in their judgment, and they are ardently devoted to the protection and well-being of the members of their kinship groups. They must be consulted by either the whole kinship group, the family, or the individual members of the family before any undertaking, large or small, is begun. Before the family members eat or drink, these spirits must be fed or given drink by one member's spilling a little on the floor. The ancestor spirits are addressed by name by the elder of each household when a big decision is to be made or an important matter comes before the family. They are consulted about everything in the affairs of life. They are said to be very jealous and very demanding at all times, and therefore they must be satisfied. The Gbandes firmly believe that the living are only happy if the ancestor spirits are made happy. Therefore, in Gbande society written rules or laws are not needed to regulate an individual's behavior, nor is anyone needed to enforce such rules or laws. The ancestor spirits' watchful eyes are forever upon every adult in Gbande society. One cannot bring disgrace upon one's ancestor; hence there is a built-in social control system in Gbandeland that needs no explicit law or policemen to enforce it.

The next group of deities, third in importance, are the non-ancestor spirits. They are, at times, unpredictable in behavior. They can be mischievous and unrestrained harmless nuisances, simply to amuse themselves. They are said to have the ability to transform themselves into any form they desire —a man or woman, a young or old person, an animal or a plant, or any other object. Because of their plasticity, they are said to be unpredictable in their behavior. The non-ancestor spirits can also be manipulated by some individuals who claim to understand them either through a friendship with such spirits or through some secret powers which they have over these spirits. Such individuals are said to have complete control over these spirits and they can use them to benefit either themselves or their friends or to harm their enemies. On the whole, these spirits are unlike the ancestor spirits in that they are controlled by those individuals who understand them. They neither punish nor reward; they only do what is requested. They may be extremely good or extremely bad depending on what their manipulator wishes. They are said to live under water or in a very thick forest, but they can usually appear to those who know them, either in a dream or in a pre-arranged meeting at some secret place.

The fourth group of deities are the natural forces or natural phenomena such as lightning, thunder, rain, rocks, trees, or a particular forest. All these are also subject to manipulation. Because of their presence in the bush, one cannot have sexual intercourse there or do anything else which might pollute the bush, thereby offending them. They are a bit more difficult to understand and they are not particularly friendly. They can be used by the ancestor spirits or non-ancestor spirits as well as by those of the living who are trained to deal with them.

Birth

The role of religion in crises such as birth, the rite of passage,° sickness, and death cannot be overemphasized. Although the Gbandes have full knowledge of conception, pregnancy, and childbirth, they still give religious significance to them by crediting the ancestors for every birth. In times past, birth among the Gbandes was a serious crisis for

---

°In a "rite of passage" the adolescent becomes fully integrated into adult status in society. The rite of passage for Gbande boys and girls is called the Poro and Sande respectively. See Chapter 7 "Educational Institutions" for a full discussion of this.

the mother, the child in particular, their relatives, and the community in general. Childbirth was considered an actual engagement in the war between man and nature because of the risk involved in having a child. Therefore, traditionally, childbirth never took place in a hut or house or within a fenced-in area, because it was thought that one could fight better in an open area rather than in an enclosure. Consequently, birth sites were prepared in the bush some distance away from the village. The sites were usually chosen by the leading woman doctor or *sowoi* in the village, or less often by the midwife if she was not already the village female doctor. A new site was picked for every birth crisis. However, a site would be used again if it was thought to be connected with good luck. When the site was prepared, the woman in labor was walked to it by the eligible women of the village. (Eligible women are those who have had two or more children.) It is believed that when they arrived they formed a circle around the prepared spot and placed the woman inside it. Then she was told to walk the inner edge of the circle; as she did this, she was beaten with branches, lightly at first, and was told to bear down and try hard. The more the labor pain progressed, the harder the beating and the louder the command for her to try hard. If she was a strong, determined individual, as most Gbande women are, she obeyed, bore the pain, and gave birth to the child. However, there were some weak individuals who could not bear the pain and who became exhausted and died. This happened in relatively few cases, but even these were far too many.°

As has been pointed out elsewhere, the Gbandes

° This account of traditional childbirth is an educated speculation, since it is difficult to make this observation at this time and equally difficult to get any adult Gbande female to discuss this phenomenon. My speculation is based upon discussing the matter with a number of adult Gbande men at different times who gave the same account or explanation.

strongly believe in reincarnation—that the newborn individual is an ancestor who has returned to his or her children in the form of a child. Therefore, a child is given deference until he assumes his adult status and self-identity, as mentioned previously. If an infant dies, which is very often the case, no mourning is permitted; rather, the family is examined seriously with the help of a doctor to determine why the ancestor chose to leave them. Many sacrifices are made and rites of purification are conducted in order to appease the anger of the ancestor spirits. The death of an infant is rarely attributed to disease but is considered witchcraft done by a person who is jealous of the child's parents or angered at mistreatment of the child, since it is still an ancestor. No one is allowed to grieve or even talk about the death of a child. One is not allowed to show a mirror to an infant or child or let him look into a mirror, because it is believed that mirrors will show the child the way back to the other ancestors from which he came. The infant must be loved, honored, and attended to at all times for fear he may find company with the ancestor spirits.

The naming of the baby is a solemn occasion among the Gbandes. As the newborn individual is considered a relative returning home from a long journey, there must be ample time for rest before any entertainment is provided. If the child is a girl, the rest period is three days; if it is a boy, four days. During the rest period, only certain persons are permitted to visit the mother and child. They are the mother's sisters, the child's grandmothers, the female doctors of the village, the midwife and her assistants, and the village blacksmith. After this, the ritual of the birth ceremony to welcome the child beings with the announcement of his or her name. This is the day the father is allowed to hold his child for the first time. The baby is given the name of one of his mother's or father's ancestors. From that moment on, the father and mother address the child by a pet name; that is, if he was named after his grandfather or grandmother, he will be called *k'ɛwāla* (grandpa) or *mamā* (grandma). For the most part, the use of such a pet name will continue until the child assumes his self-identity and his own personality. Immediately following the naming ceremony the father and especially the mother take on the name of their child; for example, the mother may be called $d>b>njee$, which means "$d>b>njee$ mother." (The word $d>b>njee$ means "bush"; hence she is now "bush's mother.") As mentioned before, a stranger coming to the village afterwards would have a difficult finding out the real names of the parents. A modest feast of chicken, rice, and palm oil is given in honor of the ancestors to thank them for allowing one of them to return. The rice is cooked separate from the chickens which are cooked in palm oil. Then the rice is mixed with the chicken and the oil, and the mixture is carried to the graves of the ancestors and placed on banana leaves which have been spread on the graves. The food is covered with banana leaves and remains covered on the graves for at least one hour, the normal amount of time taken for a Gbande meal. It is expected that the ancestors will finish eating in that time. The food is then uncovered in the presence of the husband's relatives by the elders, who announce that the ancestors have indeed eaten, although the food does not appear to be disturbed. The elders then eat from the graves, but they leave a lot of food there for the children, who are anxious to get their share. The waiting children need not be relatives. They scramble for the remaining food. After this meal, the infant is dressed with all the paraphernalia and talismans designed to keep him from returning to the ancestors' world and to protect him from misfortune. From this point on, the major responsibility for the personal care and welfare of the infant falls to the mother.

Sickness

Sicknesses that are fairly common and occur frequently are treated by individuals who are trained in the Poro and Sande schools to deal with them. However, when the sickness is an unusual one and not easily understood a *sowì* (described at the beginning of Chapter 2 "The Gbandes and Their Neighbors," subsection "Lomas"), who is also a religious functionary, is asked to come and call upon the ancestor spirits. He asks the spirits to reveal the cause of the sickness and disclose what the sick person and his relatives must do for the restoration of his health. These performances are done in secret as a rule, and it is therefore difficult to include a discussion of them. However, in one instance I witnessed an occasion such as this. A man was critically ill and a female *sowì* was called in. She came dressed like any Gbande woman in ordinary dress. She carried a homemade basket which was packed with paraphernalia. She selected a young man among the spectators to help her and she made him sit on a mat in the center of the floor of the sick man's hut. She placed a bundle of small sticks into his hands and recited some phrases which I could not understand. As she continued to do this for about twenty to twenty-five minutes, the young man began to quiver and temble and began thrashing on the mat. The *sowì* claimed to be communicating with the ancestor spirits through the young man. As she did this, the *sowì* herself tended to be in a semi-trance and began to talk with the young man in a language not understood by anyone. The young man responded in a similar manner. This went on for about three or four hours. When it was all over, she said that it was too late for her to do anything for the sick man. The sick man died the next day.

Death

The death of an adult among the Gbandes is an affair which brings together all the members of the kinship group. There are usually three reasons given for the death of an adult: the ancestors wanted him, someone witched him, or a witch within himself killed him. The third cause of death is relatively easy for the Gbande to test. A piece of the deceased's liver is placed into a receptacle of water. If it sinks, then his death was caused by a witch within himself, but if it floats, then someone else killed him. No one ever deliberately joins with a witch or buys one. Those who have a witch never know they have one. It it is found that the deceased had a witch, the family is deeply shamed. In this case, the body is usually buried very carefully by a doctor to make sure that the deceased's spirit does not wander aimlessly to harass the living. However, later there may be disturbances, especially at night. Sometimes a whole village is believed to be harassed by such a spirit. It usually starts with the members of one household who, for one reason or another, start yelling very loudly. Once such a cry is heard, the whole village joins in. If the villagers continue to be restless at night, a doctor is employed to help the situation. He usually recommends that the body be removed from the grave and burned in a designated place. The burning of the corpse, in most cases, ends the harassment of the village. It is believed that such a corpse does not join the ancestor spirit hierarchy and does not become reincarnated. Those who die because of other witches do join the honored group of ancestor spirits and do become reincarnated as children.

Let us examine a little more closely the death and burial ritual, for obviously death is usually followed by the disposing of the body. For the Gbandes, as for most cultures of the world, the dead body is usually buried, except in the situation described above. In that case, the body of such an individual is cremated and it is considered completely destroyed, meaning an ultimate end for that individual. The Gbandes bury their dead by wrapping the body in several layers of cloth and then in mats, instead of sealing their dead in coffins. The body is first bathed and dressed in clean clothes. It the deceased is a *sowoi* or other important man in the village this is done secretly by the leaders of the Poro school; if the deceased is a woman, the Sande leaders perform these duties. The common man or woman is attended to by his friends or kinsmen. The body is then buried either in a regular cemetery or beside the big hut of the family or in the yard of the deceased's family. Burial beside the family hut or in the yard of the family is a privilege usually reserved for those who die in old age or those who have supposedly been killed by witchcraft. When those suspected of having been killed by witchcraft are buried, they are provided with weapons such as sticks with thorns, bow and arrows, or swords. It is believed that with these weapons the spirit of the deceased will hunt its killer. If anyone should die within a month of another person's death, it is assumed implicitly that the second person to die was responsible for the death of the first. If another person should die within a month of the second person, the death of the third person is attributed to the same cause—that is, that he or she collaborated in causing the death of the first person. The Gbandes can go on and on with this type of reasoning as long as there are deaths occuring within a month of each other. However, if anyone dies a month or two after the last death in the village, the new death is caused by a new phenomenon; consequently, the cycle would start over again.

The dead person does not enter the spirit world at once. It takes three or four days after burial, depending on the sex of the deceased, before he enters into the spirit world. This event is consummated by a specific ritual called the "breaking of the grave" or *ka mbày wolonga*. For a woman, it takes three days to flatten out the grave and dress it and to offer sacrifices of food and other things; for a man, it takes four days. The ritual is designed, to a lesser extent, to announce to the ancestors the coming of a new individual to join them; they are asked to accept the new member. More important, however, is the assurance for the living that everything has been performed correctly; it is hoped that the new spirit will stimulate the old ancestors to give new blessings. One of the first performances in honor of the dead

is the mourning or $w>l>hày$, which starts immediately at
death. The overt mourning is restricted to female relatives.
All or most of the female relatives must cry at least three
times a day—early in the morning, at noon, and late in the
evening. But when relatives come from another village to
console the bereaved, the visiting female relatives start
yelling and crying as loudly as possible just before entering
the village of the deceased. They are greeted in a similar
fashion by the females of the deceased's family. This practice
is continued until the day of the final ritual—the flattening
out and dressing of the grave. During this period, if the
deceased was a married man, his wife or wives would shave
their heads and put on white clay during the period of
mourning. In olden times, the deceased's body was usually
kept for two days before burial. During these two days any
person to whom the deceased was privately indebted entered the place where the dead man's body lay. The body lay
in a reclining position with the head slightly raised. The man
sat down on a stool directly in front of the body and told the
relatives and friends of the deceased that he wanted to talk
to the dead person in their presence. At this announcement,
everybody fell completely silent. He began by calling the
deceased by name, addressing him as follows: "Monlū, you
owed me so and so which you promised to pay, but you
never got to pay me until this day. The amount which you
owed me is exactly so and so. As I am looking straight into
your eyes, you know that I am telling the truth. Good luck
on your journey." Those to whom the deceased was indebted
had to come in and make their claims looking straight into
the face of the deceased, because it is believed that no one
has the heart to look into the face of a dead person and lie.
Debts claimed in this manner were paid immediately by the
kinsmen of the deceased; debts not claimed as prescribed by
this custom were not honored.

   During the final death ritual the ancestor spirits are called
upon to ask God, the creator, to forgive the mourners of any
sins they may have committed which may have caused the

death of the family member. All the immediate members of the deceased's family go through a rite of purification, thus ending the death ritual. The village *sowòi* sprinkles the men, women, and children with *salèy* or medicine from a bucket. They then proceed to their respective daily bathing areas behind the hut and also bathe in the *salèy*. They put on new clothes there, leaving the old clothes to the *sowì*.

Life After Death

The Gbandes do have a concept of heaven and hell, but both heaven and hell are part of the social world shaped by the living and the dead. Heaven is designed for most people because the creator wants his work of creation to continue throughout eternity. This gives rise to belief in reincarnation. Those who are reincarnated are those in heaven, because they never die. Those whose bodies are subject to cremation are those in hell, because they are subject to eternal death by total destruction. For the Gbandes, heaven means eternal life and hell means fire. Hell does not mean everlasting fire, as implied in Christianity; for the Gbandes, destruction by fire is complete and immediate extinction. Therefore, those whose bodies are judged unfit are cremated at once, and their destruction is complete and final.

The Gbandes do not believe that death is an end to everything except for those who are cremated. They believe that there are individuals who are not ready for heaven, the spirit community, or cremation. These individuals are said to leave their community for a faraway land after death. There they remain as living persons and send gifts to their families. These individuals are ready and willing to meet any of their old acquaintances who are still living and have not yet heard of their death. At times, it is believed, these dead who return to life can send gifts and messages via these old acquaintances to their families. They may even live a happy life with a new family and pursue a business life in their new environment. They may live in such a condition as long as no one

who knows about their death sees them; if this should
happen, they are said to die again immediately and go to live
in another community. They will continue to do this until
they are ready to settle down in their own community with
the ancestor spirits. The Gbandes have no explanation for
this phenomenon. When I was in Somalahum, one of the
headmen died. Immediately, in the same hour, someone who
apparently did not know of this death came to Somalahum
and claimed that he had just met the dead man at the edge
of town carrying a large traveling bag, going away down the
road. This man maintained that the dead man told him he
was going away and wouldn't be back for some time, and
that the dead man requested him to look after his family.
The dead man also said that his family would be hearing
from him from time to time. I remember vividly, although I
was a boy of thirteen at the time of this incident, that this
man drew a very large audience to hear of his experience.
The bereaved family was sure that they soon would be
receiving messages and gifts from the dead man. This episode, as can readily be seen, served to console his family and
friends.

Islam Religion

Before discussing the Gbandes' relationship with the Islam
religion, I should indicate why I prefer the term "Islam" to
"Muhammadanism." For the most part, the term "Muhammadanism" is used as an equivalent of "Christianity." Of
course, this is erroneous and unacceptable to Muslims on the
ground that Allah (God) is one, having no partner or son,
and that Muhammad is only His prophet and messenger.
Therefore, every faithful follower of Islam must perform and
direct for himself the supplications and rites presented to
God. Moreover, Muhammad, unlike Christ, makes no claim
of divinity for himself; neither does he claim to be the door
to the kingdom of Allah or God. Instead, Muhammad insists
that every believer demonstrate his faith in Allah for himself.

In obedience to this faith, every believer prays at least three times a day to Allah, for prayer is the essence of man's duty to God [4, p. 3]. This is the view held by those Gbandes who have embraced the Islamic religion.

On the whole, the Gbandes are not enthusiastic adherents of any outside or foreign religion. Nevertheless, a large number of Hasalah, a subdivision of the Gbandes who are adjacent to the Mende people, have accepted the Islamic religion. Of course, this is not strange since most Mendes in this region have long embraced the Islamic religion. The acceptance of this religion by the Hasalah people is a reflection of their close proximity to the Mendes. As one moves from west to east one finds fewer embracers or converts of Islam. Nonetheless, Islam is widely accepted among the Gbandes. In view of their resistance to things foreign, I can only suggest reasons for their acceptance of this religion. The first suggestion is that the Islamic religion represents a source of power arising from the sought-after ability to read and write. The Islamic religion also gives one the power to tell fortunes and to make charms which are imbued with magical powers to accomplish various things. (These charms are usually amulets and talismans.) The third possible reason is that one does not have to leave home to become a follower of Islam. Whatever training is necessary to become a Muslim can be obtained at home without any tuition payment. Finally, there are no restrictions on worshipping one's ancestor spirits, having a number of wives, or using or not using a certain language. On the whole, the demands or expectations of Islam are very few because most of what is expected tends to be well within traditional limits. Therefore, it is not difficult for a Gbande to become a Muslim.

Christian Religion

Among the Gbandes there are no more than one or perhaps two Christian churches. These churches are located in the Tahamba region. The only well-known one is the church at

Boawolahum. There is a less well-known one at Kololahum.
The Christian doctrine is completely incomprehensible to
the Gbandes. They are aware of the differences between denominations, each of which has different doctrines. They
reason that all the Christian denominations cannot be right;
some must be wrong. Since it is difficult to determine which
denomination is right and which is wrong, it is best to stay
away from such a religion. Moreover, the Christian religion
preaches love, peace, liberty, and understanding, among
other things, but these are the very traits that appear to be
lacking among the adherents of Christianity. The Gbandes
firmly believe that the attributes of Christianity are not even
practiced among Christians themselves, much less among
non-Christians. Therefore, they think of Christianity as an
organization of hypocrisy that should be treated with pas-
sivity. Those Gbandes who are or who profess to be Christians do so as long as they are employed by the Christian
Mission, but once they leave, they leave their Christianity
there. Since our world has been made small by modern
transportation, many Gbandes have visited areas where
Christianity is the guiding principle of life. Here, the
Gbandes observe, Christians fail to practice their doctrines.
The Gbandes reason that if the Christians can be so light-
hearted about their religion, how can anyone be serious
about it? For this reason, among the Gbandes Christianity is
something to be used for one's advantage and nothing more.

"Witch Doctor"

The term "witch doctor" is one of the most difficult and am-
biguous terms to understand in the social sciences today. Yet
in spite of its ambiguity, it tends to convey a common
meaning and to evoke a similar reaction. What the term
refers to is never clear. Does it mean an individual who has
the ability to dispose of a witch, or one who has a witch, or
one who is a witch? This lack of clarity is perhaps common

in human behavior. Very often human behavior is guided by
what is believed to be true rather than what is really true.
But when human beings define situations as real, the consequences of those situations are real. The terms "witch" and
"witch doctor" are now used to refer exclusively to those practices relegated to non-Western peoples. Among the Gbandes, as has been pointed out, one does not join associations or
clubs of witches. A witch cannot be bought. The person who
has a witch does not know that he has one; he has to die before he can be diagnosed as witched. How then is it possible
for anyone to tell a witch from a non-witch or to tell a witch
doctor from a non-witch doctor? The term "witch doctor" has
become a superstition in Western thinking which had been
adopted by the Africans. If the term "witch doctor" means
one who has the ability to treat or cure witches, then the
concept is being used in a positive sense. If, on the other
hand, it means one who has a witch, and if witchcraft by definition is evil, then the concept is being used in a negative
sense. However, as the term is being used at present, it does
not include either of the above categories. In other words, it
is a meaningless concept if not a completely repugnant and
nonsensical one. I would like to suggest that the term either
be clarified each time it is used or be abandoned.

Magic

The use of the terms "religion" and "magic" as though they
were separate concepts is a Western creation with a Western
bias. They are one and the same to the Gbandes, and I suspect this applies to many other indigenous Africans if not all
of them. Magic is but another phase of religion, not a different realm of a belief system. Magic as religion may be
used to promote good or to promote evil. It may be used to
help, to cure, or to harm. The magician may be an individual
with epileptic seizures who, when he has a seizure, is considered to be communicating with the spirit community. The

individual may be a *towōn̄ggbē*; the most appropriate English equivalent of this word would be "fortuneteller," but the *d>b>njee* is really more than that. There are many forms of *towōn̄ggbē*. Some practitioners may use ashes; others, sand; others, calabash (a gourd) with other paraphernalia; and still others may use rocks or stones and so on. The Muslims use writing from the Koran and beads* for the same purpose. One can readily see the lack of a distinction between religion and magic. Magic, as well as prayer to the ancestor spirits, may be used to manipulate people, as in the case of love potions or harmful medicines. Magic may be used to control spirits. Charms and amulets are employed by the practitioners of magic to ward off injury and evil. A mother may obtain a talisman from a practitioner to protect her infant from harm. A person may employ a magical technique himself or he may seek the services of a regular practitioner.

Closely related to religion and magic is sorcery or *kala*. It is even more closely related to what is called "witchcraft." As a matter of fact, the distinction between witchcraft and sorcery is an academic one, because the Gbandes do not usually differentiate sorcery from witchcraft. If such a differentiation is made, it is on the basis of one's becoming a sorcerer or a witch, rather than on their function. In the case of sorcery, one has to learn the practice consciously; in the case of witchcraft, one does not consciously become a witch or practice witchcraft.

There is a great need to restudy these concepts in the context of our present knowledge about Africa. I have a feeling that we are still culturebound to some extent, despite the dramatic advances we have made in fostering an understanding of indigenous cultures. A breakthrough in objec-

* The Christian equivalent is the Roman Catholic rosary.

tivity with respect to Africa, let alone with respect to the Gbandes, awaits a new generation of social scientists. This may sound staggering to some, primarily to those who know little about Africa and who are, therefore, uncritical about material written about Africa. This type of superficial and uncritical approach finds expression in writings about African religions including writings about witchcraft, magic, sorcery, witch doctors and so on. We are still ignorant about many areas of African culture, but this ignorance is excessive in the area of religion. This is not hard to demonstrate. One needs only to look at missionary activities in Africa. These activities by implication suggest that African religion is either no religion, a bad religion, or an inferior religion that must therefore be changed. The emphasis has been on change rather than on an attempt to understand the indigenous religions and regard them for what they are worth. If they are to be studied at all, this study must be done comparatively—that is, by comparing them either with Western concepts of religion or with other African religions. In the first instance, there is no basis for comparison, because one is not converted and baptized into an African religion. One is born into an existing religious group; one's religion is practiced every hour of the day and practiced every day. It cannot become a hypocritical Sunday religion in the Western sense. One does not need law enforcement officials to control one's behavior; the religion does that. One does not do good to others only on Thanksgiving, Christmas, or other such holidays, but is expected to do good every day because one's religion demands that this be done. One does not help others because one expects immediate reciprocity, although reciprocity is built into the system as part of the way of life. There is no opportunity for hypocrisy in the Gbande religion as in Western religions. Despite all these qualities and more, Gbande religion is considered undesirable by Westerners and by missionaries in particular. In the second instance, that of comparing one African religion with another, this has been done with insufficient data. Before an attempt can be made to make such a comparison, there must be a clear understanding of the basis for the comparison. A valid comparison would be a tremendous undertaking because of the great variations—national, regional, and inter- and intra-regional variations. To accomplish such a task would require many trained social scientists.

Chapter 10
Gbande Art

The Artist

ART, ACCORDING TO one anthropological dictum, is a universal attribute of culture. However, the theory that art is a form of universal language cannot be accepted without modification. Art is a universal language only in the sense that it represents one of the salient symbolic features of every culture. Nonetheless, art differs in both form and meaning from culture to culture. For example, Westerners would evaluate both art objects and art forms by taking into consideration the artist who created them. The higher the prestige of the artist, the higher the rank or rating and the price of his creation. On the other hand, the Gbandes attend only to the art object itself in evaluating art objects and art forms. They put little or no emphasis on the artist who created them. The Gbandes consider the art object and art form, not the artist, to be symbolic of social cohesion. Undoubtedly, the artist is necessary for the production of art objects and forms, but for the most part he is not important in the evaluation of his products. Some art works, especially those dealing with religious rituals, call for partial anonymity of the artist; the artists are known only to a very few select individuals. But except in this realm of art objects and forms, artists are generally known to the members of their communities. This is true for woodcarvings to a large extent and to a lesser extent for the other art objects and forms. However, there are always exceptions, even with woodcarvings. I know of one such exception in which the artist was used as the sole criterion by which his art products were judged. I shall return to this exceptional case later; but first, it is in order at this point to set forth the aim of this chapter.

I want to emphasize that I am a sociologist and an anthropologist by training and that I am definitely not an art critic. I am not at all qualified to talk about the merits of any particular works of art, whether European or African. The aim of this chapter is not to compare Gbande art with European art or any other art. Neither is it to evaluate Gbande art per se. The primary concern here is not with what art means in general, but rather with what Gbande art means to the Gbande people. It is from this vantage point that I will describe a few Gbande art objects and art forms. The description is designed to show how these art products function in Gbande society and the extent to which they influence Gbande culture. I have arbitrarily divided Gbande art objects and forms into two broad categories in order to make this complicated subject more manageable. The first category is the decorative arts. This category includes: carving, dyeing and weaving, metalworking (the work of the blacksmith, goldsmith, and silversmith), leather work, pottery making, and basketry, mat making, bag making, and rope making, among others. The second category is what I have designated as the performing arts. It includes music, song, and dance. A limited description of some musical instruments concludes my discussion of this category.

Carving

Carving is done out of wood, ivory, animal horns, and elephant heels. Both ivory carving and heel carving are almost lost arts among the Gbandes because there have not been any elephants in Gbandeland for a very long time. The only access these people have to tusks and heels is through the system of reciprocal trading, when goods and services are exchanged with the Mandingoes, a people in West Africa who specialize in short and long distance trading. Tusks and heels may also be obtained through an exchange of gifts between Gbandes and non-Gbandes other than the Mandingoes. These acquisitions are so infrequent that they are inadequate to stimulate much interest in the art of ivory and heel carving. Artists could not be assured of a continuous supply of tusks and heels. For this reason, very few Gbandes are interested in working with ivory. Ivory has a variety of uses. It is usually carved into handles for the walking canes used by chiefs and other dignitaries. This is by far the most frequent use of ivory. To a lesser extent, it is used in jewelry, such as bracelets or armlets for females. It is also used for game pieces. In form, these pieces resemble a child's top; they are shaped like an inverted cone. These tops are spun by the thumb and one or two middle fingers. The game may be played by two, four, or eight men. The tops are spun simultaneously by the men in a grass ring covered with a homemade mat. The man whose top knocks the other tops out of the ring is declared the winner. This was an important gambling game for the Gbandes in times past. Today, it is limited to a pastime for very few Gbandes. As a matter of fact, the Gissies, neighbors of the Gbandes, play it more than the Gbandes do nowadays. As to elephant heels, I know of only one use for them. They are used to make bracelets or armlets for both males and females. The material is relatively easy to carve, much easier than ivory or wood. As a result, almost any adult male is able to carve it with his own design. Horns, particularly cow horns, are carved with a variety of designs. Such horns are used primarily as drinking receptacles. Horn carving is done by young men who have just learned to make palm wine on their own. As they get older, their interest dies.

Wood is by far the most frequently used material for carving. Wood carving is very important for the Gbande people. It is aesthetically as well as religiously significant in Gbande culture. That is to say, broadly speaking, wood carving falls into two categories—the sacred realm of religious rituals and the realm of everyday use. The first use involves the different kinds of masks and other paraphernalia used in sacred or religious rituals. The role of these masks is inestimable in the traditional formal educational institutions, such as the Poro school for boys. They are used to a lesser extent in the Sande school for girls. In connection with these types of art products, the anonymity of the artist or artists is imperative. These artists are known only to a few select individuals. The form of a mask represents a certain level of authority in the hierarchical structure of those in charge of the Poro school. These masks are the visible symbols of authority. The masks for a given rank within this upper echelon are supposed to be similar in form. However, artists are permitted to vary within limits and to be artistic in bringing out certain basic features as they see fit. For this reason, masks representing the same level of authority may vary slightly but not noticeably. Symbolically, these masks convey a common meaning to all the Gbande people. Some of these masks and other art objects connected with them form the ceremonial code in the rite of passage from adolescence to maturity. They represent the outward manifestation of inner change which transforms youths into adults.

Masks

The socio-psychological importance of wood carvings cannot be overemphasized. Their role, especially with respect to the Poro institution, is so inextricably intertwined with the total Gbande life that it is difficult, if not impossible, to estimate the influence of the carved masks. These masks create fear, anxiety, and admiration in the minds of all Gbandes. Fear is created because the beings the masks constitute part of are greatly respected and feared. Some of these beings represent life or death, good or bad, permanent success or failure. These beings are feared as they are the final arbiters who decide the future of every boy in the traditional Gbande society. The masked being is free to reprimand sharply chiefs and commoners alike, male and female, young and old. Children, particularly boys, are often told that if they do not behave, one of these masked beings will carry them away to an unknown place. Once this fear is internalized, it becomes the regulating force which controls the boys' lives until they enter the Poro school. Seeing the masked beings rebuking chiefs and other important individuals publicly increases the children's fear of these beings, because only a powerful being can act in this manner. Moreover, since every boy must one day be placed at the mercy of the masked beings, the women are anxious about the masked beings and about the day their sons must face them, for each woman fears that her son will be consumed by these beings and never return. The artists are aware of this fear and anxiety and take them into consideration in their carvings. Therefore, the artistic part of these beings is designed to portray what is believed about them. For example, the faces of some are designed to have a mean and horrifying expression. This is particularly the case with the *landáy* (Poro super leaders). Others have an almost smiling and pleasant facial expression, for example the $\beta > tu$ (women doctors). The very appearance of these masked beings indicates something significant and is often marked with rituals of some sort. These rituals reinforce the fears and anxiety of all uninitiated boys.

Furthermore, those who are involved with the performance of the *landáy* or other masked Poro leaders, such as the musicians, interpreters, or guardians, soon share the respect and admiration of the community because of the high respect accorded to the masked beings. Such popularity gives rise to individual popularity, so that those who are so distinguished gain the status of a privileged group. The social status of these privileged groups is directly related to the type of masked being they are associated with. The more complex the mask's carving, the greater the feeling of fear the mask inspires in those who see it and the higher the status of those who accompany it. For example, the *landáy* and the *ñāgbày* are both masked beings, but the *landáy* is much more complex and fearful than the *ñāgbày*.

Wood carvings for everyday use include: bowls, spoons, combs, handles for various things such as knives and spears, and different types of toys. The artist has great latitude to elaborate his carving with imaginative symmetrical designs. However, the opportunities to exhibit special talents are limited at times by moral values. It was mentioned at the beginning of this chapter that, for the Gbandes, artists are unimportant to the evaluation of their work. There is at least one exception to this. It has to do with K>yon, a man I considered to be truly the greatest Gbande carver of his time. He was so completely involved in his carving that at times he became less than prudent. It was at one of these times that his carvings became enigmatic to the Gbande people. K>yon was a self-trained and self-styled artist who was particular in bringing out fine detail in his work. He specialized in carving animals and human forms exquisitely. His ability in bringing out the finest details in his work was the factor which led to his expulsion from Somalahum, his village. The women of Somalahum led the way in expelling him. His sin was no other than carving a male and female expertly in the nude with striking details to their sex organs. It was this work which offended the Gbande people, especially the women of Somalahum. Gbande morality demands that each sex remain or is supposed to remain ignorant of the sex organs of the other. K>yon's works were hailed and admired by the missionaries at the Bololahum Holy Cross Mission. The missionaries in this institution were so much impressed with his carvings that they accepted his works in exchange for refuge or asylum for him as long as he lived. The missionaries kept their word and K>yon spent the rest of his life with them. K>yon produced many exquisite works of art in wood carving for his adoptive institution before his death. His works were exhibited constantly for foreigners, especially European and American visitors. While this episode is also important as an example of a benevolent act of the missionaries, it is the change in the Gbande mode of evaluating art that is crucial here. K>yon was identified with his art products, which was a radical departure from Gbande practices. Having been thus identified, he was forced out of the village of his birth. This is the strongest punishment that could possibly be meted out to anyone.

Dyeing

Dyeing and weaving are important decorative arts. In this portion I will discuss dyeing only. Weaving of cloth is discussed thoroughly in Chapter 3 "The Gbande Mode of Making a Living," subsection "Cotton: Source of Clothing." (Weaving of fibers into mats, receptacles, and rope items is discussed later in this chapter.) The Gbande people are self-sufficient in supplying themselves with all of their apparel from special indigenous cottons. Each family is responsible for the cultivation of its cotton for cloth. Like most Africans, the Gbandes take care to be fashionable by African standards by creating elaborate designs in their woven cloth. These designs are made by two methods: the threads may be dyed with different desirable colors to form the base of the design and then woven into cloth, or the designs may be added to the material after it has been woven. Fabrics in which the design is woven are striped in a variety of colors; fabrics that are dyed later have symmetrical designs of different colors. The making of the dyes to produce the desired colors is the most important step in making the designs. Dye is produced from three sources and provides three basic colors—red, brown, and blue. The first color, red, may be obtained from the stump and roots of a specific tree. Both the stumps and roots of these trees are red. They are dug out and cut into small pieces. These pieces are placed into a large earthen pot which is sunk two-thirds down into the ground to give it firmness and support. Each family reserves three or four of these large earthen pots for this purpose. The pot with its contents is filled with cold water and covered with banana leaves, which are held in place by sticks or rocks. The second source of dye is the bark of a special tree which produces a reddish brown or mahogany dye. The bark is stripped off the trees and cut into manageable pieces. These pieces are placed into a wooden mortar where they are pounded with a wooden pestle until they are mashed. Then this substance is put into a large earthen pot as described above. The third dye, blue, is from the leaves of a special vine. The leaves are picked in large quantities by the men and boys and brought home to the village. The women and girls spread the leaves out on homemade mats, where they are mashed under foot, a few at a time, until they are soft. The mashed leaves are likewise placed in the earthen pot. Each dye is left to stand two days in the pot. Each can produce a number of different tints and shades in material added to the pot. Darker shades are made by adding fresh coloring agent to the contents of the pot. Sometimes it is necessary to extract some of the old agent from the pot to make room for the fresh one. The dye can be made more or less concentrated in this way. Another method is to allow the material to remain longer in the coloring agent. The longer the material remains in the dye, the more effectively it is dyed. Moreover, the different dyes may be mixed to produce other distinct hues.

If the design, which is suggested by the oldest man in the family, is to be woven into the material, the threads are dyed by the women in as many colors as the design requires. Sometimes it takes several weeks to make the suitable colors. The thread which is to be dyed is unwound from spools, wrapped loosely into skeins, and put into the dye pots. Two days later the women return to examine the strands carefully to see whether they are evenly dyed and are the shade or tint desired. Slowly, daily, the women inspect the strands trying not to get the skeins of thread tangled. When the thread is the desired shade or tint, the skeins are removed and hung to dry on a rattan line strung between two wooden poles. After the skeins are dry, the thread is again wound on larger sticks inserted into the spindle base on which the thread was originally spun. When it is agreed that the different colors are now available, the men who are responsible for working out the design arrange the threads in such a way as to permit the designs to be woven directly into the material. (This weaving process is described in detail in Chapter 3.) However, if the designs are to be imposed on the woven material, it becomes the work of the women. Such designs are produced by making as many small folds in the material as are necessary to produce them. Each of these folds is knotted tightly in order to permit only a given amount of dye to reach the folded areas. It takes several weeks to complete the design, by this technique of tie dyeing. When it is finished, the cords are cut away and the folds smoothed out, revealing the complete design. If it should be decided that the finished product needs more design, such as embroidery, it will be added by hand and may be done by male or female. These cloths usually last from four to six years or longer before they show signs of wear. The arts of spinning and dyeing belong to the women, but the blending of colors and weaving are reserved for the men.

Metal and Leather Work

Next in importance are the metalworking artists. They include the blacksmith, the goldsmith, and the silversmith. The blacksmith is by far the most important among these artists. Unlike wood carving, goldsmithing, or silversmithing, which can all be learned by any Gbande male who wishes to

do so and who has the talent, the blacksmith trade must be
inherited from ancestors on the father's side. The blacksmith
may, at times, learn the trade from his uncle. In an extremely
rare case, an individual may be granted the privilege of
becoming a blacksmith by divine grace. In such a case, the
new apprentice is revealed to the eldest blacksmith of the
village. Blacksmiths are highly respected by all. They are ex-
empt from all public work and are among the few individuals allowed to participate in both male and female organizations, including the Poro and Sande schools. They are
strictly forbidden to strike anyone with their hands. The
Gbandes believe that such an action brings the curse of undesirable fortune on the individual being struck. Metal-
workers are believed to possess a special ability in indigenous medicine as well as in other areas of life—areas
restricted to women or to special men—which cannot be understood by ordinary men. For this reason, blacksmiths are
feared, honored, and respected. Each adult in the blacksmith's village (every village has its own blacksmith) must set
aside a day to work on the blacksmith's farm; at the end of
the farm season, every adult has served his term. The
villagers are neither asked nor forced to work by the blacksmith; they work voluntarily as a gesture of appreciation for
his services to all. Iron plays a vital role in Gbande life, as it
does in the life of any people who rely upon agriculture as a
way of making a living. The blacksmith fashions the iron
into the various implements necessary for farming in
Gbandeland. Iron is also used as a medium of exchange. It is
also used in making instruments of war, such as swords, ar-
rowheads, and spear heads. These are usually artistic in
design. Here the blacksmith uses wood or ivory, and he
alone designs and makes the handles for these products. If
the handle is to be ivory, he is responsible for making it; if it
is to be wood, he carves it. When villagers want farm tools or
personal items made, they bring the materials to the blacksmith and tell him what they want made. Although the
blacksmith is busy all year round, his busiest time is the

beginning of the farm period around February. It is during this time that many farm tools are made and repaired. At times, an individual may not have the necessary material to get what he wants made. In this case, the blacksmith will make it out of left-over materials previously given him by others. Other useful items, such as hunting and fishing gear, are also fashioned by the blacksmith. In short, metal is always fashioned by the blacksmith for a particular purpose, and in some cases he makes specific sizes for different users, whether the items are for males, females, or children.

Goldsmiths and silversmiths are not differentiated by the Gbandes. I made the distinction merely to show that the Gbandes do use both of these metals. Both smiths are referred to as goldsmiths. Both metals are used primarily for jewelry for women—jewelry to be worn on the arms, wrists, ankles, neck, fingers, etc. Although these are skillful artists who are creative in their own right in making many intricate designs, they have little or no prestige in Gbandeland. Most of them live in the largest cities, and all of their products are made for sale. Their work is looked upon with suspicion because they are considered unreliable. The Gbandes believe that since the motive which influences the gold-smiths to produce their artistic products is to make a profit, they cannot be in earnest. One can never be sure about the quality of their work. For this reason, they are respected as individuals but held in low esteem as artists.

Closely related to metalwork is leather work. Although leather workers do not share the privilege and honor of blacksmiths, they are closely related because their works are interrelated to some extent. For example, both swords and spears require decorative leather shields and strips which are made by the leather workers. In traditional Gbande society, mores demanded that swords and spears be kept in shields at all times unless in use. Moreover, they should be hung up immediately when one arrived at one's destination or when one was at home. For this reason they had to have strips with which they were hung up on other objects or with which they were carried by strapping them on the shoulder. However, the artistic nature of the leather workers is attested to mainly by their leather jewelry, such as leather anklets, bracelets, necklets, and waistlets (not belts). Earrings are designed in a multiplicity of patterns for females by age group. In this sense leather jewelry is also made to indicate social status. For example, among the most aesthetic leather work are the waistlets, which are worn in great quantities by adolescent unmarried girls around their waist. These are made of leather dyed in many colors and are about half an inch in diameter. It used to be the wish of girls of pretentions to status to own many sets of waistlets. It was a mark of distinction for a girl to wear the most elaborate set of leather jewels on various occasions. The leather worker with imagination and special abilities in making designs and patterns and colors was usually awarded the highest esteem and prestige. The leather workers, unlike the goldsmiths, produce many artifacts of practical utility which are considered desirable and obtainable by any Gbande. For example, in addition to what has been described, the leather workers produce leather hats, slippers or house shoes, cloth, bags, belts, masks, and so on. Any male can become a leather worker provided he has the stamina to endure the tedious years of apprenticeship under the direction of a master leather worker. In passing, the reader should note the Gbande emphasis on apprenticeship. A people who do not have a written language to record their knowledge and experience must rely on experts instead of textbooks. Only such experts can disseminate the required knowledge to those who desire it.

Pottery

While the professions of goldsmithing and leather working are exclusively male professions, pottery making is exclusively female. Pottery making is very important artistic work among the Gbandes. It is reserved entirely for women, including the decorating and designing. Pottery containers are used in most cases as receptacles for drinking water or for storing items of value, such as palm oil. Although pottery is used by all households in Gbandeland, pottery making is not a widespread art. It is done mostly by the Gbandes who occupy the Western region adjacent to the Mendes. The lack of widespread pottery making is due to a number of factors. One factor is that since pottery making is a purely female occupation, it is less prestigious; too, since girls are by and large not given in apprenticeship, the art becomes a localized one. An even more important factor is that the uses of pottery containers are limited to their use as receptacles for drinking water for the household and places to store palm oil. Once these two demands are satisfied, there is little or no incentive to acquire more pots. The only subsequent need would be for replacement of a broken pot. Notwithstanding, pottery making requires sophistication. For example, the pottery worker must know the type of soil that can be used for pottery making. She must also learn different intricate designs to be engraved upon her work. In addition, she must know the length of time her pottery must stand in the sun before it is ready to be baked. Perhaps the most complicated aspect of pottery is that which involves baking. Here, the knowledge of the right temperature, which must be kept constant, and the number of days the pottery must bake is imperative. After it is baked, each piece of pottery is examined carefully and tested for leaks before it is put on the market. The decorative designs do not determine the value of the pottery. The value of any piece of pottery is determined by its quality—that is, whether it is solid enough to take abuse. This is the most crucial point, since the purpose of pottery is utility rather than appearance. Yet there is no pottery without designs and decorations. At this point of our knowledge we can only assume that the decorations and designs serve a latent function.

Weaving with Fibers

Other significant works of art include the making of mats, baskets, bags, nets, and hammocks. Mats are made from a tall tropical grass in the sugar cane family, but much smaller than sugar cane. The Gbande term for this grass is *sabày*. The same name is used for mats. Mats play a very important role in Gbande culture. A mat, instead of cloth, is used as a bed cover to sleep on. It is used to sit and to play on. In addition, the wedding ceremony is performed upon a mat, and mats are given or exchanged as gifts between the bride's and groom's kinsmen because a mat symbolizes stability and fertility. Mats are used as coffins in which the dead are buried. In this case, a number of extra mats are usually buried with the body. Mats are not adorned with different colors but are decorated by plaiting the bark or outer layers of the *sabày*. The *sabày* grows only in swampy places where the men cut it and gather it into large bundles to take to the village. The outer layer of each cane or rod is peeled off lengthwise, in small pieces, with a knife. These pieces are made very thin by scraping each piece from the inner side until it is perfectly smooth. Then these pieces are allowed to dry in the sun from three to five days, after which they are ready to be plaited. As a rule, mats do not vary in size or design. They are approximately 8 feet by 6 feet. These mats are easily worn out and therefore their frequent production is a necessity. It is for this reason that every adult Gbande male is a mat maker.

A basket which is called *kambày* is made by the men from rattan, the Gbande word for which is *balwī*. Here too the fiber is cut by the men and gathered into bundles. The bundles are brought to the village, where the outer layers are peeled off the canes lengthwise in similar way the *sabày* is peeled. These pieces are made smooth from both within and without with a small knife, after which they are ready for plaiting. Note that rattan does not have to be dry to be

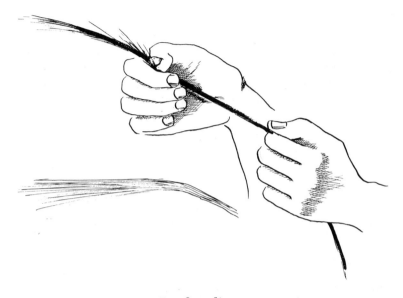

Leaf peeling

plaited as does the *sabày*. Although baskets are very important in the life of every Gbande family, they do not have the
same prestige as mats. Baskets serve primarily as receptacles
for storing or conveying other objects. Like mats, they do not
have special decorations except those which are due to the
plaiting. Baskets are usually used by women, although they
may be used occasionally by men.

Bags called *sīlō* in Gbande are made from piassava palm
fiber. These piassava palms resemble coconut trees and they
grow wild in swampy places. The young leaves are stripped
from the stalk in large quantities and carried to the village.
Each leaf is then carefully folded over at its upper end, between the thumb and the first finger. The top end is then
pulled with one hand, breaking the outer fiber, which is
gradually separated from the inner fiber held lightly with the
other hand. The inner fiber, which may or may not be further refined, is the one used in bag making. Bags are made

by both males and females. They resemble drawstring
pouches and vary greatly in size. They may or may not have
decorative designs. These fibers are much easier to dye than
thread and are usually dyed in many colors. Bags are used
primarily for carrying small items or for storing such items.
For this reason, almost every adult Gbande owns a bag or
number of bags as personal property. Both baskets and bags
are essential to the members of the Gbande communal
household, but whereas baskets are owned by the household,
bags are never owned by the household but belong to individuals.

Net is made from palm fiber instead of piassava fiber.
The process of obtaining the fiber from the palm leaves and
preparing it is the same as that described above for the bag
making. *Tuwī* (the Gbande word for "net") is made and used
by both male and female as fishing gear. Twine, which the
Gbandes call *gesáy*, is also made from the palm fiber. It is
used primarily as a fishing line. This kind of twine is made by
men only. When the palm fiber has been prepared in the
same way as the piassava fiber, the maker takes a few strands
and splits them in half. The halves are then intertwined by
rolling them up and down on the thigh with the palm of the
hand. This process is repeated again and again until enough
twine is made. The twine may now be used to make net by
weaving several strands of twine together, or a single strand
of twine may be used as fish line.

The methods and processes described above also hold
true for the manufacturing of hammocks or *bowaín*. This is
strictly work for men. Hammocks are made from piassava
fibers. (The piassava tree is called *duhúi* to differentiate it
from the palm tree, which is called $t>gb>\bar{y}$.) Here again,
since the piassava fibers are easily dyed, the hammock
maker like the bag maker is able to decorate his hammock
with different colors of twine. Although it is not difficult to
make hammocks, they are not widely owned. They are
usually found in the home of chiefs and other important indi-

viduals. The hammock has three basic uses in Gbandeland. It is used as a bed, as a place for temporary relaxation, and as a conveyance in which important people are carried from one place to another. It takes two or four persons to carry another person in a hammock. In the case of two persons carrying it, the hammock is fastened to a long horizontal pole which projects far enough beyond the hammock to permit the carriers to put the ends on their shoulders. It is this pole that holds the hammock and supports the person in it. When carried by four persons, the hammock is mounted on two short perpendicular sticks, each of which is carefully mounted on specially prepared boards at each end of the hammock. The boards project far enough beyond the two perpendicular sticks and are spaced far enough apart so that two carriers can walk abreast in front and two abreast in the rear. The boards supporting the hammock are placed on the heads instead of the shoulders of each carrier. Unlike mats and bags, hammocks are not easily worn out. If they do wear out, they are easily repaired; this is usually done by men.

Dance and Music

The remainder of this chapter will focus upon what has been designated as the performing arts. It will cover music and musical instruments, song, and dance. Although music and song are for all practical purposes interwoven, they must be separated if we are to understand their separate roles as well as their relationship in Gbande culture. Dance is related to music and song but is on a slightly different level. The role of music is enormous in Gbande culture. It is part of almost every exuberant activity in which the Gbandes engage. Whether the activities are being performed by a group or by an individual, by males or females, music always forms an indispensable part. There are very few if any chores without their appropriate music. Music is so important that every undertaking by a group must have its musicians. For example,

there are songs especially designed for blacksmiths, leather
workers, farmers, and so on. The blacksmith song, "n͡gge
mōy lītī n͡ggā ay ya n͡gga fō n͡ggāy yā jāā vō n͡gga," means
"The blacksmith has gone wild because I am blowing the fire
for him, but he keeps putting it out with water." In the
blacksmith's shop, the homemade leather bellows are
mounted on a specially designed wooden apparatus which
inserts them into the heating device. As the blacksmith's
helper blows the bellows, the fire becomes very hot and the
blacksmith has to cool it down by putting water on it with a
homemade brush. The leather worker's song is a song of
praise for two professional leather workers, Yen͡ggbē and
Mānjo. ("Yen͡ggbē gbēlē Mānjō gbēlē kolo gbā tea ndā
wān," meaning "Look! See? Yen͡ggbē and Mānjō have made
me beautiful leather jewels.") The song for the farmer has a
double meaning. It has to do with the evening sun; the
farmer is tired and wants to go home, but by Gbande
custom, he cannot go home until the sun has set. On the
other hand, the farmer may want to complete a piece of work
but is afraid that darkness will prevent him from doing so.
Therefore he sings, "O yāveli yāveli yaa gbombō, folo ya lī ve
li mà." This means "Oh! Sun, let me know before you disappear" or "Sun, tell me good-bye before you disappear." In
addition to these cases, when a task requires a group of
workers to act as a unit, they are almost always accompanied
by a musician whose sole responsibility it is to furnish music
—usually a combination of song and instrument. As a rule,
the musician is to call out the name of each worker with loud
praise and at the same time beat his instrument as loudly as
possible. Music and dance catalyze most activities in Gbande
society.

Aside from the role of music in work, whether it be of a
group or of an individual, music is also important as a pastime in everyday life. This type of activity usually takes
place on the night of the full moon and consists of singing
(accompanied by musical instruments) and dancing. It may

or may not be segregated by sex or age. If there are no sex or age distinctions, anyone who thinks he or she has something significant to contribute either to the singing or to the dance may do so by stepping directly up to the instrumentalists and telling them that he or she can contribute something. It is like an amateur talent show in which each person wants to outdo the others. This activity may go on into the morning hours. For this reason, it is an activity of the dry season when there is no farm work. Songs for dances of these sorts are few, because most activities in this realm are segregated by sex or by age group. By far the most interesting activity is the one performed by certain age groups of boys and girls together. This activity also has a limited number of songs. It, too, takes place on the night of the full moon. The participants form two columns, the girls forming one and the boys the other. They face each other and pretty soon the singing and the clapping of hands begins. Then one of the girls dances between the columns for about one or two minutes, at which time she touches one of the boys; having done this, she immediately returns to her place in line. The boy whom she has touched dances between the columns as the girl has done for about the same length of time. He touches another girl, any except the one who touched him, and immediately returns to his place in line. This is repeated over and over again until they are exhausted. Aside from these two activities, most activities of this nature are strictly segregated by sex and by age.

Music, singing, and dancing are also part of every important event in the life of this people except birth. For example, festivities of any sort require at least some singing; sometimes singing and dancing with instrumental music are combined, depending on the importance of the event and whether such an event is group- or individual-oriented. Among the festivities requiring an exuberant exhibition of musical talents, in instrumentation and singing as well as dancing, are those dealing with the Poro and Sande institutions, marriage, and death. These fall within group-oriented activities and each is important in its own right. Poro and Sande institutions have been covered elsewhere; I will not devote any further discussion to them. Marriage calls for rejoicing involving singing, dancing, and instrumental music because it is through marriage that the patrilinear lineage is perpetuated. Marriage is the time one entertains in an attempt to illustrate or assert one's family's well-being and one's own popularity in the community, as well as the status of one's family. This is the time when family pride is on trial before the community, foes and friends alike. Therefore, marriage requires many types of music and musicians as well as participants.

Similarly, the death of an important person requires instrumental and vocal music with dancing. The duration of such activities depends upon the status of the deceased. Here again, family pride is at stake before the living and the spirit world. It is believed that the larger such a festivity is, the greater will be the reward from the ancestor spirits to the family of their descendents. There is no such festivity for less important people. There is a simple grave-breaking ceremony for such individuals, for the purpose of presenting them properly to the spirit world.

There are also tribal festivities which may take place periodically. Very often, the tribal festivities are male festivities —that is, they include only initiated males. Here, most of the music and sometimes the musical instruments are secret. This type of festivity may take place every year, every fourth year, or every seventh year. Musicians who perform at such festivities are all experts who are especially charged with the responsibility of playing. Such responsibilities are passed from fathers to their male children.

Strangely enough, there is no overt rejoicing about birth. Everyone is happy about the addition to the family. It is considered a blessing that one of the ancestral spirits has seen fit to return to the land of the living, but at the same time, the imperfection of the living and their world pose unpredictable difficulties for the infant. Therefore, covertly, everyone is glad, but given the above circumstances, there can be no rejoicing of any kind.

In addition to the occupational songs already described, there are a number of other types of songs. However, before describing these songs, I would like to say a few words about the tunes and melodies of Gbande songs. Most Gbande songs are monotone songs—chants sung at relatively high pitches. The words are repeated at regular intervals. There is little, if any, variation in the tunes or melodies of different songs. The fact that there are hardly any new songs may account for the lack of variation over the years. New songs, when they do appear, are usually phrased in familiar old tunes and melodies. The consistency of tunes and melodies is the distinguishing characteristic of Gbande songs.

There are many different kinds of songs. For example, there are love songs, such as: *"Ai lai ndèe na lɛ n̂ggulu bēgēlēhon na gol, ēa ge na lɛ n̂ggu bēgēlēhōn."* which means, roughly: "What kind of tree shall we climb in order to be ourselves for a moment so that we can just sit down and look at each other?" There are songs designed as jokes or songs ridiculing a village leader by describing his beloved wife as follows: *"M>le n̄ā hai n̄a nde jū man̂ggi lái gu n̂gg>y pɛpēy ma,"* roughly translated as: "The leader's most beautiful wife has a mouth which smells worse than half-dry crayfishes." There are also songs for circumcision. One of these songs, already mentioned in an earlier chapter, is sung by adolescent boys who have been circumcised previously but who have not yet been educated in the Poro school. Another circumcision song is the one sung by those newly circumcised: *"Ya ya gbōlō lē n̂gga kē n̂gg>i waya n̂galʔ a gba lɛ̄!"* translated as: "Ah! this is indeed a circumcision, it feels funny, but Man! The thing can hurt." There are songs designed to express joy on behalf of one's younger kinsmen, for example: *"Gaagē nun̂g gāāi dày wan njenje ke la wén nindāi ye?"* trans-

lated as, "If I have always shown enthusiasm about other's
joys, how much more about my own kinsmen?" There is a
song telling of the wish fulfillment of an adolescent girl. She
had a secret love for two men but could not marry either of
them because she was already bethrothed to another man by
her father. The best she could do about her secret love was
to promise herself that if she ever had girl children she
would surely give them to her lovers as wives. So she sings.
"Na n̄ggaandoole n̄ggāā fee Jī M>lē yɛ ma tài aa lo gā fe
G>nd> Bala da nāi na," translated as, "When I am grown
and have my own girl children, I will first give many to J ī
M>lē as he wants for wives, and if there more girls than he
wants, I will give the rest to G>nd> Bala." It is obvious
from these examples that Gbande songs in these categories
are designed to do two things, namely to tell a story or to
praise.

However, dance among this people serves other functions. It is usually an acrobatic celebration in which the accompanying musicians must follow the dancer rather than
the dancer's following a set musical pattern or rhythm.
Dancers, particularly male dancers, are loudly applauded for
their exuberant acrobatic exhibitions, which may involve entirely new steps or a combination of old steps to produce
new ones. Female dancers are expected to exhibit similar
characteristics, but to a lesser extent. For this reason, it is impossible to teach dancing in Gbande society. Dancers using
the same music may dance quite differently from each other.
If, however, a certain individual style of dancing is
applauded over and over again, younger dancers may try to
imitate this style and perhaps add a little more of their own
creation to it. Gbande dances take place outdoors. A Gbande
dance is an open type of affair in which any individual who
wishes to dance may do so. It this case, those who are
watching form a big circle around the musicians, both vocal-
ists and instrumentalists (these may or may not be the same
persons). Anyone who feels like dancing will go into the

circle directly in front of and facing the musicians to attract their attention. Having done so, the dancer turns abruptly and goes around the circle rapidly. As he does so, he picks up momentum. As he becomes excited by his own performance, the dancer becomes more exuberant and the applause becomes louder and louder. When he leaves, another person immediately enters the circle and attempts to outdo those who have preceded him. This is the pattern the dance will follow until everybody is tired and the musicians can play no more. Up to now, I have been talking about singing and dancing, but I have yet to describe the musical instruments.

Musical Instruments

Gbande musical instruments may be divided into five categories. There are those that fall into the drum family, the stringed instrument family, the horn family, the rhythm or maraca family, and the xylophone family. The drum is, by and large, the most important musical instrument among the Gbandes. All drums are made out of wood. There are two general types of drums, namely those that fall into the category of *taaninggi*, usually called the "talking drum," and those in the category of *sagbày*, the regular drum. *Taaninggi*, the talking drum, is a hollow wooden cylinder constructed in the shape of an hourglass. The drum heads are covered with specially prepared skins (monkey skin is preferred) which are held together lightly by numerous strings made from palm fiber. The *taaninggi* is played with a stick resembling the head of a walking cane. The drum is put under one arm and the player makes higher or lower tones by squeezing or releasing the strings holding the drumhead, thereby tightening or loosening it while he beats the drum. This gives a rhythmic combination of high and low tones. The *taaninggi* is to some extent a basic instrument in that it usually accompanies other instruments. Moreover, this is the instrument chosen by the Gbandes to entertain and to ac-

company chiefs and other important individuals. The players
of this instrument are expected to be good and gifted vocal-
ists. The singing and drumming function together in giving
praise to their patrons. The *sagbày*, the next general type of
drum is also made out of hollowed wood like a bongo or
conga drum. It is made much the same as drums seen in
Western society, being covered with a cured deer skin held
in place by a number of strings. It is played with the hands
instead of sticks. The *sagbày's* uses are limited to evening
pastimes and affairs relating to festivities. In most cases, it is
accompanied by at least two *taaniñggís*. The player of the
sagbày is not expected to be a vocalist and usually does not
sing. Notwithstanding, his task is as strenuous as that of the
player of the *taaniñggí* if not more so. The player has to play
usually for long hours with all his might with little or no
respite. There are also a number of other kinds of drums
which are more or less like either one of the two general
types discussed above.

There are not many stringed instruments in Gbande society. By far the leading stringed instrument is the *mbakáy*.[°]
It is made out of a small forked stick carved neatly into
shape. A hot iron is used to make seven holes in each of the
tines of the fork directly opposite each other. The lower end
of the stick, where the two forks join, is inserted into a
specially prepared gourd backwards so that the open end of
the gourd faces away from the fork. Strings made out of paissava fibers are affixed, one in each of the seven holes, to form
tones to suit the musician. The *mbakáy* is played by placing
the open end of the gourd directly against the stomach. At
the same time the player touches the strings, he presses on
the slightly open or slightly more open end of the gourd
away from his stomach. This action controls the tones which
are produced from the strings. The *mbakáy* is usually played

----

°For another stringed instrument, used for communication, see
Chapter 8 "Communication," subsection "Gbεkáy."

informally as a pastime by a male, for his own amusement or for a group's amusement. Almost every adolescent and adult Gbande male knows how to play a *mbakáy*, more or less. There is only one major formal role in the playing of the *mbakáy*: it is the major instrument accompanying the *ñāgbày*, one of the Poro leaders.

The horn is used much less as a musical instrument. A wind instrument resembling a flute is usually used by lone male adolescents to amuse themselves rather than played as a part of group music. Horn instruments are used by adults to summon all males or village leaders together. The horn may also be used to announce the arrival of an important personality. Aside from these uses, the horn is used in a very highly secret ceremony to furnish secret music.

Mbakáy

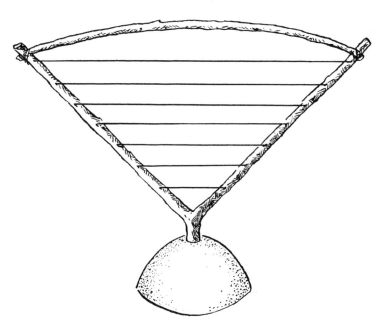

Similarly, the maraca, a rhythm instrument, is limited to female activities. Only females play it. It is usually played on occasions which call for the exclusive participation of women, such as Sande celebrations or good-time activities in the evening or at night when the moon is shining. The maraca is made from specially prepared gourds which are small with long narrow necks. A small hole is made at the larger end of the gourd. The seeds are emptied through this hole. When all the seeds are out, the gourd is dried in the sun for about three or four days. Strings of beads are plaited artistically to form a net into which the prepared gourd is inserted. The net has strings extending beyond the bulbous end of the gourd, while the neck of the gourd sticks out at the opposite end of the net. The maraca player holds the strings in one hand and the neck of the gourd in the other hand. She wiggles the hollow gourd inside the plaited net of beads to produce any rhythm she wishes.

The xylophone is strictly a male adolescent instrument. It is played for the amusement of the player to help him es-

Maraca

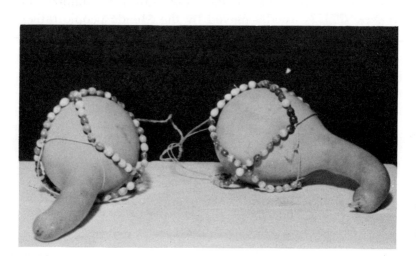

cape the loneliness of boys' farm work. It is played during the period when the rice is about ready to be harvested (as described in Chapter 3, "The Gbande Mode of Making a Living," subsection "Subsistence Crops"). It is the responsibility of the boys to keep away the birds and other pests from the rice. This is a job which starts at dawn and lasts until dark. It may last for six to eight weeks. The boys are pretty much confined during this period. It is during this period that the xylophones are made by the boys and played by them. They are made out of a special type of lightweight wood on the order of balsa wood. The boys first cut this wood and let it dry from two to three weeks; then they split it into the desired lengths and sizes. Seven bars are then delicately shaped by hand into very thin slats of various sizes. The longest and largest slats yield the deepest tones, whereas the shorter, smaller ones yield lighter tones. Then a special kind of dry grass is carefully placed upon two larger parallel sticks made out of the same wood. The slats or bars are then tied lightly but securely across these sticks with rattan to form a ladder. The Gbande name for xylophone is *kēlēn̄ggī*. There is a form of xylophone called a *mbakēlēn̄ggī* which is played in the village to entertain large numbers of groups. This is usually played by the Mende people rather than by the Gbandes, except for those Gbandes who share a common boundary with the Mende people. There are a number of other instruments of music in Gbandeland which I did not include here, but I have included those that are most significant.

Chapter 11
Gbande Folklore

FOLKLORE PLAYS A significant role in the Gbande traditional
system of education. It enforces conformity to social norms;
it validates social institutions and religious rituals; and it
provides a psychological release from the restrictions imposed by society. Folk tales are forms of verbal art which are
important in preparing individuals for adult life in societies
such as the Gbande's, where schools which teach reading
and writing are lacking. They provide a medium for the
transmission of knowledge and values, and thus contribute to
the continuity of culture. Myths and legends may contain
detailed descriptions of religious beliefs and dogma, accounts of the origin of the people and their migrations, and
so on. Proverbs, on the other hand, have often been characterized as the distilled wisdom of the ancestors and are un-
mistakably so regarded by all Gbandes. The transmission of
the judgments expressed in proverbs and of the information
contained in myths and legends is considered important in
itself. Even folk tales which are regarded as fictitious by outsiders are recognized by Gbandes as important in the education of children, because so many of them are moral tales.

Gbande folklore, like most African folklore, has not been
the object of significant scientific interest in the Western
world for obvious reasons. No known study has previously
been done on the Gbandes or their folklore. It is the conten-

tion of the author that, in the absence of historical material, an understanding of the folklore of a people who have no written records will greatly enhance understanding of that people's culture.

Legends

This chapter focuses on legends and myths, folk tales, proverbs, and riddles. Legend provides a logical starting point for this chapter, because people everywhere and at all times have used legend to explain their origin as well as the origin of their culture and their being. This is no less true of the Gbande people.

"Legend of the Origins of the Gbande People"

In the beginning, after the Creator had created everything else, he came to create the most important thing in his creation—man. He created everyone out of the same stuff. He saw to it that every man was good and equal. God had only two requirements for everyone: to be earnest and to obey him. Notwithstanding, he gave every man the freedom to choose whether or not to be earnest and obedient to these rules. After men had lived a very long time together, one day the Creator decided to test man's earnestness and obedience to his rules. He summoned everyone before him, and divided them into two groups. He placed one group on his right-hand side and the other on his left-hand side. He then informed them that they must follow the instructions of his word explicitly if they were to receive his blessings. He instructed the two groups to go to two different but identical caves—the group on the right to the cave on the right-hand side, and the group on the left to the cave on the left-hand side. He told them that the caves were full of good things, such as kings, soldiers, slaves, women, children, iron, fine huts, clothing, jewels, horses, cattle, sheep, goats, and every other imaginable good thing. "However," God told them, "you must wait patiently until everything has come out of the cave. Then let the oldest male among you be your spokesman. Let him give the kings who were the first to come out of the cave this message: 'The Great Creator of all things, both seen and unseen, has sent you to us with all these peoples and things. He has sent you in order for you to serve us. He alone is able to reward you well, but you must be earnest and obey us at all times.'" The group on the righthand side was the first to depart for their cave. This group did exactly as it was instructed by the Creator. For this reason, this group was greatly blessed by the Creator and its members lived harmoniously and happily. This group represents the Gbande people. Next the group on the left-hand side departed for the cave on the left-hand side. The members of this group were so preoccupied with personal greed and selfishness that they completely forgot the instructions which the Great Creator had given them. When they arrived at the cave and saw the kings, soldiers, slaves, women, and children, they decided on the rule of "everyone for himself" instead of following instructions. As a result, they began to quarrel and fought among themselves over the things that had come out of the cave. The Creator, who sees everything, became very, very angry with them. In his anger, he told them, "Since you have deliberately chosen to behave in a disorderly manner by fighting among yourselves over all of the good things which I have freely given to you, I will take everything away from you immediately and you will never get anything free. From now on, you will have to work for everything you get. From this day on, you will be marked by selfishness, dishonesty, distrust, and rivalries." This group represents all the other people of the world. The Gbandes believe that they are truly blessed with everything in the world including a good climate, an abundance of foods, good health, and peace. They consider themselves the chosen people of Kgala the Creator, who is also referred to as Kgaiwolo Kgala.

"The Legend of Kɛsukɛkula"

"Vengence is mine," says Kɛsukɛkula, the professional rogue who avenges wrongdoing. Kɛsukɛkula is believed to be a man from among the Loma people, neighbors of the Gbandes. He was greatly admired by all the Gbande people. He traveled freely among them and was both loved and feared by all. He was a man who loved peace and justice and went about seeing to it that they came to everybody. In order to ensure the enforcement of peace and justice, he developed the skill of being a professional thief. Using this skill, he was able to retrieve anything of which a person had been cheated and restore it to the rightful owner. His constant insistence upon justice and peace restored honesty in Gbande society at a time when things seemed to be deteriorating by Gbande standards. It is said that a European and his wife doubted the ability of Kɛsukɛkula as a professional thief. They challenged him to prove his skill by stealing from them. Kɛsukɛkula accepted the challenge and told them that he would visit their hut before the sun came out the next day. The European and his wife had their guns ready and sat up to wait for Kɛsukɛkula. About midnight, they became very, very sleepy and could not keep their eyes open. Kɛsukɛkula came and undressed them, put the woman's clothing on the man and the man's clothing on the woman, took their guns away, and gave them sugar cane sticks instead. He carried them into the center of the village, where he kept them in a deep sleep until the whole village had gathered to see them sleeping in the center of town. When they awoke from their deep sleep and saw the whole village standing around them, they were very much ashamed and embarrassed. From that day on, they never doubted an African.

"The Legend of Haalē"

Another name which is very important among the Gbandes is that of Haalē. Haalē may or may not be a legendary figure. He is said to be a man who gave his own life to

save the Gbande people from destruction. It is stated that
the Gbande people were threatened with a dreadful strange
disease which was killing people the world over. The Creator revealed to the Gbande people through their chief
diviner that they would be spared from the plague if a
healthy young man from a chief's family would give himself
to be shot with many arrows and buried alive in the center of
any Gbande village. Haalē offered himself because he was
the son of a famous chief in Gbandeland. He was shot with
forty arrows and, while still grunting from the pain of these
arrows, he was buried alive in Somalahum. Because of this
noble deed, all members of his immediate family were freed
from taxation of any kind and from all public work.

Folktales

"Why the Soles of the Feet and the Palms of the Hands Look Pale"

One day the Creator, Gew>l>ñggala, told everybody
to go down to the stream and take a bath. The Gbande people and other Africans were in no hurry to get down to the
stream, while all the non-Africans were rushing to the
stream. Those who got to the stream first washed themselves
thoroughly until they looked pale all over. Today, the
children of this group represent the very pale-looking people
of the world. The next group arrived in time to find enough
water to bathe in but not enough to play in as the first group
had done; therefore they did not get quite as pale as the first
group. The children of this group represent the intermediate
peoples of the world who are between the very pale people
and the Africans. Last to arrive at the stream were the
Gbandes and all other Africans. To their surprise, they found
the stream almost dry. They tried in vain to squeeze water
out of the stream bed with the soles of their feet and the
palms of their hands. Their efforts produced only enough
water to cover the soles of their feet and the palms of their

hands. This is the reason why the soles of the feet and the palms of the hands of Gbandes and other Africans look pale.

"A Woman Who Stayed Pregnant for Forty Years"
Once there was a king who had many wives and daughters. He was very unhappy because he did not have any sons. It was the custom of his subjects to pay him tribute once every year. The gift was made by the head of each household. One year a very poor man, who had nothing but one ugly daughter, brought her to the king as his tribute. When the king's other wives saw her, they laughed at her so much that she decided to keep to herself. Notwithstanding, the king was impartial to her. She received the same consideration as any of the king's wives. In the course of time, she became pregnant. The king was very happy at first that his ugly wife was pregnant, but the king's other wives hated her more. She stayed pregnant for one, two, three and four years without having the child. The king became very sad again, but the other wives began to laugh at her again. She went ten, twenty, and thirty years without having the child. Then the king had a special hut built for her at the edge of the village where she lived by herself. She became very sad and hated herself every time she looked at her stomach. On the very night she was forty years pregnant, she became very sick with labor pains and cried for help. The king's doctors went to her aid and she gave birth to a handome young man who was already forty years old at birth. He was wiser and stronger than anyone in the kingdom and braver than anyone known to the king and his people. At once he began to assume many of the responsibilities of the aging king, who was very pleased with him, so much so that all the people in the kingdom loved and respected him greatly. His mother was very happy that her son was loved by all the people in the kingdom. When his father, the king, died, he became the most beloved king of the people. He had a special beautiful hut built for his mother next to his own. His mother was very

kind to all of the people, especially to the women of the kingdom. Her ugliness was at once transformed into beauty to such an extent that her past life became forgotten.

"The Elephant and the Goat"

Once an elephant quarreled with a billy goat who always stood under the bushy trees which the elephant wanted to eat. The elephant told the goat that he must not always stand under the bushy trees, because the trees were very good to eat. The billy goat replied by saying that he liked to stand under the bushy trees because he found nice tender leaves there which were good to eat. The elephant responded by telling the billy goat that *his* need for food was much greater than the billy goat's. "What I can eat in one day is enough for you in your whole lifetime," continued Elephant. Billy Goat was becoming quite irritated with Elephant and he said to Elephant, "My need for food is as important as yours and it is nonsense for you to think that you can eat more than I." This statement annoyed Elephant to the point that he challenged Goat to an eating contest which, of course, Goat willingly accepted. They agreed to meet early the next morning by an enormous rock which was close to the bushy trees. When they met the next morning, Elephant suggested that he start eating on one side of the rock and Goat on the other side.

At once Elephant started pushing over trees and eating everything in sight. About noon, he had leveled things on his side of the big rock as far as one could see. But Goat was standing in the same place they had met that morning and eating one leaf at a time. When the afternoon shadow of the bushy trees fell cast over the big rock, Billy Goat climbed it, lay down upon it, and continued to chew on the leaf he already had in his mouth. Toward evening, when Elephant could eat no more, he came to look for Goat and see just how much he had eaten. He found that nothing was disturbed on the side assigned to Goat. While looking around, he saw

Goat on top of the big rock chewing something. "Are you still eating?" he asked Billy Goat. "Yes, I am," said Billy Goat. "What are you eating when there is nothing on the rock? Elephant asked. Billy Goat replied, "I am eating the big rock and as soon as I am through eating it, I am going to eat you too." Elephant was very frightened when he heard the threat made against him by Billy Goat and he ran away into the forest.°

"The Princess Will Wed a Man Who Can Tell an Endless Story"
    Once there was a king who had many sons but only one daughter. She was very beautiful but was spoiled by her father and her brothers. As she grew up, the family became concerned about the type of man who could make her a good husband. After they had discussed this matter for a long, long time, someone suggested that the man who could best suit the princess's personality would be one who was wise. This suggestion was accepted by the king. The question remained how to find the wise man, for what could distinguish this man from other men? They discussed this matter in turn for a long, long time without coming up with any good suggestion. The king decided to let his daughter indicate her own criteria or criterion for judging wisdom in a man. Without any apparent effort on her part, she answered, "A man who can tell me a story that never ends is one I would consider a wise man." The king, therefore, proclaimed throughout the land that anyone who could tell an endless story would marry the princess. Many, many men came, old and young, all with their stories, but each of these stories came to an end. In the meantime, the beautiful princess was

°Even today the Gbandes firmly believe that elephants are afraid of goats and that the best deterrent against elephants is the bleating of a goat. When they travel in places where elephants are supposed to be, particularly at night, they usually bleat like a goat.

aging and there appeared to be no more storytellers left in
the land.

However, one day when the princess was very
depressed, a young man who was very unimpressive in appearance came to the king and begged to marry the beautiful princess. They laughed at him and wanted to throw him
out. But the king would not have him thrown out of his hut.
Instead, he told the young man that if he could tell an
unending story, he would not only get to marry the princess,
but he, the king, would also give him a portion of his
kingdom. The young man was very happy to hear the king's
promises. He, in turn, promised the king that he could tell a
story without an end and that he wanted to start his story
the next day.

The next morning, when the sun had come out, he went
to the king and the king's sons and began to tell his story. He
told them that he was a farm boy; therefore it was appropriate for him to tell a story about a farmer. "Once a farmer
made a big, a very big, rice farm," he began. "The rice grew
very well and yielded much, very much, rice. The farmer
built a very big hut to store his fine crop of rice. He built the
hut so well that there was only one little hole or opening in
the whole hut. This hole was so small that it could only let in
one grasshopper at a time, which must come out again
before another could go in. When the farmer had stored all
of his rice in this big hut, the dry season came and everything became dry. Then very many locusts came to look for
something to eat, because they were very, very hungry. The
locusts smelled the rice in the big hut and began to examine
it. One of the locusts discovered the little hole or opening to
the rice in the hut and went into the hut and took a grain of
rice and went away. Then another locust came and went into
the hut and took a grain of rice and went away. Then
another locust came and went into the hut and took a grain
of rice and went away." The young man kept repeating this
part for two years. The king asked him to go on with the rest

of the story because he had heard enough about the locusts and the rice in the hut. But the young man begged the king to be patient with him because he really wanted to tell the story exactly as it was, therefore he could not go on with the rest of the story until all of the locusts had been fed, or all of the grains of rice were gone, or all of the locusts had had enough to eat and had gone away. The young man continued for three more years, after which he told the king that there were still very many hungry locusts and a whole hut full of grains of rice to feed them. The king was very tired of the repetition of: "and then another locust came and went into the hut and took a grain of rice and went away, and then another locust came and went into the hut and took a grain of rice and went away." He again asked the young man to tell him when the locusts would stop coming and when the grains of rice would be finished. The young man said, "There are more locusts to come than those that have gone into the hut and the hut of rice still seems to be filled to the top. It will take many, many years for all of the locusts to come and finish the grains of rice." The princess told her father, the king, that by the time all of the locusts came and the grains of rice were finished she would probably have no need to get married; she would be too old. Therefore, she was willing to marry the young man from the farm. When the young man heard this, he was very happy because the princess was very beautiful. He was given a portion of the king's kingdom where he and the beautiful princess lived very happily and had many children.

"A Woman Who Did Not Want Her Daughter to Get Married"

Once there was a woman who loved her daughter so much that she did not want her to get married. This fact became apparent when the daughter came of age and yet had no husband. The people of the village summoned the mother and demanded an explanation why her daughter was

not married. She told the village elders that she was willing
to let her daughter marry, but the man she married must be
able to build a hut for her upon the big rock.° The men of
the village thought she was being unreasonable; nonetheless,
they attempted to build the hut. Each man went and got the
hardest sticks he could find, but all to no avail, because the
rock was very hard and the sticks could not go into it. Finally, all of the men of the village gave up the idea of marrying the unreasonable woman's beautiful daughter, because
none could build her a hut upon the rock. One day a young
man clothed in rags came to the woman and proposed to her
beautiful daughter. He told the woman that he knew the
requirement, which was to build a hut for her upon the big
rock, and that he was prepared to do so. At once, he began to
work and cut all kinds of sticks and brought them to the big
rock. He did this for three weeks and accumulated a big pile
of sticks. All of the sticks were of soft wood. The villagers
laughed and laughed at his foolishness. After he had accumulated enough sticks he went fishing for crabs and
caught a whole lot of crabs. He brought them to the woman
and told her that he was ready to start building the hut that
day. However, he said that he was very hungry for crabs, he
had a few with him, and he wondered if she would cook
them well-done for him. The woman did not consider this an
unreasonable request. She proceeded to cook the crabs. In
the meantime, the young man was busy sharpening the
points of the sticks to make them ready for piercing into the
rock. At noon, the woman called him to come and eat, but
when he took one bite of the crab, he jumped up with pain
and told the woman that he was suffering a toothache and

°A Gbande hut is built by first sticking several sticks into the earth
vertically to form either a circle or a trapezoid. It would be impossible
to pound sticks into a rock of that size. Hence, the woman was sure that
her daughter could never get married because no man could build the
hut.

that this was why he had wanted his crabs well-done so that the whole crab would be soft, including the shell. The woman cooked the crabs for five days, but each time the young man attempted to eat the crabs, the shells would crack in his mouth and he would jump up and tell the woman that they were not yet done, and that he would not start building the hut on the rock until he had had his well-done crabs. The woman cooked and cooked for two, three, and four weeks, but the shells of the crabs still cracked in the young man's mouth and he still jumped up with pain saying that the crabs were not well-done. Finally the woman became convinced that the crabs could not be cooked soft. She told the young man that she was a very good cook, but that she found it impossible to cook the crabs soft. "Likewise," said the young man, "I am a very good hut builder, but I find it impossible to build a hut upon a rock. If you are reasonable with me and do not insist that I build you a hut upon the big rock in order to marry your beautiful daughter, I will also be reasonable with you and will not insist that you cook the crabs soft." The woman agreed and the young man clothed in rags got to marry the woman's beautiful daughter without building her a hut upon the big rock.

"The Man With Three Plaits of Hair"

Once there was a king who forbade the growing and plaiting of hair by men in his kingdom. One day a man was found who had long hair plaited into three plaits. He was brought to the king, who asked him if he had not heard the decree forbidding long and plaited hair to be worn by men. The man answered the king by saying that, indeed, he knew of the decree. "Why then did you not obey it?" asked the king. "You shall be punished very severely for your disobedience unless you give me a very good reason why you should not be punished." The man told the king to have mercy on him, to be patient with him and to let him keep his three plaits of hair. He told the king that each plait had a name and a deep meaning. The king demanded to know the name of each plait. "The one directly over my face," the man said, "is called 'A woman is not to be trusted;' the one above the right ear is called 'Sleep has no mercy;' and the one over my left ear is called 'Another man's child is not your own.'" The king was sympathetic with him and let him go with his three plaits of hair.

Soon afterward, the king's brother died, leaving a very beautiful wife with a young son. The king immediately took this beautiful young woman as one of his wives, for such was their custom. The king loved her and her child very much. However, one of the least of the king's servants fell in love with this beautiful young wife of the king and began to have an affair with her. The king trusted her completely because she was very beautiful and shy and never left the king's court. She was above suspicion in the king's court among the king's wives. But one day the king decided to take a journey to a faraway country. After many days he returned, arriving at night. He went straight to the hut of the beautiful young wife, because he loved her very much and was concerned about her. He was surprised to find her sleeping in bed with one of the lowest servants in the king's court. He was enraged with anger and called both of them to wake up and get up. They were very much surprised and full of fear when they saw the king himself standing over them. The king had the servant arrested immediately. The commotion woke all of the royal family up, including the beautiful young wife's son, who had now grown into manhood. He came to see what the commotion was about and, behold, he saw the king beating his mother. He flew into a rage and knocked the king down, away from his mother. The king said to him, "Son, your mother has done a very bad thing; that is why I am beating her, because I love her." The young man said to the king, "I am not your son and do not touch my mother anymore." Then the man with the three plaits of hair sent words to remind the king of the names of his three plaits: A woman cannot be trusted, Sleep has no mercy, and Another man's child is not your own. From that day on, the man with the three plaits was given a position in the king's court as a wise man.

"The Disgusted Band Leader"
    Once there was a band leader who was very disgusted with the members of his band, because each time he suggested a song for them to play, a long, tedious argument ensued before they finally played it. One day he told them that if anyone argued with him about the next song, that person would no longer be a member of the band. As they reached the next village and were about to start whatever song the band leader might suggest, a pepper bug flew into the band leader's eye and he yelled, "Oh oh yeow yeowee!!" The band members picked it up and started to play, "Oh oh yeo yeowee!!." When he realized what was happening, he yelled, "There is something in my eye burning like pepper." And they started to play, "There is something in my eye burning like pepper." He again tried to explain, "This is not a song; there is something buring in my eye!" The band members again picked it up and played, "This is not a song; there is something in my eye," because they wanted to avoid anything that might be designated as an argument.

"The Trickster and the Woman With Her Baby"
    Once a woman took her little baby with her when she went to work on her farm. She was working so hard that she forgot all about the time. When she looked up to see the sun, it was already gone down and the moon was shining. She quickly picked up her baby and her things, including her fish net, and tied her little baby tightly on her back. She started walking very fast to get home before it got too dark and too late, because she had to walk through a thick forest which had a stream of water running through it. Her feet began to feel very heavy under her. When she got to the middle of the

thick forest, she met the Troublemaker—the Trickster, who asked her to cook for him. He asked her to cook his food without fire because he, the Trickster, hated fire. If she did not cook his food without fire, he would take away her little baby. The woman became very worried and perplexed because she did not know how to cook without fire and she did not want to give her little baby to the Trickster. After much time had been spent arguing with the Trickster, the little baby on the woman's back told her to tell the Trickster that she could indeed cook for him without fire, but she could not cook without water. "Tell the Trickster to fetch you some water with your fish net from the stream and you will cook for him without fire," the baby said. The Trickster agreed that the little baby was making sense. He took the fishing net from the woman and departed for the stream with it. But each time he dipped the net into the stream of water and pulled it out, it was completely empty. He tried over and over again without success. When at last he realized that the little baby had out-smarted and out-tricked him, he ran far away into the deepest part of the forest, where he remains to this day. He never again bothered the woman and her baby or any other person in their village.

"The Deer and the Woman"

Once there was a woman who made a small farm. She planted lots of okra, among other things, on her farm. Each time she went to examine her crops, she discovered that her okra and other crops were mysteriously being consumed. Upon closer examination, she saw deer tracks all over the farm. While she was there, a deer came to the farm and began to eat the okra. The woman was obviously annoyed and told Deer not to come to her farm anymore. But Deer replied by telling the woman that the site on which she had made her farm was his road and had always been his road, long before the woman made her farm there. Therefore, if the woman did not want him to walk on her farm, she should move her farm away from his road. In fact, Deer *insisted* that the woman move her farm away from his road. The woman was at a loss as to what step she should take next. Fortunately for her, she had her little baby girl tied on her back, who was listening to the whole dialogue between her mother and the deer with interest. The baby then suggested to her mother, "Deer is right and it is not a bad idea at all to move the farm away from Deer's road. But you will not want to carry your farm away with Deer's messy tracks all over it. Therefore, tell Deer to remove all his tracks from the farm and you will gladly remove your farm from his road." Deer agreed to pick his tracks up from the woman's farm. But as he picked up his tracks, he made more behind himself. When he found out that he could not successfully retrieve his tracks, he ran away into the forest and never again bothered the woman and her baby.

"The Raccoon and the Dog"

Once Raccoon met Dog at the edge of the village and said to him, "Dog, you are really blest. You do not have anything to worry about. You always get good food to eat and a good place to sleep, and nobody hunts you. Besides, you are loved by everybody in the village, it seems, because your name is heard all over the village day and night." Dog said to Raccoon, "Some of the things you have said are true, but I can assure you that I am not always treated with love." Dog invited Raccoon to be his guest that evening. He told Raccoon to wait for him at a designated spot under the kola tree and he would come there to get him when it was dark. Raccoon was very happy and waited eagerly for night to come so he could go with Dog. Dog kept his promise and came for Raccoon as soon as it was dusk. He asked Raccoon to get on his back each time they were about to enter a hut, so that Raccoon would become inconspicious in the light provided by the fire. The first hut that they entered was the hut of the chief's wives and they were all busy cooking. Dog made a mistake and stepped on one of the main fire logs supporting several pots, which sent these pots crashing down in every direction on the floor, putting out the fires. Everybody became enraged with Dog and started beating Dog with anything they could lay hands on. Of course, Raccoon received all the beating. This kind of treatment was repeated over and over again. Finally Raccoon begged Dog to take him back to the edge of the village and let him off his back. He told Dog that he, Raccoon, was actually better off than Dog, and that he would rather be a raccoon anytime than a dog.

"The Leopard and the Deer"
        Once there was a clever little deer whom Leopard wanted to eat very much. He tried every way possible to catch the clever little deer, but failed. One day he told all the other animals that he was now very old and that he would die that very day. The news went around that the old leopard was dead and that he would be buried the next day. The clever little deer had some reservations about the quick death of the old leopard. Nonetheless, early the next morning, he went to pay his last respects to the seemingly dead leopard. However, he refused to go through the main door like the rest of the animals. Instead, he climbed through the window. He quickly observed from the window that the leopard's mouth was closed. He said to the other animals, "I have seen many dead leopards in my lifetime, but I have never seen one with his mouth closed." When Leopard heard this, he gradually began to open his mouth. When Deer saw what was happening, he exclaimed, "In all my life, I have never seen a dead leopard who understands what is being said about him. This leopard is not dead." And he ran away again from the old leopard.

"The Little Bird With the Big Beak"
        Once there was a little bird with a big head and beak who stayed in her tree hole and demanded food from all the

other birds, telling them that if they did not feed her, she would come out and drive all of them away from their favorite spots. They were all afraid of her. One day, all the birds were gone except for one little bird who stayed behind. Pretty soon, the bird with the big head and beak called out to the little bird and demanded food, but the little bird refused to provide the food. The bird with the big head and beak became so angry with the little bird that she came out of her tree hole after the little bird, but the wind carried her farther and farther away from her tree hole because she was so skinny. When the other birds came back and saw the skinny bird with the big head and beak, they laughed and laughed at her. From that day on, she never got any more free food.

Spider Tales

"Spider at the Feast"

Once there was a meeting of all the animals for a big feast. When Spider heard of the meeting, he went and made himself an enormous wood carving which looked very frightful like a bad animal. He got into this carving and went to the meeting. All of the other animals were afraid of him and they gave him the best of everything, including the food. One little animal observed that the big frightful animal could not bend any of his members even when he went to sleep. When they began to investigate, Spider knew that he had been discovered. He ran away from them into the bush where he remains to this day.

"Blind Spider"

Once there was such a long, dry season that the people did not have enough food from their farms. Nevertheless, they were always kind and were willing to share with strangers and the handicapped whatever they had. Spider pretended to be a blind man. Every afternoon, he would go to a certain place in the woods close to the village by a big tree.

There he would take out one of his eyeballs and pretend that he was an old blind stranger. The people gave him the very best food they had. He continued to do this until one day he was accidently discovered by a little boy, who saw him take one of his eyeballs out and hide it under the big tree. The little boy went and got some hot pepper and sprinkled it over Spider's eyeball, which was hidden under the big tree. Then he went and told the elders of the village what Spider was doing. The old men of the village went with the little boy and hid themselves behind the big tree where Spider had put his one eyeball. When he came back from the village and tried to put his eyeball back in place, it burned so badly that he began to weep loudly and call for help. All the old men of the village came to Spider and helped him clean off his eyeball and put it back, but then they drove him away from the village forever.

"The Reason For Spider's Tiny Waist"
Once Spider heard that there would be a big feast on the same day in two neighboring villages. He went and got himself a very long rope, fastened it around his waist, and gave one end to a boy in one village and the other end to a boy in another village. He told each boy to pull the rope as soon as the drums began to beat, so that he would be pulled to each feast in turn. It so happened that both villages started their drums at the same time, and moreover the two boys were of equal strength. When they began to pull, they almost cut Spider in half and he never got to go to either of the feasts. This is the reason Spider has a small waist.

"Spider's Punishment"
Once spider committed a very bad crime and was to be executed. It was decided to find the most appropriate method to put Spider to death. Someone suggested death by fire. When Spider heard this, he was very happy or pretended to be so. Then someone suggested that since Spider appeared to be happy with this method of punishment, they

should put him to death by drowning. When Spider heard this suggestion, he began to cry and weep bitterly, so much that the people decided to kill him by water. When he was thrown into the river, he just walked on the water over to the other side and laughed at his accusers.

"Spider and Dog"
Once Spider and Dog were guests together at a place where they brought their dinner. Spider looked at Dog for a long time in an attempt to find Dog's mouth. All that he could see was Dog's nose. So he decided to take a walk and told Dog to go ahead and start eating without him because Dog's mouth was so little. When he returned, he found all of the food gone. He started beating Dog because he thought Dog had given the food to someone else. Dog finally opened his mouth and barked at Spider. When Spider saw Dog's mouth, he became so frightened that he climbed the wall, and there he remains even today.

"The Obedient But Stupid Servant"
A servant was once told to go to bed early because the chief was to send him on an errand to the next village early the next morning. The servant got up at midnight and went to the next village, came back before daybreak, and waited. When the chief called for him, he told the chief that he had already been to the next village and back; the only problem was that he had forgotten to take the chief's message.

Proverbs

The chicken whose eyes are bright (a symbol of good health) does not escape being sacrificed to the medicines.

A man's greasy mouth after eating indicates the nature of his good food.°

A wise man is one who gives his son a big bone with a

° This means: What one eats is a measure of one's social status.

little meat on it and gives the servant's son a little portion of meat only, because it is not good for the master's son to beg the servant's son for something to eat.

The outward appearance of a man's servant is a measure of a man's social status.

A hunter looking for game does not whistle until he has found his prey and killed it.

An animal which is destined to die does not hear the hunter's whistle.

He who has once been bitten by a snake will be frightened at the sudden sight of a hut lizard until he has had a second look.

He who is a latecomer to a dance should not suggest a song—it might already have been sung.

He who is lucky enough to recover from a serious sickness is the one who complains of being skinny and looking bad.

If you want something to be a secret, keep it from everybody, even your wife and your closest friends.

He who cannot dance is the one who finds fault with the beating of the drums.

When a blind person says that he will stone you, you can be sure that he already has the stone in his hand.

The anatomy of a mosquito is like that of any other living thing, but we never take the time to examine it when we are bitten.°

When you tell a little boy to keep out of the grass because of snakes when the sun is hot, and the little boy tells you that he is looking for a snake, what other reason will you use to get him out of the hot sun?

When a crocodile's son dies of thirst, then surely there must have been a catastrophe.

°This means: When we are angry, we do not take the time to reason things out.

One's words are like the shells of the palm kernel—they never rot.

Only those who have teeth worry about toothache.

A man who is completely bald does not worry about head lice.

Riddles

What goes into the mouth by itself and comes out in the company of many? (A palm kernel.)*

Once a man who considered himself the fastest met another man who also considered himself the fastest. One day as they were going to visit the neighboring village, they came to a big river which had one small log as a bridge. Only one of them could cross at a time. The first man was almost across the river when he slipped from the log; but before he hit the water, he completely undressed himself, because he did not want his clothes to get wet. The other man looked up just in time to see his companion falling off the log bridge. He quickly dashed across the log and took the clothes from the one who was falling before he hit the water. Who was the faster man?

Once there were two men, each of whom considered himself the best thief. One day, as they were walking in the woods together, they saw an eagle sitting on her nest with two eggs. One of the men quietly climbed the tall tree where the eagle had nested and stole the two eggs from under the eagle without disturbing her. He put them securely in his pocket. When he got down from the tree, he discovered that the eggs were gone. The other thief had stolen them. Who was the better thief?

Once there were two men, each of whom claimed that he could sleep longer than the other. The first man climbed to the top of a hill overlooking a river, lay down, and went to

* This riddle also refers to the fact that one word may have many meanings.

sleep. The second man went into an open field, lay down, and went to sleep. They went to sleep during the dry season; but when the rainy season came, the one who was sleeping on the hill was washed away by rain water running down the hill into the river. As soon as he reached the river, he was swallowed by a very large catfish. He continued to sleep in the catfish undisturbed. Meanwhile, the one who went into the open field to sleep was completely buried by a colony of ants who came and built their hill on top of him. He too went on sleeping undisturbed. After many years, the people decided to build new huts in the open field. While some of them started digging the soft clay from the ant hill to cover the huts, others went to the river to fish because there was no meat for the workmen to eat. One of the men who went to fish caught the large catfish and brought it to be cooked for the men. As they cleaned the catfish, the knife touched something in the catfish's belly, and the man who was still sleeping in the fish awoke and said, "Who is disturbing me? Please keep quiet. I am very sleepy." Simultaneously, the workmen at the ant hill touched something with their hoes, and the man who was asleep in the ant hill awoke and said, "Who is disturbing me? Please keep quiet. I am very sleepy." Who was the longer sleeper?

Once three men were going on a journey when they were caught by a rainstorm. They ran and came to a hut, but only one of them could go into the hut because it was a small hut. The first man to get to the hut went in and the other two men remained outside. When the rain stopped, the man who went in came out completely wet and the two men who did not go in were completely dry. Who were they? (The male sex organs.)

Jokes

Once a young man who was a practical joker was having an affair with an experienced married woman. Whenever he was in bed with her, he teased her by saying, "Your husband is coming!" He did this repeatedly until one day the woman got fed up and invited him to her farm. She told him that her husband had gone to hunt and would not be back until very late in the evening. The farm hut was located right in the middle of the farm, so that anyone leaving it would be seen by any other person on the farm. While the young man and the woman were in bed, she spotted her husband coming to the farm hut. She told the young man, "Look! My husband is coming!" The young man did not know what to do. The woman told him, "Hide quickly under the pepper bush and I will cover you with rice straw," which she did neatly. When her husband came, she said to him, "I have never seen you shoot anything. Do you think of yourself as a good marksman? If you do, I want you to prove it to me by shooting into that pepper bush over there with the rice straw over it." The young man could see them and, of course, he heard all the woman had said to her husband. He saw the man level his gun at the pepper bush. However, before he could pull the trigger, the woman told him that she did not want him to waste his bullets on a pepper bush. By this time the young man had messed all over himself because he was very much afraid and had thought that that was the end for him. From that day on, he never again joked with the woman about her husband.

Once a man who was having an affair with another man's wife was surprised by the husband, who came home unexpectedly. He climbed up into the attic of the hut because there was no back door or window. The top of the attic was too low for him to stand up. He sat down flat on the crossbars of the attic and his testicles hung down through a hole in the ceiling. When the woman's husband saw them, he asked his wife what they were, and she told him that they were a new set of bells she had just gotten. "Well, I'd like to hear them," said the husband, so he proceeded to strike them with a little stick. At each blow the man above, in pain,

would cry out, "Ding dong!" until the husband had had
enough fun. Then he went away because he did not want to
make his wife feel bad by making a liar out of her.

Once there was a woman who used to climb out the
window onto the shoulders of her lover to get away from the
hut as soon as her husband was away. Her husband learned
of her trick from another person in the village. One day he
fooled her and pretended to be the lover, after telling his
wife that he would not return until the next morning. He
went to the window as the lover did and knocked three
times. At once the woman came and climbed down upon his
shoulders, and as the husband carried her away, she said,
"Am I not clever, my love?" The husband answered, "Yes,
but I am more clever than you because I am your dear husband." The woman was so shocked, she fainted.

Mother-in-law Jokes

Once a man went to pay a visit to the parents of his wife. He
was very hungry at the time of his visit. His arrival was a
welcome sight for his father-in-law, who was busy at the
time weaving cloth for his family. The father-in-law at once
turned over the weaving to him and went to check his bird
traps. In the meantime, his mother-in-law was cooking some
sweetheart beans (lima beans) which were almost done. She
decided to go to the creek for water to heat for her husband's
bath. The beans smelled so good that the son-in-law was
tempted to taste them. He took the lid off the pot and began
to eat the beans. While eating, he took off his hat and placed
it beside the pot lid. When he looked up and saw his mother-
in-law coming back from the creek, in his haste he put the
pot lid on his head and his hat on the pot.

Once a son-in-law visited his in-laws at the time of the
evening bath. His mother-in-law gave him a pot of warm
water to take a bath in behind the hut. He took off his pants,
and as he commenced to bathe, a dog came and started

sniffing at his pants. Pretty soon, the dog began to drag the pants toward the center of the village. The harder he tried to retrieve them, the farther the dog moved toward the center of the village with his pants.

Once a son-in-law visited his in-laws on a rainy night. He was very hungry. The mother-in-law, knowing that the night would cool, got out a large white cloth for the son-in-law to use during the night. She put it in a large gourd in order to keep it dry and took it to the son-in-law's sleeping place. When the son-in-law saw it, he thought it was food. As soon as the mother-in-law left, he opened his calabash (gourd) of palm oil and emptied it on the cloth. Only when he tasted it did he realize his mistake and he was very ashamed.

Once a son-in-law visited his mother-in-law at a time when one of her hens was setting. His mother-in-law asked him to look after the hen while she went to fetch water from the creek. While she was gone, he decided to boil two of the hen's eggs. As the eggs boiled, he saw his mother-in-law approaching. He hid the hot eggs in the seat of his pants. He said good-bye to his mother-in-law, but the mother-in-law followed him down the road to send a message to her daughter. He attempted in vain to get away because the eggs were very hot. Finally, he told his mother-in-law that it was time for all good men to lay eggs like chickens and he dropped the hot, hard-boiled eggs.

Once a son-in-law visited his in-laws who had just built a new hut. The place where they had dug up the dirt to plaster the hut was filled with water from the rain. As he walked by it, he fell into it. When his mother-in-law came to express her sympathy, he told her he was practicing his swimming.

Once a greedy son-in-law visited his mother-in-law at mealtime in the night. The hut was pretty dark because the firewood was wet. This son-in-law, who had a large hand, was invited to eat with them. (As a rule, the Gbandes eat with their hands, and a man who has a bigger hand would naturally get more food. However, as a rule, this natural advantage is seldom used for fear of public disdain.) The son-in-law was observed with a huge handful of food when a litttle boy threw a bunch of dry leaves into the fire and suddenly made it light. The son-in-law in his embarrassment asked, "Is there a dog in this hut?" (meaning, of course, that he wanted to give his huge handful of food to the family dog).

Once a young man, newly married, wanted to impress his young wife and her parents by catching a cow fly which was sitting on a piece of wood. He missed the fly but jammed a big splinter into his hand; it went through two of his fingers. He was in great pain but very embarrassed and said, "I got the fly, but it is too big to kill here. Therefore, I am taking it somewhere to kill it." And he ran away.

A List of Insults in Gbande Culture

Your backside looks red like the setting sun.

Your teeth look like sweetheart beans. (When these beans—lima beans—are dried, they turn yellow.)

Your mouth looks like a water fence which has been broken through by flood water, or like broken fish traps. (This refers to those persons who have one or more front teeth missing.)

Your mouth smells like spoiled shrimp.

Your belly looks like a goat's when it has drunk dye water.

Gbande Compliments

Your teeth look like elephant tusks.

Your legs look like ceramic work.

Your neck looks like ceramic work.

Chapter 12
Hygiene and Sanitation

ALTHOUGH HYGIENE AND sanitation differ, they are sufficiently related to be considered together in one chapter. Hygiene is concerned with the maintenance and preservation of both physical and mental health. It is the system of principles for the preservation of health and, by implication, the prevention of disease. Sanitation refers to the study and application of hygienic measures, among which cleanliness and the disposal of wastes are most basic. In this sense, the Gbandes share common meanings of these concepts with the rest of humanity. However, when these concepts are examined in terms of their content and application, the Gbandes are unique. One reason for uniqueness of their practices of hygiene and sanitation is the fact that, for the Gbandes, sickness, misfortunes, and death are not caused by germs or mishaps but by witchcraft. Of course, this approach to hygiene will defy the imaginations of those enculturated in urban industrialized societies. The fact is that the Gbandes employ as rigid precautionary measures to prevent or deter the practice of witchcraft as Western societies do to ensure hygienic practices. The Gbandes believe that if witches and/or the practice of witchcraft could be controlled, diseases, sickness, misfortunes of various kinds, and even untimely deaths could be reduced if not completely prevented. It is not difficult to see that Gbande thought patterns about the causal relationship of disease and witches are equivalents of the germ theory of Westerners. In both cases, the debilitating condition is caused by agents external to the organism. To combat spread of the causes is the essence of any preventive method designated by the term "hygiene." It is from this point of view that a discussion of Gbande hygienic and sanitary practices has been formulated.

Gbande hygienic and sanitary practices operate at three levels, namely the communal, the familial, and the personal. For purposes of clarity, discussion of hygienic practices at these three levels will precede discussion of sanitary practices at the three levels.

Water

It has been pointed out elsewhere in this work that among the Gbandes, as among other Africans, there is no known club or any other organization of witches with a known membership. No one wants a witch and/or knowingly accepts a friend who is a witch or belongs to a group of witches. In fact, witches or fear of witches and witchcraft is the most important single factor determining all Gbande hygienic and sanitary practices. This fear demands full participation of the members of the whole community, who must put forth their best efforts to control witches so as to prevent the practice of witchcraft. The quickest ways of being witched or getting a witch include coming into physical contact with the carrier of a witch and eating or drinking a witch in food or water. Therefore, it becomes imperative for the entire community to have a common source of water for all domestic needs. This common source is usually one or two streams of water near the village. It is believed that no witch will wish to witch herself or himself in this water since this is the only source of drinking water for everybody in the village. (Witches are not limited to women or old ladies on brooms, as witches are often portrayed by Western people.)

Water for cooking, bathing, and laundry is provided by these streams for the whole village. For these reasons, such water areas are considered relatively safe. Because of this feeling of safety, a certain area of one of these streams is used by the females of the village for bathing and laundering as well as for fetching drinking and cooking water and bath water for those who must take hot baths, such as the old people and guests. Another area in the other stream is reserved for the menfolk to bathe in and to sharpen their tools in,° among other things. It is a common practice that bathing, fetching water for household use, and laundering—that is, activities involving the use of the streams—are regulated so that they are always performed in groups and at a given time. Anyone found alone in any of these spots at noon, (when the sun is overhead), between 12:00 and 2:00 P.M. in the afternoon, or anytime in the night would be suspected of being a witch. If the suspect was a woman, and if any misfortune befell the community or a member of the community within three days after the time she was seen, she was automatically blamed. If the suspect was a man, he was usually held under suspicion for four days. Any member of the community—male or female, child or adult—is absolutely duty-bound to report such a suspicious person to the head of his family, who in turn brings it to the attention of the village elders if anything unfortunate happens within the designated period (whose length is determined by the suspect's sex, as indicated above). If nothing happens within that period, the suspect is exonerated and the matter never gets beyond the members of the household who have seen the suspect.

The second level at which Gbande hygienic practices operate is that of the family (the extended family), which I have referred to as the familial level. The fact that there is

---

°Water washes away the dust between the metal tool and the stone it is sharpened against, so that the two make better contact and friction is improved.

usually one big house—a common house for all women,
married and unmarried, and their children—and that each
married male has his own sleeping house has been pointed
out elsewhere in this volume. Almost all important domestic
familial activities take place within the women's house. It is
in this house where drinking water for the entire family is
kept, bath water is heated, and food is prepared. The devices
employed at the familial level as control mechanisms against
witches and witchcraft are unquestionably impressive but
are difficult for Westerners or Western-trained individuals to
accept as hygienic practices. What is impressive is that the
rules governing the system of controls apply equally to everyone in the household, without regard to age or sex. In
order to deter witches and the practice of witchcraft adequately, the following rules must be regularly observed.
Every household has only one water pot—a large earthenware pot—which holds water for cooking, bathing, and
drinking for the entire family. The drinking utensil is a
gourd split in half, which is sometimes called a "calabash."
This calabash is the only drinking utensil which each
member of the family uses to draw and drink water from the
large earthenware receptacle. The large earthenware pot
and the drinking calabash are only cleaned once in a while,
because it is believed that water is the best cleansing agent
and therefore nothing can clean it better than itself. This
logic, the logic of having only one water pot and one
drinking utensil for all members of an extended family, and
the fact that these utensils are not washed regularly would
be considered totally unacceptable in terms of resulting
hygiene by Western standards. However, the logic behind
these practices is very sound by Gbande standards since the
practices reduce the opportunity of any family member to
put a witch in the drinking pot or calabash. Strangers are
fed separately in the strangers' house and do not have an
opportunity to visit the big house where the water pot
and drinking calabash are kept; hence the likelihood of a

stranger's putting a witch into either of these utensils is slim.

By Gbande standards, the absence of witchcraft means the absence of diseases and misfortunes, and a reduced death rate. Protection against witchcraft gives everyone in the household confidence that each of them is being protected against disease and misfortunes. The Gbande's strong belief in a control mechanism that will eliminate the causes of sickness is bound to have appropriate effects on their behavior making methods used to prevent witchcraft a way of life.

Preparation of Meals

The next important category at the familial level is the preparation of meals. Food (that is, staple food) is kept in the attic of the women's house, where it is measured out daily by the head woman to whoever is the cook for the day. The actual cooking is done in two pots. One pot is used for the main staple and the other for meat, fish, vegetables, and so on. If a household or a family has more than one adult woman, the preparation of meals is by assignment, each taking turns for three consecutive days. Each woman may do the cooking herself or supervise one of the younger girls of the household who actually prepares the meal. The adult woman is fully responsible for any irregularity which may result from such a meal. Just as there are two pots for cooking, there are two dishes for serving, one for the females and the other for the males. These may be large wooden bowls or gourds. The staple food is placed in the bowl first and the meat, fish, and vegetables are added to it. The boys eat with the men and the girls with the women. It is absolutely necessary that everybody eats together. It anyone is away, that person has to be found before the eating starts. This practice is a protection of that one individual against witchcraft. However, there are cases in which cooked food is conveyed to certain individuals, for example, to guests and sometimes to elderly people who cannot wait to eat at the regular eating time. In this case, the person who carries the food to such an individual must sample it before them by tasting the food as well as the water to assure the guest or elderly person that the food is "witch-free."

Wine

The Gbandes are makers of wine from the palm tree and piassava tree as mentioned before. Wine is usually served to superiors and honored guests and is used for the entertainment of friends. If it is served to a superior person or an honored guest, the giver is obligated to take a swallow in their presence. If it is used for the entertainment of friends, it is drunk out of the same calabash by everybody, beginning with the giver of the wine. This practice is a standard procedure throughout Gbandeland regarding food and drink.

Personal Hygiene

This brings us to the third level—the level of personal hygiene. In terms of personal hygiene, the Gbandes are meticulous about cleanliness. Each Gbande is enculturated to take a bath twice daily, in the morning and in the evening, as a minimum prerequisite of cleanliness. In other words, one may take more than two baths a day, but one cannot take less than two. A soft vine, which the Gbandes call *duwì*, is used to fulfill a dual role. It is used as a wash cloth as well as bath soap. The vine is cut into short pieces, and these pieces are then beaten until they look like excelsior. This material is used to scrub one's self until it is worn out. The Gbandes take a lot of time scrubbing with it under their arms, between their toes and around their heels. It is also used to scrub the body generally. The material is replaced when it does not foam anymore. The hair is washed only periodically because the Gbandes believe that hair has its own nutrients and the frequent washing of it will rob it of these nutrients. Nevertheless, since cleanliness and neatness are a way of life for these people, haircutting for the men and boys and hairdressing with different styles for the women and girls are regular routines. Men keep their hair short and comb it as often as is needed with a homemade wooden comb. Women keep their hair long and plait it in various styles in order to keep it clean. Most Gbande males are clean-shaven. An unshaved man is considered not only dirty but lazy, unless such a man is a member of the Islam faith. Fingernails and toenails are trimmed regularly and polished. The children are trained to brush their teeth at least once a day, usually in the morning before eating anything. (Toothbrushes are made out of rattan vines that are chewed on one end to soften and loosen the fibers there, which become the bristles to scrub the teeth.) Hands must be washed before eating. No one is allowed to spit or blow his nose during mealtime or around the place where the meal is being prepared.

Let us now examine Gbande sanitary practices in a similar manner—that is, on communal, familial, and personal levels. In discussing Gbande sanitation, I have arbitrarily decided to limit the discussion to two phases, namely cleanliness and the disposal of wastes. The elimination and disposal of bodily wastes is a major problem of sanitation which concerns any society. The concern is much more acute in Gbandeland. This acuteness is due to the fact that there are no manmade latrines or lavatories for individual or public use. If a village has a large body of water close by, it is a welcome natural lavatory for the community. In the case of a river, the upper part is used by the womenfolk and an area downstream, about a quarter of a mile from the women, is reserved for the men. No man is allowed to wander into the area designated for the women and vice versa. These areas of the river are off limits for fishing. There are usually schools of catfish living unmolested on the excrements of the adult

community of the village. Let me point out that such rivers
are not used for other domestic purposes, such as drinking,
bathing, and so on. If a river is a large one, fishing is allowed
about one mile from the point of defecation. There are a
number of serious disadvantages in the use of this natural
communal facility, but I shall mention only two in passing.
In the first place, such a river is almost always some distance
from the village; consequently, it is not easily accessible at
night. The fear of witches (who are believed to walk at
night), the fear of predatory animals, and the fear of simply
falling into the water keep villagers from using it at night.
The second disadvantage is that during the rainy season, or
whenever it is raining, it is impossible to use the river. In the
first place, it is impractical for anyone to walk half a mile in
the rain to and from the river; in the second place, at this
time the rivers often swell to overflow their banks. In addition, there are many villages in Gbandeland without such
natural facilities for the disposal of wastes. The people of
these villages, as well as those people who cannot use their
river at a given time, resort to one place. This place is usually
under the banana trees or some similar growth close enough
to the village. The banana leaves are broad and strong
enough to protect the users of the place under them from the
rain. This is feasible and poses no great problem to the community, because the community dogs are only too eager to
clean up these deposits as fast as they are made. Each village
has a clearance of about twenty-five to thirty yards around it.
This clearance is to keep away unwanted guests, such as
snakes. It is the area beyond this clearance that is used for
the elimination of feces. Children between the ages of two
and five can eliminate anywhere and at any time they feel
like doing so. There are always some dogs around to clean
up.

　　Disposal of the dead is both a communal and a familial
obligation. The body may be buried deeply in the center of
the village or by the side of the big house, the women's

house. At any rate, graves are about six to eight feet deep. The question of death and the dead is discussed adequately in Chapter 9 "The Gbande Religion" subsection "Death." Therefore, Gbande sanitary practices at the familial level will be considered next.

Every extended family has two bathing places, one for the males and the other for the females. They are built either around a specially constructed wooden platform or around a pad of specially prepared gravel or rocks. In the first case, a wooden platform is constructed about two feet above the ground. It is enclosed with a circular fence woven lightly around it in order to provide privacy for the user. A similar circular fence is built around the gravel or rocks for the same purpose. The gravel serves the same purpose as the platform, which is to keep the feet away from the mud. These places also serve a vital function as places for discharging urine. Urine is discharged against the fence from within a given corner. This corner is constantly washed off by dumping left-over bath water over it. This is not necessary during the rainy season; the rain water does the cleansing since there are no roofs over these bathing areas. The male members of the family are responsible for keeping these structures in good repair. A few small drainage ditches are usually made to allow water and other wastes to drain away from the structures.

Dishwashing and Garbage Disposal

With the exception of the main water pot and the water calabash out of which everybody drinks, other cooking utensils—that is, pots, spoons, and sticks—are washed each time they are used. The pots are soaked and scrubbed carefully with the hands and fingernails or with a piece of stick until they are clean. The Gbandes do not believe in using a cloth to wash dishes because the cloth is considered dirty. Houses, particularly the big house, are swept twice daily; the garbage and other rubbish resulting from this cleaning is hauled and dumped beyond the clearance of the village. Here, again, the dogs become the ever-ready disposal agents. The Gbandes do not believe in lawns. Every bit of grass is cut off with hoes and dumped in the same place as the garbage and rubbish. This is done as often as needed, because grass grows the year round.

Imperative Sanitary Care

At the third level, the level of personal sanitary methods, we meet face-to-face the problem of the fear of witchcraft. Every adult Gbande personally and secretly disposes of the hair from any part of his body, his fingernail or toenail clippings, anything else directly connected with his body, and any article of clothing which he wears close to his body. It is firmly believed that witches are capable of manipulating any of the above items to work their will upon the person to whom the item belongs. For this reason, each person is careful to sweep his or her hair up from the place where it has been cut or dressed. It is then secretly buried with great care. The same is done for fingernail and toenail clippings. Women who have reached the age of puberty and all women subject to menstruation are vulnerable to the manipulation of witches. For this reason, each woman carefully disposes of her own menstrual materials secretly, probably by burying them.

The practice of hygienic or sanitary measures is a defensive mechanism which protects not only the community but each member of the community. As a result, cleanliness is the accent or pivotal point upon which Gbande society and culture depends. Mental illness and the uncertainties which surround the business of living are believed to be mitigated or deterred by a strict observance of these rules which I have taken the liberty of calling "hygienic and sanitary rules."

Chapter 13
Gbande Government

IN GENERAL TERMS, political organization comes into existence whenever a society becomes segmented into functional entities—kinship, economic, religious, and other groups. Moreover, whenever there are groups that are discrete entities within the society, there is political organization—a system which regulates relations between the groups as well as between members of the different groups within the society at large. Implicit in the idea of a governmental system, wherever it may be found, are these three elements: a territory; a people; and a government. These three form the core of any human community, including that of the Gbandes. The members of a community often share a common culture. In this sense, the term "community" means a commonality in which diversity exists but unity prevails. To the Gbandes, the term "community" means a feeling of oneness, a sense of entirety and esprit de corps extending to the whole territorial society. It means that the culture sets values that regulate behavior in the direction of communal interests as well as of individual or subgroup interests. As we shall see, the Gbande community is the essence of the political entity of the Gbande people. Political organization, therefore, is that part of Gbande culture which directs the activities of the members of the society toward community goals. When all of the communities are considered as a unit, we have what is known as the Gbande state.

The state, in this sense, includes all of Gbandeland; it is
the composite structure within which the communities find
expression as political entities. But it is not the society, the
state, or the community, per se, which makes government an
important institution for Gbandes; rather it is the complex of
behavioral characteristics that members of the Gbande communities exhibit in their political lives. As a group, the
Gbandes constitute a social entity characterized by a community sentiment that arises from a common cultural heri-
tage. For them, government is a working instrument of justice designed for Gbandeland. When one speaks of a Gbande
political entity, one really means the organization of which
government is a part and which includes the administrative
institution of the land. From this point of view, while it is obvious that all Gbandes are citizens of Gbandeland, it is
equally obvious that only a few Gbandes may be part of the
government, since only a few members of most societies
belong to the administrative institution. Indeed, the people
who staff the Gbande government are the specialists and
functionaries who transact Gbandeland's business with outsiders. (The term "outsiders" refers to all non-Gbandes,
including the Liberian national government.)

Politics and Allegiance

This brings us to the problem of politics and allegiance
within and towards two different forms of government. This
phenomenon is common to most if not all African states,
varying only in degree. For instance, the Gbandes are faced
with the demands of two loyalty groups. First, they are concerned with the loyalty necessary for continual integration
and perpetuation of the Gbandes as a cultural and linguistic
group; second, they are concerned with the loyalty necessary
for them to form a part of a larger whole—the Liberian national government. The Gbandes are only one of twenty-
seven such cultural and linguistic groupings in Liberia, a

small country of only 43,000 square miles. As indicated
above, this phenomenon is a common one for the African
continent as a whole. The issue is obvious but sensitive and
at times is raised unnecessarily; it is very difficult for Africans to discuss it, much less resolve it. The fact is, the term
"tribe" has been so much misused, usually with a derogatory
connotation, that it has become a taboo word. All the national governments of the African continent are made up of
just such cultural and linguistic groups. This is a fact that no
African can deny. Hesitancy to use the term "tribe" is due to
a number of related reasons. The term has been used for peoples held in the lowest esteem, the so-called "pagans," and
for people who were outside the tribe of the Biblical character Abraham. It was not used for descendants of one of the
three divisions into which the ancient Romans were divided
but was used for the gentiles, pagans, unsaved, and
unpolished peoples. Nonetheless, regardless of how ashamed
the Africans may be of the concept of tribe, it is a factor
which cannot be ignored because, on the whole, tribalism
still controls the majority of sub-Saharan Africans in their
allegiances, sentiments, and thought patterns. The fulfillment of political destinies and other aspirations are very
much dependent upon tribal support. Even modern cities are
structured in tribal ghettos, whose members band together
to aid members of their own tribe. These tribal ghettos serve
to maintain tribal ethnocentrism in the urban milieu.

Staff of Gbande Government

The staff of the Gbande government and the functionaries
who perform Gbandeland's business with groups external to
the Gbande people include, beginning with those at the local
level: the headmen; the town chiefs; the regional or district
chiefs; and the paramount chiefs and their various aides. It is
apparent from this listing that only a few Gbandes represent
all of the Gbandes in both internal and external rela-

tionships. It is therefore necessary that these few individuals be distinguished from the mass of the Gbande people by some criterion recognized by all Gbandes. This criterion is the political order which persists within Gbande traditional political institutions. After all, it is always within an institutional framework that men acquire power, wield power, or influence the distribution of power. The term "power," as used here, refers to the characteristics of those individuals who can influence the conduct of others, even against their will. Even in a situation in which everyone is declared equal, there will be politics. The game of politics usually involves subordinates and superiors. Moreover, the functioning of an institution involves a distribution of power, and it is exactly this distribution which is the essence of politics. Power implies that an actor can carry out his will; it implies the obedience of those over whom it is wielded. The general problem of politics is then the explanation of the varying distribution of power and of obedience which defers to it. Once this is understood, the question becomes one of political psychology: Why do men, by their obedience, accept other men as powerful? Any answer to this question must take into account the type of reasons given for obedience—that is, whether power is publicly or privately recognized. The former is the case here. An understanding of publicly recognized reasons for obedience (legitimations or symbols of justification) is crucial to the understanding of authority, and it is authority that characterizes enduring political order. Power, in this sense, is synonymous with but not identical to authority. Power is nothing more or less than the probability that men will act as another man wishes them to act. This action may rest upon fear, rational calculation of advantage, lack of energy to do otherwise, loyal devotion, indifference, or perhaps, motives other than these. On the other hand, authority, or legitimated power, involves voluntary obedience based on some idea which the obedient person holds of the powerful or of his position. The strong man is strong not only because he has power but also because he has authority. This fact was recognized by the 18th-century philosopher Jean Jacques Rousseau in his theory of the social contract. Rousseau held that "the strongest man is never strong enough to be always master, unless he transforms his strength into right and obedience into duty [1, p. 141]."

To facilitate a broader understanding of present-day Gbande government, it is necessary to make explicit the influence and roles of the traditional Gbande government and of the Liberian government and to point out that these are becoming one and the same. Before President W. V. S. Tubman took office in 1944, Gbande territory was a district in the Western province of Liberia, controlled indirectly by a District Commissioner appointed by the President. The District Commissioner was directly responsible to the Secretary of the Interior. He was the link between the traditional Gbande government and the Liberian national government. But since the District Commissioner could not possibly interact with every Gbande, it became necessary to create new functionaries, other than the traditional ones, who would form a liaison between the Gbandes and the District Commissioner or between them and the Liberian national government. These functionaries were, as mentioned earlier: the headmen; the town chiefs; the region or district chiefs; and the paramount chiefs. I shall discuss each of them in the order they are listed.

Headman

The position of headman is a relatively new one among the Gbandes. The functions delegated to the headmen were once the tasks of the traditional elders. Each Gbande village normally has two headmen. Each headman is responsible for one half of the village. He serves as a local liaison between the village as a whole and any visitors, strangers, or Liberian government officials. If a visitor or stranger comes to the

village, it is the headman's responsibility to approach him
and to inform each household of its turn in caring for the
stranger. When anyone from the Liberian government enters
the village, he deals with the headman. It is in this capacity
that the headman does all he can to protect and preserve the
Gbande social order and the established social relations
within Gbande society. He is usually the first to make himself available in time of crisis or when any danger threatens
an individual or group. He will suffer any indignity, any insult, and any injustice to preserve relations between his
village and the government. For it would not be one lone individual who would bear the brunt of an insult to the government but the entire village. Very often, the headman is
willing to assume the blame for any wrongdoing by anyone
in his village and is willing to take any punishment necessary. For these reasons, village headmen are chosen for their
courage, strength, intelligence, and tact. They are usually
young, swift, and strong. As each group of Poro students
graduates, the elders and leaders of the Poro school select
two promising young men to serve as headmen. Each serves
a minimum of two years or a maximum of three years.
(Worthy headmen who have served well sometimes later
become town chiefs.)

In 1946 when I was in the village of Gbageehilbah, I
saw a headman being beaten unmercifully by two members
of the Liberian Frontier Force, simply because he did not
have cooked food prepared for them prior to their arrival.
The fact was that he had no way of knowing that they were
coming, and furthermore, in Gbandeland, no man cooks
because it is not proper for a man to cook. He was knocked
down, kicked, and struck several times. He never fought
back, although he was quite capable of doing so, since he
was much larger than either of the Frontier Force men. He
did not fight back because, had he done so, however right he
might have been, it would have brought the wrath of every
Frontier Force man in Gbande territory upon the village of
Gbageehilbah, and perhaps the District Commissioner

would have imposed a very large fine on this village. The position of Gbande village headman is one of service to his village and villagers. His compensation lies in the satisfaction of doing his job well. There is absolutely no material reward for him; instead, he gives himself willingly in service to his community in order to preserve the dignities of both the living and dead members of the community. He is therefore willing to absorb abuses of all sorts for his community; indeed, he considers such abuses inestimable honors. It is his privilege to be of service to his community because the community is far more important than the individual. He answers directly to the town chief and at times refers problems to him.

Town Chief

Like headman, the position of town chief is a relatively new one to the Gbandes. It originated in much the same way as that of headman. The town chief's duties are on a somewhat larger scale than the headman's, but he has approximately the same jurisdiction—the local village. (Formerly, chiefs were assigned to each of the five subdivisions of Gbandeland —Tahamba, Goolahum, Wawoma, Hasala, and Yawuyahum; the villages or smaller communities were controlled by village elders, who were not called chiefs and did not claim to be chiefs.) The town chief coordinates all of the public activities of his village. He supervises the communal farms. He sees that the communal huts for strangers are built and repaired. He is in charge of keeping roads and bridges between his and other villages in good condition. And, of course, he supervises headmen and handles any problem of larger scope than a family dispute, while serving as the main liaison between his village and the Liberian government. Qualifications for the position of town chief are identical to those for the position of headman, with one exception: chiefs are usually older than headmen. The chief does not expose himself to physical humiliations and abuses as the headman does. He is responsible to the district and paramount chiefs, but more so to the former. Like the headman, the chief forgoes any material reward. His reward lies in discharging his responsibilities as a representative of his people. As a matter of fact, the headman and the chief are not addressed as "headman" or "chief" by their community. They are referred to by their regular names, like any other person in the community. The chief is responsible for his own farm work and does not live in a better hut than other members of his community. Neither does his family enjoy any more privileges than other members of the community. Both the town chief and the headman are selected by their local community. This recognition by their community members tends to be more rewarding to them than any material reward. Unlike the headman, the town chief has indefinite tenure. He may serve as long as he is physically able. A retired chief is most respected by all, especially if he has served for a long period of time and in times of crisis. His accomplishments are often made the subject of songs of praise by members of his local community. A few characteristics of a typical town chief are wisdom, maturity, good judgment, temperance, kindness, understanding, and good speaking ability. These characteristics are the minimum requirements for a chief according to Gbande standards, and they are very easily verified, since the communities are usually of the "gemeinschaft"° type in which the members know each other intimately.

District Chief

The position of Gbande district chief is much more difficult to describe than that of headman or town chief. Most of the

---

° "Gemeinschaft" refers to an "in group," "primary," "face to face," or "informal" group relationship, in contrast to an "out group," "secondary group," or "informal" group relationship.

district chiefs, who now find themselves integral parts of a larger whole, are marginal men in that they represent the old traditional order. Most of them are assigned positions in their district because they are chiefs' sons or grandsons. In former times they were responsible to no one except the Gbande king.* Today they are responsible to the paramount chief, to the District Commissioner, and to their people. Their major duty is to coordinate the activities of the town chiefs in their regions and to serve as liaisons between the local communities and the paramount chiefs. In contrast to the town chief, the modern district chief must be literate, in addition to having the characteristics required of the town chief. In this marginal position, he has to play two roles: that of being the representative of his ancestors and therefore being respected by his people, and that of being a subordinate to the paramount chief and the District Commissioner. The district chief, instead of being able to be himself, has to play politics—the politics of reconciliation, which do not really satisfy him. He is a traditional leader of his people; his position was offered to him by the gods and the ancestor spirits. Therefore, he ought to be interested mainly in pleasing the ancestor spirits and his people, rather than having a divided allegiance. This, indeed, is exactly what he would like to do, but he finds it impossible. He is forced to take orders from the paramount chief and the District Commissioner, who show little or no sympathy for his dilemma. The district chief has only two alternatives. He can follow the indigenous practices in the traditional way, or he can deviate

---

*The Gbande kings were the children of a man known as Hardi. He was supposed to have allowed himself to be buried alive with four arrows in his body so that all the Gbande people might be saved from calamity. This event took place in the city of Somolahun. I saw the grave in which he was supposed to have been buried, but no one living at the time of my investigation remembered exactly when this event took place.

greatly from these practices and follow the course set by the
Liberian government. From all indications, the latter choice
is widespread. The district chiefs are now members of the
Liberian Senate and House of Representatives.

The membership of the district chiefs in the legislative
branch of the Liberian national government creates a new
set of problems. The children of these new congressmen are
far better educated than their fathers. Most of them have
received their education in Europe or the United States;
many have gone beyond the bachelor's degree. The difficulty
arises when these young men return home and discover the
inadequacy of their parents in their role as statesmen and
lawmakers. (Even the method of parliamentary procedure
used in the House of Representatives and Senate is quite
foreign to these tribal people.) Very often these young people with their superior education are forced to work under
their elders, "uneducated" in the Western sense. These
elders are ready to employ both traditional and modern
methods to keep these young people in check. For example,
if a father could not convince his son to agree politically with
him, he would remind him of his duty to respect and obey.
(Traditionally, a son must respect his father at all times and
in all places, even if he believes his father to be in error.) Of
course, this traditional, unwavering obedience has no place—
or rather, should have no place—in a democratic, bureau-
cratic government. Essentially, then, the problem is that
these district chiefs in Congress are unable to differentiate
between the modern form of government, in which the
governing members are independent of one another, and the
old traditional society, in which the older men were considered the wise men of the community and therefore accorded
respect and obedience at all times. The Liberian national
government, by including these tribal fathers in the
governing process (although they do not understand it), has
been able thereby to control the indigenous sector of
Liberia. These tribal men are made to believe that the way

of the national government, the modern method of government, is better than their traditional tribal methods. Firm in this belief, they can then exploit and control their own people for the national government. Ironically, both the chiefs and their educated children must depend upon the traditional Gbandes for support in their new political roles; but at the same time, they are finding themselves further from their indigenous brothers. Indeed, this is the dilemma of modern chiefs throughout Africa, and this problem will remain for some time.

Paramount Chief

The paramount chief is selected by the people, but the selection must be approved by the national government. The District Commissioner submits a list to the district chiefs from which they can select names for the position of paramount chief. The District Commissioner suggests his priorities by the manner in which the names are listed. The paramount chief is responsible to the District Commissioner and the Secretary of the Interior. He works very closely with the District Commissioner. The paramount chief's major duties include: collecting taxes for the District Commissioner; seeing to it that each district chief provides the full quota of working men for government projects such as road or bridge building, constructing government buildings for officials in the interior, and providing food supplies for government officials; providing a labor force for foreign entrepreneurs; and, if any of these duties are not fulfilled, fining the district chiefs for their offenses. Here we face the problem of traditional versus modern government. Both the district and the paramount chiefs are rewarded with tax payers' money, and they enjoy all the benefits and privileges of other government officials, though to a lesser extent. But the paramount chief does not feel any obligation to the people at all because, very often, he is not a traditional chief. His position is an acquired one, and therefore he tends to explore every avenue for gain. Today, the position of paramount chief is decided by vote. He is no longer selected only by peoples of his region but rather by all of the Gbande people, as indicated by the ballot box. The position of paramount chief requires a college education and postgraduate work. The paramount chief is also a marginal person, but his marginality is of different type than that of the regional chief. He is not tradition-bound in conscience, as is the regional chief, but the fact remains that he is a tribal member. This he cannot change. He is never fully accepted into the clique of those who consider themselves other than tribal members. He is tolerated insofar as he keeps in his place, and he may even rise to a high economic position above the other members of his tribe. At the same time, he cannot find his place within the indigenous group from whence he came— but then, it is never too clear whether he wants to be identified with them. Usually, the paramount chief is a man admired by the Gbandes, but not loved. He is said to be more closely related to the District Commissioner than to his people.

Liberian National Government

William V. S. Tubman, president of the Republic of Liberia during 1944–1971, clearly saw the disparities between the peoples of the hinterland and those of the coastal region, a region divided into five counties and one territory. This region was the mainstay of the Liberian national government. All positions of any significance, whether they were political patronages or otherwise, were held by people from this region. The peoples of the hinterland, including the Gbandes, were never considered. Accordingly, the Liberian peoples were very class-conscious prior to 1944. Since then, any discussion of the indigenous hinterland groups has brought to mind the word "unification." The goal of the unification program was to get all elements of the Liberian population working harmoniously together in a new spirit of unity, equality, and brotherhood; for the first time, Liberians would be proud to be Liberians. President Tubman urged his countrymen as follows: "We must now destroy all ideologies that tend to divide us—that is, 'Americo-Liberianism' must be forgotten and all of us must register a new era of justice, equality, fair dealing and equal opportunities for everyone from every part of the country, regardless of tribe, clan, section, element, creed, or economic status." In line with this unification program, he inaugurated the practice of requesting chiefs to confer the title "Honorary Paramount Chief" on visiting dignitaries from foreign countries. (Richard M. Nixon, then vice president of the United States, was among those who were robed in indigenous array and made honorary chiefs.) [12, p. 19]

The program also affected the status of the hinterlands. The hinterlands, as indicated elsewhere, were formerly designated as provinces, and the Gbandes are located in what was known as the Western Province. President Tubman's unification program eliminated Gbandeland's provincial status, thereby elevating it to countyhood; that is, Gbandeland has now achieved a rank formerly held only by areas inhabited by "Americo-Liberians." The new status carries with it wider responsibilities for the new counties. These responsibilities include selecting members of the House of Representatives and the Senate. Therefore, it has become reasonable that the present indigenous members of the House of Representatives be selected from among the district chiefs. As yet, I know of no chief who has been selected from among the Gbandes for the House of Representatives. Nevertheless, their chances are as good as those of any other indigenous group. Perhaps I should make it clear that for the Gbandes, having a chief as a member of the House of Representatives does not necessarily mean drastic or positive change with respect to their standard of living. I think that one of the satisfactions, or perhaps the only satisfaction, which is shared by all Gbandes is the feeling of having a Gbande occupy a position once taboo to them. Besides this, I see no other reason for them to be jubilant. In the first place, such a representative tends to be more interested in himself than in the people he represents, because he does not understand the significance of his new office. Moreover, he does not understand most of the issues introduced on the floor of the House of Representatives. Hence the position becomes an end in itself rather than a means to an end for the representative and his people. The danger of such representatives' being used as instruments in exploiting their own people is always present and should not be ignored. However, this situation need not be so if these representatives have at least the equivalent training of the other members of the House; otherwise, their positions are not much more than political tokens and, at worst, a political mockery.

Today, more Gbandes travel to work for different foreign companies than in times past. This has had many results, two of which, I think, are definitely disadvantageous to the Gbandes and to the Republic of Liberia. First, the Gbandes, are less self-sufficient than at any other time in their known history. Second, the Gbandes as a social unit are no longer able to control their destinies as Gbandes without interference from the national government, as they were in times past. The end result is that both the Gbandes and the Liberian national government are becoming poorer to such an extent that the importation of foodstuffs from other countries has for the first time become a government policy. The over-all pattern is that the Liberian national government is diminishing the usefulness of the Gbandes' traditional government. Hence, there tends to be more distance between such leaders and the mass of the Gbande people than there was with the traditional leaders.

In spite of these difficulties involving the diminishing of

self-sufficiency and the apparent lack of control over their destinies, the condition of the Gbandes need not be bleak. They are caught between two social systems, like most indigenous African peoples. The real problem, I believe, is essentially one of change, which is occurring rapidly everywhere in Africa and especially in the Gbande social system. It is obvious that whenever a change occurs in a system, it tends to permeate the component structures, thereby disturbing the whole system. But a social system does not and cannot exist for long without borrowing new elements from other systems and discarding old ones. The process of borrowing and discarding involves the adaptation of the whole system to what is borrowed and to the absence of what is discarded. The whole process is one of reorganization. Such reorganization is often on a different level, which may be a "high" or a "low" level depending upon the position of the observer. However, the direction of the reorganization, although very important, need not concern us too much. What is important is the problem of adjustment to the new order of things for the Gbandes and all parties concerned. There tends to be a concomitant relationship between the type of adjustment the indigenous hinterlanders make to the reorganization process and the success of the "unification" program. The future of this program is bright indeed, but as is the case with every situation involving change, valid assessments are always difficult to make during the actual change. We must therefore wait until the reorganization has had more time to develop.

Chapter 14
The Law, the Court, and Deviant Behavior

THE GBANDES DO not have an elaborate law and court system. With the Gbandes, the law is nothing more than a vague statement of patterns of behavior. The judgment of what is right or what is wrong is always subject to related factors. The same act or behavior may be judged right under certain conditions but wrong under other conditions. Moreover, if the law is to be enforced by individuals, the chance of error is always present. Hence the court, rather than the law, is the deciding instrument. The court, therefore, is made up of elders who are believed to be wise and impartial and whose duty and right it is to pronounce judgment. All disputes which extend beyond family matters, however trivial they may be, must be settled in court.

In each village the oldest graduates of the Poro school make up the group of elders. These elders may range in number anywhere from six to twenty or more. As the oldest men die off, the newest graduates take over. Only graduates of the Poro school can approach the court for a decision. Women and children can serve as witnesses and spectators and are not barred from the proceedings unless the proceedings are of a peculiar nature. They do not, however, bring cases before the court. If one of the men has a dispute, he first approaches one of the elders. The elders then try to determine whether the case can be settled within the family. If not, a court session is held in the general meeting house or court house located in the center of the village. This house consists of a thatched roof supported by poles. Generally, meetings are held here, and newcomers are often introduced here. During trials, the elders in their everyday dress squat under one end of the roof. The contestants face them. The spectators stand or squat around the outside as the case is presented. In Gbande court there are no lawyers. Each person in dispute with another person is responsible for arguing his case before the tribunal. The case is argued back and forth after each contestant has given his opening statement. Then each contestant is cross-examined by the judges, after which the case is decided. However, if there are elements of doubt, the contestants may be asked to produce witnesses. These witnesses take oaths on the ancestor spirits and are given *salèy*, a medicine. Then they are permitted to present their evidence. If the evidence is found wanting or unsatisfactory, then the contestants are given another medicine called *gafwén*.

Court Cases

The following two cases are examples of two different trial procedures.° Because the cases involved adolescents, losing did not carry quite the stigma it usually does in cases in-

---

° I have a special interest in these cases because I knew the participants personally; that is, I knew the main contestants, the witnesses, and the six elders who presided over them as judges. I was able to talk with each of the participants before and after each case was decided. Before the trials, none of the main contestants would predict the outcome, except that each believed that he had a strong argument in his favor. After the decisions, I talked with all of the participants—the winners, the witnesses, the judges, and the losers, in that order. I found it uncomfortable if not difficult to talk freely with the losers about the decisions. However, in general, the decisions of the judges were ac-

volving adults. Nevertheless, the procedures followed in
these cases are exactly like those followed in most court cases
in Gbandeland. The cases took place in Somalahun, a village
about seven or more miles southwest of Kololahum, the district headquarters (then the Kololahum District of the Western Province, which has since acquired the status of a
county). The first case involved Nagbày, a young palm wine
maker, and Dagb>, a young trapper, as principal contestants. Āmā and his son Váni were key witnesses. In this first
case, the path which Nagbày made to his palm wine tree was
the same path Dagb> used to set and examine his traps at
least two or three times a day.† Soon, Nagbày noticed an irregularity in the wine yield of his palm wine tree. The gourd
which was the receptacle for the wine was almost
overflowing sometimes but almost empty other times. This
irregularity occurred time and time again so that Nagbày finally decided to watch his wine tree. He went farther away
from the tree to a place where he could view it from all sides.
Āmā and his son Váni were nearby cutting palm nuts from
the other palm trees. About midafternoon, Dagb> came to
examine his traps, and on his way back to the village he
stopped to drink from Nagbày's wine tree. He cautiously
climbed up into the palm tree because he was aware of the
presence of others nearby cutting palm nuts. To his surprise,

cepted by all parties, on the grounds that the judges were old, wise, experienced, and honest men. A similar opinion was echoed by the witnesses. As for the judges, they were sure that their decisions could
stand any acid test of Gbande jurisprudence. While the reactions of the
main contestants and other participants to the decision are important,
the instruments and processes by which decisions are made are of
primary concern here.

   †It is necessary to note here that palm wine trees are generally
publicly owned. However, if a tree is discovered to be a good wine-
producing tree, it then belongs to the palm wine maker. Such was the
case with Nagbày and his palm wine tree.

Nagbày was standing under the tree waiting for him to come down. When he came down, he attempted to get away from Nagbày as fast as possible, but Nagbày decided not to let him go until he admitted that he was responsible for the previous irregularities in the yield of his wine tree. This Dagb> refused to do. Nagbày, being bigger than Dagb> refused to let him go and insisted that only Dagb> could be responsible for the behavior of his palm wine tree. If Dagb> therefore admitted his guilt and promised not to repeat the action, the matter would be settled. Āmā and Váni heard them and came to investigate. Both Nagbày and Dagb> explained the situation to Āmā and Váni. Āmā urged Dagb> to confess as was suggested by Nagbày if this would settle the matter. Again, Dagb> refused to do any such thing. Nagbày had no alternative but to take Dagb> to court. In court Dagb> confessed that he was guilty only the day he was caught by Nagbày. He refused to admit and to accept blame for any previous irregularities in the yield of wine by the tree. The witnesses, Āmā and Váni, were called in one at a time. Each testified that Dagb> used the path to Nagbày's palm tree more often than anyone in order to examine his traps. On the evidence, the case was decided in Nagbày's favor since Dagb> could provide no evidence to prove that anyone used the path besides the two of them. Dagb> apologized to Nagbày and promised not to repeat his action. The case was settled.

The second case consisted of a fight between Gb>le and Kpēle over firewood. Among the Gbandes, as indicated elsewhere, boys are responsible for gathering firewood. Every evening boys of the same village and approximately the same age go together to fetch firewood. It was on one of these trips that the four boys Gb>le, Kpēle, Gbēse, and Táygili had gone. Once the boys arrive at the place where the wood is to be cut, they often go off in pairs in order to offer mutual aid to one another if this becomes necessary. Each accumulates his own wood (small dried sticks) into a pile until he considers it large enough for a big bundle. The wood is then tied together with vines for easy transportation. When Gb>le tied his wood into a bundle he noticed that some of his wood was missing, and since Kpēle was the only one with him, he accused him of taking the wood. Kpēle denied the accusation. Gbēse and Táygili offered to help Gb>le get more firewood but he refused and insisted on getting his wood from Kpēle's pile. This led to the fighting between the two boys. Thanks to Gbēse and Táygili, the fight came to an end. When the boys got back to the village, Gb>le took the matter to court. In court, Kpēle still denied taking any wood belonging to Gb>le. The witnesses, Gbēse and Táygili, testified that they could not tell whether or not Kpēle took any wood from Gb>le's pile because most of the wood in this area was alike. Since the witnesses were of little help to the judges, the court decided to resort to the use of *gafwén* (an ordeal). When it became apparent that *gafwén* would be used, Kpēle confessed taking only two of Gb>le's sticks. He was told to apologize and to get a bunch of wood for Gb>le.

Gafwén has a tremendous psychological effect. Very often, when it becomes obvious that *gafwēn* will be used the contestant who is less sure he is right confesses he is wrong. Such a confession terminates the case. *Gafwén* may be a poison which each person is asked to drink. It may be hot oil or water into which each contestant is asked to put his hand, or it may be a hot iron which he is asked to touch with his tongue. It is small wonder why somebody confesses. The presence of *gafwén* acts more as a deterrent to lying than anything else since it is rarely, if ever, actually used.

In court cases involving adults, decisions are taken more seriously than in these two cases. The following case involved Māsā Gb>le and Aigūjiamá, both of whom were moderately rich by Gbande standards. Each of these men had acquired a few cows, goats, and sheep. As a rule, the Gbandes do not fence in their animals but are required to tie their cows at a particular feeding place or have someone to guide and keep them from possibly ruining property which belongs to others. When property damage occurs, it may lead to a serious law suit, especially between people who are already at odds with each other. This was the source of the problem between Māsā Gb>le and Aigūjiamá. Māsā Gb>le sued Aigūjiamá for damage done to his farm by the latter's cows. The damage included his whole farm because Māsā Gb>le claimed that the whole farm was a total loss. The trial went on for a whole week. Each side presented fourteen witnesses, and each witness was examined and cross-examined over and over again. The questions included, for example: "Where were Aigūjiamá's and Māsā Gb>le's cows on the day in question?"; "How do you know whose cows were at the place you are now describing?"; "How many cows did you see?" After careful examination of the evidence, the case was decided against Māsā Gb>le. In fact, it was shown that Māsā Gb>le let his own cows loose on his own farm and blamed it on Aigūjiamá's cows. Māsā Gb>le was asked to pay four cows to Aigūjiamá and to restore the latter's good reputation. This case was tried in Somalahum. Māsā Gb>le later left town in shame, never to return. In all adult cases, the social significance of winning or losing a case is great. One's social status may be diminished to such an extent by losing that the person who loses usually moves away as Māsā Gb>le did, to another region or village. One whose status is enhanced by winning may be greatly honored and perhaps made a minor chief or one of the elders for his display of wisdom.

Foreigners

Another function of Gbande law is to provide for strangers or foreigners within a Gbande village. Each Gbande village is divided into two halves. Each half is required to make a communal farm and to build a communal house in which to house the strangers. The harvest from the communal farm is stored in a separate hut for the women to use as necessary. Each half of the village is also assigned specific months; when a stranger comes to a town, he is immediately sent over to that half which is responsible for strangers that month. Each hut in the half has a number from one up. Each household is responsible for taking turns in preparing food and baths for the stranger. This is usually a one-day service for each household. If the stranger stays until all the huts in that half have taken a turn, the stranger is simply transferred to the other half where the process is repeated. There is no charge or cost to the stranger for these services. The more foreign a stranger is, the greater is the honor accorded to him. This practice is based upon the belief that the ancestor spirits are capable of transforming themselves into strangers in order to visit their relatives, to test their relatives' sincerity toward other human beings. There are two types of strangers: Africans with African mannerisms and characteristics and Westerners with Western mannerisms and characteristics. The word for stranger is sotā n̂ggī. Westerners are included in the term sotā n̂ggī, but they also have the additional name of wīngī. If the stranger has a light skin, he or she is called wī ̄īkōlē. All wīngī, regardless of skin color, are treated alike.

It is illegal for anyone to mistreat a stranger, for the reasons stated previously. It is feared that failure to entertain a stranger properly will evoke the judgment of the ancestor spirits. Such judgment is not limited to the individual directly responsible for the mistreatment but includes the whole family or whole village. The justice of the ancestor spirits is unequalled by any human justice; therefore the law and the court must be ready to deal with any deviation from the traditional established pattern of accommodating strangers. It is obvious that in traditional Gbande society, it is not necessary for one to have money or to know someone in order to travel. One need only have one's own clothes; all other necessities. are supplied by the host or hosts. Strangers are not required to pay anything, not even a penny. The fact that imminent justice is dispensed by the ancestor spirits for treatment of strangers makes the practice of entertaining strangers a reciprocal obligation. The very idea of charging strangers for accommodations is abhorrent to traditional Gbandes. For this reason, whenever Gbandes find themselves in the midst of strangers in a strange place, they consider other Gbandes brothers and sisters. This holds true whether or not they knew each other at home. Such Gbande brotherhood is even stronger among Gbandes living in Western cities or working for Western companies.

To the Gbandes, *wīngī* (Westerners) are heartless; they are considered just a little higher than wild animals because of the way they treat each other and "human beings" (*Gbandes* means "human beings"). This is one of the many reasons for the uncompromising determination of the Gbande elders to resist encroachment of the Western mode of life on their people. These elders firmly believe that Western types of laws are unenforceable by their courts because these laws are based on individual rights. The Gbandes consider this a calamity for any society; for them, there can be no individual rights per se, only individual rights based on tradition and approved by the group. Only the group has rights; but since these rights become rights supported by every member of the group, they become individual rights because of their reciprocal nature. Such rights need not have an agent to enforce them simply because they are reciprocal rights. Every individual becomes an enforcement agent and a friend of the court, because any infraction would result in punishment of the whole community rather than only the offender. Consequently, everybody is expected to obey these laws.

Because of this belief, the Gbande people think they are more law-abiding than Westerners. They associate human suffering with Western culture. They are quick to point to the inhumanity, suffering, confusion, and chaos of the cities as classical examples. They argue that these are the result of far too many laws and restrictions which in themselves are self-defeating, simply because no one can remember all such laws and restrictions. Even if they are remembered, these laws and restrictions are in many ways senseless to many people. What is more, Western laws are thought to be partially enforced with different degrees of intensity. Therefore, Western laws and courts are considered nothing more than an intellectual mockery composed of "book laws" and "book courts"; the purpose seems to be to display oratorical talent and thus gain money and prestige for the self rather than to serve group welfare in the name of justice. Western peoples are looked upon as makers of many laws as well as breakers of many laws. In short, the Gbandes unreservedly believe that Western laws and courts are unreliable and structured on false premises and are therefore unfit for guiding human conduct. Gbande laws are consistent with normative Gbande behavior, and the interpretations of these laws by the courts are also consistent with the expected mode of behavior.

Although Gbande culture tends to be homogenous and integrative, with a high degree of conformity, there are many kinds of deviant behavior. I shall limit my discussion to the most common ones, namely theft, lying, selfishness, rape, witchcraft, sorcery, murder, and laziness. These eight are the most talked about and most abhorred forms of deviant behavior in Gbandeland (except for sorcery, which is respected though feared). In times past, anyone accused of one or more of these acts was partially or completely ostracized by his neighbors, his community, his kinsmen, or all of these groups. A discussion of each of these asocial acts follows.

Theft

Theft is linked to all the other acts mentioned above, either directly or indirectly. It is considered one of the worst crimes and in the old traditional Gbande culture carries the penalty of death by burning. The Gbandes believe that anyone who steals does so with deliberate planning and meditation with the intent to deprive another person of his belongings. A case involving K>lĩ and Kelénde will illuminate this. While Kelénde was an unimpressive old man who lived by himself and raised chickens at the outskirts of Kololahum, K>lĩ was the nephew of Māsā Gb>le, an influential and respected man among the Gbandes in Kololahum. While Kelénde was coming home one evening, he heard his chickens making noises. When he went to investigate the noises, he met K>lĩ with two of the chickens. He asked K>lĩ to put the chickens down or else he would take the matter to K>lĩ's uncle and then to court. K>lĩ became ashamed and afraid that his uncle would find out about his foolish behavior. He knew that it would bring shame to his uncle and to the whole family. The very thought of this made him angry, and as a result he jumped on the old man Kelénde and beat him almost to the point of death. The old man was saved by the voices of people coming to buy chickens. When K>lĩ heard them he ran away; in his haste he dropped his new cap, a recent gift from his uncle. Old man Kelénde was carried to the nearby hospital in the Holy Cross Mission of Boawolahum. The next morning the news came that Kelénde had died the very night he was admitted to the hospital. The people of Kololahun would surely be punished by the ancestral spirits for Kelénde's death unless someone confessed the crime. K>lĩ heard the news but did not come forth to confess. Within a few days, it was reported that the white medicine man had brought Kelénde back to life and that Kelénde had told the people in the hospital the name of the one who beat him. It was also told that Kelénde had concrete evidence to produce against the person who beat him. Still K>lĩ did not confess to the crime. Kelénde came home the following week and, as expected, went straight to Māsā Gb>le and told him what his nephew had done. Māsā Gb>le dismissed whole thing as some sort of joke. He told Kelénde to get out of his yard quickly or he would get the beating he deserved. A word or two is in order here to explain the relationship between Māsā Gb>le and K>lĩ. K>lĩ was the only son and the only

child of Māsā Gb>le's older brother, Dagb>. Dagb> was
killed in a fall from his palm wine tree one rainy afternoon
when K>lī was less than a year old. Since Māsā Gb>le then
married his deceased brother's wife, K>lī's mother, K>lī
was both a nephew and a son to Māsā Gb>le. He was more
a son than a nephew by Gbande standards, which maintain
that one's father's brother is one's father. (See Chapter 2
"Kinship Terminology," subsection "Father.") The Gbandes
believe that the children of one's deceased relatives should
be treated with utmost care in order not to anger the dead.
For these reasons, Māsā Gb>le was ready and willing to
protect K>lī at any cost. The matter was brought to court
and the evidence, K>lī's new cap, was produced. It was
then that K>lī confessed to the stealing of the chickens and
the beating of the old man Kelénde.

K>lī was ostracized from Gbandeland by his uncle
despite the relationship. He was sent away to Bo boy school
in Sierra Leone and told never to return home by both his
uncle and the people. A few years ago, I met K>lī at an
American university working on a master's degree in for-
estry. He has since finished and gone back to Liberia. He
told me that he intended to go back home to work with his
people, the Gbandes. I have heard nothing of him since, but
my speculation is that if he did return he would never be
wholly accepted. The Gbandes reason, "Nwi áa ñgui yá w>
āl> aa nu và aa ndé le," that is, "He who steals is one who
is also capable of killing and lying." A thief must use every
possible means of vindicating himself in order to save himself
and his kinsmen from disgrace.

A thief has always been considered a very dangerous
person; hence, he must be annihilated without delay. For
this reason, every possible means to inhibit or prevent
stealing was provided for in the Gbande customary, "unwrit-
ten" law. For example, anyone who was hungry and away
from home or from his farm was allowed to eat anything
from another person's farm or garden without permission

from the owner. This was not considered stealing because of the saying "*Kesúi si ñgali á su ey h>mß⁻ >lo,*" that is, "An empty bag cannot stand up or a bag that is emptied will crumble." The action described above becomes stealing only if one yields to the temptation to take some of the produce for future use. The customary law says, "Do not go hungry; eat, but do not take away from another's farm or garden that which you cannot eat at once." As pointed out elsewhere, nobody goes hungry or in want of any basic thing because what one's kinsmen has, one has. Therefore, stealing was considered an extreme deviation for the simple reason that it was unnecessary and could be avoided so easily. In the olden days, Gbande women believed so strongly in the needlessness of stealing that they used to place their goods for marketing at the entrances to the village, leaving them unattended. Such goods were usually piled in units, each unit signifying a specific value of exchange. Those wishing to buy an item or exchange an item did so honestly because they were Gbandes, and to be a Gbande is to be honest. Therefore, they could not afford to take more or less than required. These women usually returned every evening to count their earnings and to check such earnings against the unsold merchandise. The Gbandes trusted each other to such an extent that in times past they never locked their huts during the daytime. Their huts were locked only at night when it was unwise or dangerous to leave them open. Nowadays everything is changed or changing in Gbandeland. It is not so terrible to steal today; what is important is the person or group of persons from whom one should or should not steal—that is, it is permissible to steal from a non-Gbande.

Truth

A liar is considered a deviant because in a small, closely-woven, homogenous group like those in which the Gbandes

live, it is an absolute necessity for the members to trust each
other. A liar is said to be untrustworthy because his words
are like quicksand with a depth of evil that is incalculable.
Therefore, a liar is a potential murderer and should not be
trusted. A liar is both feared and ostracized. In the first
place, no one can ever tell when a liar will deceive him. For
this reason, the traditional punishment for lying was the
same as the one for stealing, that is, either death by burning
or banishment from the group. In times past, the Gbandes
were very quick to impose the maximum punishment on
such a person in order to make an example out of him, in the
hope of deterring others from similar deeds. Knowing the
consequences of lying as described here, anyone who lies
must be an extreme deviant. Lying is closely related to
selfishness or stinginess; therefore, an examination of
selfishness is in order.

Selfishness

Anyone who fails to share his product with others is considered less than a human being. Such a person is usually
referred to as kāāfōlī or suwáy, which means a good-for-
nothing person or an animal of the lowest degree. Although
there is no specific punishment designed for a stingy person,
the fate of such a person is isolation in the midst of kinsmen
and neighbors. He can expect to rely on no one but himself
in case of emergency and no one relies on him. Whenever
such a person is in need or in trouble, both his relatives and
his neighbors employ every means to indicate to him that
any help they give him is, in fact, grudgingly rendered, and
that the help is being given out of pity and love—the kind of
love that one feels for one's pet or any lower animal. It is not
difficult to demonstrate the tragedy of a stingy individual in
Gbandeland. Although Gbande society is heterogeneous and
diversified in many respects, it is a cooperative, communal
group in which no one is self-sufficient. Without such depen-

dent and cooperative relationships, it is debatable whether the society could survive for long. Gbande society is one in which the success or failure of anyone is considered the success or failure of his kinsmen, neighbors, and relatives. To be kind to a stingy person is like throwing one's valuables into a river where they will never be recovered. Moreover, such kindness is not encouraged since it serves only to postpone the miseries which must come eventually. Therefore, the act of sharing is one of the first principles in the socialization of the child. One works not only for oneself but also for one's kinsmen and neighbors, and one's kinsmen and neighbors in turn also work for each other. Life becomes a cycle of reciprocal obligations. These reciprocal obligations are the life strings which integrate the community. Therefore, any person who fails to follow this pattern of sharing is a deviant and must be treated as such.

Rape

Rape is classified into two categories in Gbande customary law, and each has a specific punishment. These categories are: raping a virgin and raping a non-virgin. In Gbandeland, tradition demands that every girl be a virgin at the time of her wedding; anyone who dares deprive her of that honor and thereby bring disgrace to her, her parents, and her expected husband is a very dangerous person. Such a person was usually tried immediately and executed within three days. In such a trial, only one witness was needed—the victim. The girl was required by law to identify the rapist. When such identification was made, the accused was usually asked if he was guilty and why he did it. His response usually went as follows: "Yes, I did it and my reason for doing it is stupidity. Do not prolong my agony if you please. I am ready for the punishment." The punishment was usually death by burning. In this case, the guilty one's family and close friends were the first to bring firewood; they were followed by the rest of the adults in the community. The wood was then neatly arranged into a big pile, and palm oil was poured over the entire pile until it was sufficiently wet. Then the prisoner was helped to the very top of the pile, where he was tied to the wood. He was asked once more if he had anything to say. The typical answer to this question went as follows: "I am sorry that I did wrong to her, her family, her expected husband, and the whole community. I have brought disgrace to my family and my friends; I therefore do not deserve to live another minute. I am ready; will you please set the fire."

The second type of rape is raping a married woman. This crime is seldom committed and is not as severe a crime as raping a virgin; but it is serious enough, considering the punishment for it. In times past, anyone guilty of such a crime was punished by banishment from the community. This punishment was almost as bad as the one for raping a virgin, except that the guilty one could live a little longer than one who raped a virgin. As has been indicated earlier, life is almost impossible without one's kinsmen; therefore, to banish a Gbande from his kinsmen and community is equal to capital punishment. Rape is a very serious offense because it is considered unnecessary criminal behavior. One can always have an affair with a kinsman's wife, provided such a wife is not forbidden by incest taboo. It was in this connection that "name calling" was discussed in Chapter 4 "Family-Kinship Groupings," subsection "Regulation of Sexual Behavior." (A woman tells her husband the name of her lover, who may then be fined by the husband.)

Witchcraft

Witchcraft is a subject much discussed by the Gbande people. It is called *kàlā̃ggī*. The general rule is that every adult suspects every other adult of being a witch. Suspicion exists even between husbands and wives, friends, and neighbors.

For this reason, when food is prepared by the wife she must taste it in the presence of her husband and of all others who are to eat the food, to indicate that she did not put a witch into it. This testing is necessary because no one has ever willingly bought witchcraft, learned it, or been initiated into it. Witchcraft is always given to one by another person in a disguised manner. As mentioned before, it is never certain whether or not a person has a witch until he is dead. For the Gbandes, witchcraft is always considered evil and therefore undesirable. It is considered bad because it controls the behavior of the one who has a witch without his desire or consent. Whatever he is told to do by the witch in him he must do, whether he likes it or not, even if it is against his kinsmen and neighbors. Therefore, witchcraft is greatly feared because a witch person's behavior cannot be predicted.

A sorcerer is a deviant in the sense that such a person is capable of invoking either good or evil upon whomever he wishes. Sorcerers are individuals whose characteristics approximate those of a lunatic. The Gbandes believe that at every new and full moon, a sorcerer may be expected to deviate enormously from the normal pattern of behavior. In Western culture, such individuals cannot escape the mental hospital. But their extreme deviation and fanatic impulses make sorcerers highly respected and feared among the Gbandes. Some of them are even epileptic and may indeed have many seizures in a given period. The more severe and frequent these seizures are, the higher the honor bestowed upon that sorcerer, because of the belief that such an individual is in constant contact with the spirits or with the supernatural world. Sorcerers are highly individualistic, and in most cases their services are sought on a contractual basis rather than a reciprocal one, which is the basic mode of Gbande behavior. Their extremely contractual and individualistic behavior has earned them the classification of "behaving by Western standards." From the point of view of the general code of Gbande behavior, they are considered

deviant. Although such persons are considered deviants,
they are not considered sick; for this reason there are no in-
sane asylums or mental hospitals in Gbandeland. Rather, sorcerers are considered very useful to their community and to
their society in general. In this sense, there are many
rewards for this deviation or insanity and no punishment,
not even in the form of confinement behind hospital walls.

Laziness

Laziness is a characteristic which no Gbande wants to claim.
A lazy person is a liability to his kinsmen and community
rather than an asset. Anyone who earns himself the reputation of being a lazy person is to be avoided whenever possible because a lazy person cannot be trusted. The Gbandes
believe that such persons will steal, lie, and cheat even their
best friends when they are given the chance. A lazy person
cannot find a wife or a husband because he or she lacks a
sense of responsibility. Such persons do not command the
respect normally given a Gbande by those who are younger
or his peers. They are the laughing stock of the community.
The ridicule for being lazy is great, and the indifference and
contempt others show towards a lazy person are unparalleled. A lazy person's life is not worth living because it
is a parasitic life. His life is parasitic in that he is expected to
reciprocate less than his kinsmen and other members of his
community. He contributes little or nothing to the work of
his kinsmen and his community. He expects others to share
the fruits of their labor with him, but he does not want to
share the labor. He is not given equal shares and, in some instances, he is given nothing. This does not mean that he
starves, but rather that he does not share in the group life.
There is no formal punishment for being lazy except this almost complete disregard by kinsmen and neighbors. As has
been stressed before, Gbande society is a communal society
and its functioning depends upon the full participation of

every member. Every person has his or her place in the functional hierarchy of the community. Consequently if anyone fails or refuses to accept this functional structure, he is likely to be forgotten, the exceptions being those who are sick or those who were born abnormal.

Murder

Murder is not a worse crime than stealing, raping, and so on. There are types of murders which do not involve punishment at all. Such murders include killing someone when one is extremely angry, especially when it can be shown that there had not been any previous quarrel between the victim and the accused. If a Gbande is caught beating someone who is younger or smaller and weaker than himself, he can be killed in the name of justice. The person who kills the bully is not punished. If a person is killed by a thief and the thief is caught, he must be killed by burning. Killing one's wife out of jealousy or killing one's kinsman are punishable by death, unless the killer can justify or legitimize the murder.

Misdemeanors

The eight types of deviant behavior described are by no means the only kinds of deviant behavior. I limited myself to these eight because I feel that they are sufficiently diverse to be fairly representative of the various types of deviation among the Gbandes. (As noted before, the first four acts of deviation are more serious than the last three; that is, stealing, lying, selfishness, and rape all carry severe punishments, whereas witchcraft, laziness, and some types of murdering are not so serious. Sorcery, although a deviation, carries no stigma whatsoever.)

There are also misdemeanors, for which there are lesser punishments. For such crimes, there are many types of punishment, one of which is being put in jail. Gbande law

provides jail sentences for lesser crimes which may run from
five days to a month. The Gbande jail does not physically
isolate the prisoner from the rest of the community, but does
prevent the offender from moving freely. The jail is a piece
of log three feet long to which the offender's left foot is fastened by means of a horseshoe-like iron ring. The log has a
rope or strip fastened to each end. With this strip, the prisoner can raise the log from the ground, which enables him to
move around. There is no escape from this type of jail.
Therefore, the prisoner does not need a guard. It is not a
disgrace to be jailed, because jailing usually indicates a
minor offense. The prisoner is kept in the open public meeting hut where trials are held. He is allowed to talk with anyone including members of his family and kinsmen. Prisoners
are usually fed by their family and kinsmen, but they are not
allowed to go to their hut at night or any other time regardless of their marital status. Prison terms are usually a month
or less. Momóluñgguyàn, an old wise man in Somalahum,
told me that the longest prison term he remembers being
given anyone was from one new moon to the next. He bitterly disapproved of such a long jail term on the grounds
that it might fail to accomplish its purpose: to make the prisoner uncomfortable to the extent that he regrets his action. A
long term creates a condition in which the prisoner becomes
adjusted to prison life. His discomfort is no longer a discomfort to him but a way of life. Once he accepts this way of life,
the whole aim of the punishment is lost. The Gbandes
believe, therefore, that prison terms should be short because
the shorter the term, the greater the discomfort.

Chapter 15
Social Change and
Social Reorganization

THE PROBLEMS OF social change and social reorganization are among the most interesting areas of investigation since these two phenomena are the least understood as they affect the Gbandes. It is crucial to bear in mind that all forms of social change come within the province of culture, and that a statement about the nature of culture, its structural features, and its mode of culture change is generally regarded as essential to the discussion of socio-cultural reorganization. From this perspective, one might even say that there is a general lack of knowledge about social or cultural change as it affects not just the Gbandes but the entire continent of Africa. For most people of the Western world, Africa is still the continent of enigma. In their book *Cultures and Societies of Africa*, under the heading "Africa and Its Peoples," Professors Simon and Phoebe Ottenberg maintain that since the early years of European contact, a number of myths have grown up concerning Africa. Two such myths will help to illustrate the lack of knowledge and understanding about social or cultural change in Africa.

According to the Ottenbergs, the most unfortunate of these myths is the belief, "Africa was an area of a kind of cultural stagnation in the days preceding European colonial rule." Such a belief still persists in many quarters, particularly in the Western world. The second myth, equally popular, is the belief, "All African cultures are basically alike [9, p. 3]." This implies that once one knows about one of these cultures, one knows about all of them. While it is true that there are elements common to all African cultures and to the social life of many groups in Africa, there are also enormous differences which can easily be seen with a little effort of insight. Resistance to the acceptance of change in Africa and in Gbandeland is, perhaps, based legitimately on the extraordinary technological success of the Western world. Although technological success is a vehicle of change, it is only one among many change agents; the other agents are equally important and should not be ignored.

African Exploration

One serious misconception about socio-cultural change in Africa is the acceptance of the absolute isolationism of the continent. This mistake pervades most, if not all, previous investigations of and in Africa. From this point of view, most of what is called African history is in fact a European history of Africa. In this regard, Basil Davidson, in his book *The African Past*, observed that there are many anthologies of African exploration, but most of them conform to the same pattern. They are anthologies of the European discovery of Africa, conceived as companion books to a study of Africa which has regarded that subject as no more than an extension to the study of Europe and the New World. Using sources which, according to Mr. Davidson, are largely from the 19th century, they aim to show why and how it was that Europe opened up a continent which was soon to become a European possession. Their attitude is therefore strictly European, and their value lies less in any light they may throw on African life than in what they reveal of European penetration and conquest [3, pp. 3–4]. The accent was clearly European, and whatever changes occurred were those noticed in Europe. While it is true that World War II played an enormous role in the acceleration of change in Africa, as it did throughout the world, it cannot be taken as the beginning of change in Africa.

Modern investigators of African exploration often begin with the year 1600, just as those who are interested in the African independence movement begin with the year 1960, the year the Gold Coast became independent and acquired the name Ghana. The year 1600 represents the beginning of the era of partitioning and domination of Africa by European powers. Yet much of Africa had been opened to the outside world, or to a significant part of it, many hundreds of years earlier. These earlier years are not without important records of their own about socio-cultural change. Mr. Davidson points out from an older record that a most valiant mariner of Portugal, Diogo Cão, sailed his little ships up the waters of the Congo as early as 1482. The book of the Portuguese sailer Zara, which relates tales of the discovery of sub-Saharan Africa, was written in 1453. Mr. Davidson maintains that many contacts were made between Europeans and Africans but that few accounts of such contacts were made public because they were regarded as commercial secrets [10, pp. 53–55]. In a similar vein, Margaret Shinnie writes about the fame of Mansa Musa, the Mandingo King of Mali who came to the throne in 1307 A.D. His name was known throughout the Mediterranean and European worlds.

In spite of the rich records of contacts between Africans and Europeans, the colonial powers were not concerned with Africa's past as much as with producing a record which would reflect the colonial situation and meet its peculiar requirements. One of these requirements was that no serious consideration could be given the period before the beginning of European exploration. To go back earlier would be to plunge into fruitless mythology. This viewpoint was well expressed by Sir Reginald Coupland, writing more than thirty years ago of British penetration into the heart of

Africa: "Up to the middle of the 19th century, the main body
of the African continent had had no history, but had stayed
for untold centuries sunk in barbarism so that the heart of
African was scarcely beating [3, p. 28]." African history
could not be an adequate subject for scholarly investigation
in this period because no such history existed. If Africa had
no history prior to the arrival of the European, then there
could be no social or cultural change in Africa because
change is inherent in and expressed by history.

Africa Today

The last twenty-five years have promoted an entirely different attitude to the African past. This attitude has
displaced what may be called the "colonial stereotype"—that
Africa was in social chaos and stagnation before the time of
European conquest. There is now a significant awakening of
scientific interest in Africa. This interest has been augmented
by the growing discontent, agitation, and aspirations of indigenous Africans and the rapid emergence of independent
African nations; these events are frequently treated by the
public press, television, radio, and other communication
media. This is indicative of the growing public awareness of
the strategic importance of Africa to the security of the
world and its importance to themselves, the Africans, and
the scientific community. Man is becoming more aware of
the fact of the common enterprise of all human beings as
members of the same family in the world community. The
close of the second global war and its effects on international
politics were instrumental in developing a new type of broad
public interest in Africa. There has been notable development of university teaching programs in the African field, a
growing trend among university students to single out a
phase of this field for their concentration, and a consequent
increase in scholarship relating to Africa. This intellectual
awakening is, at least in part, a response to the political

preoccupations of our time. It is also a response to the growing intellectual interest in the problems of Africa and African people.

Today, more than ever, Africa is playing an increasingly important role in world affairs. The continent is involved to an ever greater extent in the complex network of communications, both internal and external. In some areas transformations of the social, cultural, and ideological phases of traditional African life are taking place. In the course of these changes, the relations between African nations and the great centers of organized urban cultures are being reshaped and re-aligned. In effect, we are now witnessing in Africa a new form of social and cultural change, which, according to some writers, is mirrored in the weakening of traditional systems and erasing of ancient social forms and sanctions. The development of new types of economic, social, and political structures has brought about these new problems. Peoples who were once relatively isolated from one another are now being brought into a complex web of contacts. As a result there are reorganizations, insecurities, tensions, conflicts, and the emergence of new relationships, social types, and movements which are not easily (if at all) contained within the framework of traditional social systems and the established order. The Gbandes are no exception to this general rule of the dismantling of tribal ways of life by cultural change. The only thing static about the Gbandes, or for that matter about the entire continent of Africa, is the attitude held by those who do not wish to change their views even in the face of massive evidence to the contrary.

Many factors are necessary for social and cultural change. Some of these factors are apparent while others are much less apparent. Both socio-cultural change and reorganization in present-day Africa are the result of concrete objective factors. Two of these objective factors, urbanization and industrialization, although related, will be discussed separately. Urbanization in Africa, although modern, still re-

tains rural roots because of the uncertainty and undepend-
ability of the city. For the Gbandes, as for most Africans,
one's village with one's kinsmen is irreplaceable. Nevertheless, urbanization of the modern type is one of the chief
agents of socio-cultural change. The Gbandes, once inex-
orably entrenched in their environs, are now looking beyond
Gbandeland for the fulfillment of many wants and obligations. For the old Gbandes, a journey of fifty miles from
Gbandeland was considered a journey into a foreign land,
because Gbandeland was self-sufficient. This is no longer
true for the new generation of Gbandes. Gbande young men
and women are semi-urban dwellers without being urbanized in the Western sense. The characteristic features of
the modern towns are distinctly different from those of the
old ones. The modern towns tend to separate the young people from their elders (in new ideas and skills, if not in space);
they lead the minds of the young outward from the primary
to secondary groups; they make necessary the learning of a
personal skill which can be sold anywhere. Urbanization
calls for the reorganization of social relations by permitting,
even encouraging, geographical and social mobility among
the Gbandes. Towns make the traditional inherited capital
and family ties less important as determinants of a man's career and make intelligence, personality, and will power more
important [6, p. 61]. The new generation of Gbandes look
beyond their immediate environment for the gratification of
their wants, as a result of the exigencies of modern living.
Consequently there is a tremendous migration of young men
and women to the towns and to places where money can be
earned to pay taxes and buy things of symbolic value. For
the Gbandes, this is a new social process which involves
social and cultural change and reorganization. From the
point of view of social organization, one of the most striking
characteristics of these modern towns is the very large
number and variety of voluntary associations as well as of
the more traditional mutual aid groups. What generally dis-

tinguishes the latter kind of association is its more formal constitution and the fact that it has been formed to meet certain needs arising specifically out of the urban environment of its members. It is modern with respect to both its aims and the methods employed to attain them. Obviously, then, one of the centers of change is the town. I shall return to give an illustration of the concept of the Gbandes' being semi-urban dwellers without being urbanized. But first, it is in order to introduce the other "intrinsic" factors which also affect social relationships in situations of modern change.

Industry

The factor of industrialization, which is clearly related to urbanization and even overlapping in its basic characteristics, may or may not be considered urban. The first industry of any large and significant scale in Liberia was the Firestone Rubber Plantation Company. The coming of this company marked the first time a number of Gbandes traveled long distances away from their homeland in order to work. The number of Gbandes traveling out of their indigenous environment to the plantation was limited and their initial stay was brief and temporary. Their number was limited because a Gbande belongs to Gbandeland and, therefore, to travel and to stay away from Gbandeland is "un-Gbande." Their stay was brief and temporary because the acquisition of material outside Gbandeland was not an indigenous mode of behavior. One of the incentives motivating them to work outside Gbandeland was to earn enough money for the hut tax and for fines imposed on them by the Liberian government. Hut taxes were increased and fines imposed more frequently for the Gbandes in order to force them into working for the plantation, because the government had an agreement with the Firestone Rubber Plantation Company to supply it with "native" laborers. When these needs and wants were met, and perhaps the purchase of a few strange

items was made, the excursion came to an end. This abrupt
ending of wage labor by the Gbandes, a common characteristic among most indigenous Africans, is a constant point
of criticism of African workers. Such a criticism reflects a
lack of understanding of the African economic principle. It
operates on the principle of reciprocity rather than that of
contract.

> The rationale of the contractual principle is that all
> the factors of production as well as the products
> themselves change hands according to the principle
> of contract at a price determined by the law of
> supply and demand. It involves the exchange of
> goods and services between people who are bound
> in market and in hierarchial relationships with one
> another. Whether the market is selling oneself, i.e.,
> one's labor for a given price, or buying someone
> else's services for a given price, the relationship is
> based on a formal contract. Most behavior in west-
> ern industrialized societies is characterized by the
> contractual principle on the one hand. On the other
> hand, the principle of reciprocity involves the
> exchange of goods and services between people
> who are bound in non-market and in non-
> hierarchial relationships with one another. In other
> words, the exchange does not create the rela-
> tionship as it does in the contractual system, but
> rather, it is that part of the behavior that gives it
> content. The most vivid example of reciprocity, but
> not the only one, is that relationship based on
> kinship obligations and the type of interdepen-
> dence one finds among hunting groups [2, p. 230].

An economic system governed by the principle of reciprocity requires the participation of all able-bodied workers
in the production of whatever is considered basic for sur-
vival. Therefore, Gbande workers did not stay on their jobs
to gain seniority or promotion or both. These concepts were

foreign to their vocabularies and meaningless in their culture. To them, one does not gain such recognition by working in a foreign land or for foreigners. Seniority and high social status were intrinsic in the Gbande culture and were congruent with one's age and one's family's position as well as one's position within the family. The earning of money in a foreign land and from foreign peoples was proper only in so far as such earnings went for payment of taxes for one's hut and for those of one's kinsmen, and for other kinship obligations such as the payment of fines. But to turn such earnings into a means of gaining a high social status was considered madness by Gbande standards. Farm work as a family project was not only the most important work but also the most desirable work. The recognition of high social status within the family comes with one's performance on the family farm. Gbandes became wage earners divorced from the family farm as the result of extreme conditions—the imposition of innumerable fines and the increase in hut taxes as well as the creation of new taxes by the Liberian national government. These conditions forced them to more or less abandon their traditional standard—the standard of "staying at home." At this time the Gbandes were part of the Western province and Kololahum District. A district commissioner was appointed over them, and several members of the Liberian Frontier Force were assigned to the district commissioner to serve as law enforcement agents, hence change agents. Both the district commissioner and the members of the Frontier Force took from the Gbandes whatever they wanted and whenever they wanted it without the Gbandes' consent and without compensation to them.

The Concept of "Americo-Liberians" and "Aboriginic-Liberians"

Strangely enough, most of the members of the Frontier Force who were in direct contact with the Gbandes as law enforcement agents were themselves hinterland people and were well-acquainted with the general behavioral patterns of other hinterland peoples, including the Gbandes. From this standpoint, although the Frontier Force knew little or no more about Western culture than the Gbandes, they were effective agents of social change. Such a change called for a reorganization in terms of structural relationships with others and with non-Gbandes. The position of district commissioner was one of the lowest echelon jobs among government appointments, from the point of view of training and salary. It required no training at all, and the salary was appropriately low. Notwithstanding, it was a most sought-after position because of certain rewards that went with it. The structure of the Liberian National Government, which divided the Liberian peoples into "Americo-Liberians" and "Aboriginic-Liberians," gave latitude to whatever policy the district commissioner and his Frontier Force chose to pursue. But such a classification also gave the Liberian peoples strong symbols of identification which carried far-reaching implications. In the first place, this was a classification symbolizing superordination and subordination. In the second place, it legitimized the superior and inferior relationship between Americo-Liberians and Aboriginic-Liberians. From this point of view, Americo-Liberians or their Frontier Force could do no wrong to the Gbandes. In other words, the Gbandes had no rights which an Americo-Liberian needed to respect. A Gbande was not free to visit Monrovia (the capital) or any other city on the coast without fearing intimidation of some sort, unless he was a member of the Frontier Force, a policeman, a messenger, or a houseboy in the home of an Americo-Liberian; otherwise he would generally be manhandled, fined, or both for trespassing. Because of the uncertainty regarding their physical well-being on visits to the capital or any other city on the coast, the Gbandes were reluctant or even afraid to visit these areas or any others dominated by Americo-Liberians. Many of my Gbande friends who have gone to these coastal cities have cited to me cases of extreme intimidation, some of which resulted in physical violence, for treading upon the domain of Americo-Liberians. A Gbande young man, in roughly his mid-twenties, who calls himself Koryau, told me of an incident which happened to him and to the members of his party. Five of them were on their way to Monrovia, the national capital. They were arrested, beaten, put in jail, and held there for five days at hard labor without a trial for walking through a certain district on Sunday. The main road passed through this district, and although the trucks and cars passing through on Sunday did not violate the Sabbath, these Gbandes did. Another Gbande young man, who calls himself Sōmā was similarly arrested for sitting down to rest on a roadside bench near one of the cities on the coast. According to him, he was detained for ten days at hard labor. Kēmba, another Gbande, told me that he was arrested while walking with his wife in one of these towns. He was detained for two months, and during this period he did not see his wife. I was told that at a particular season of the year, around Christmas, it was the custom that an indigenous person "disappeared." Of course, it was impossible to check such a statement since it was not possible to find a person who had disappeared and especially since the Gbandes were reluctant to discuss such matters. Nevertheless, these conditions seriously limited the participation of the Gbandes in urban life and activities.

Change in Government Policy

Change in government policy toward the Gbandes and other indigenous peoples of the hinterland did not come about until a young jurist, Dr. William V. S. Tubman, became president of the Republic of Liberia in 1944. In the entire history of Liberia as a nation, there was never a deep concern about the rights and dignities of the people in the hinterland. Dr. Tubman, who served until 1971, was the first president to express such a concern in theory and in practice. His "open door" policy at first glance appeared to have been designed only for foreign businessmen and technically trained persons. However, on closer examination it becomes clear that this policy has a broad perspective and has become the focus of various types of social and cultural change now apparent in every part of Liberia. As indicated above, there were really two Liberias before Dr. Tubman became president. One Liberia consisted of the seats of the national and county governments, to some extent; the other consisted of all the peoples of the hinterland. These two Liberias had always been separated by a symbolic wall with an invisible door, which could be opened only by the chosen members of the national and county government elite. President Tubman weakened, if not destroyed, this wall to the extent that his open door and "unification" policies reinforced each other. Under his leadership, active support and consideration were given the Gbandes and the rest of the Liberian peoples, without regard to place or region of residence, to ensure their representation in the functional organs of nearly all parts of the government on most levels. The position of district commissioner has been abandoned in Gbandeland and in the hinterlands as a whole because they have risen from the status of provinces to the status of counties (equivalent to states). It is the practice today that if any government employee wants any item or personal service, he must be prepared to pay for it rather than squeezing it out of the people as was the case prior to the election of President Tubman. This new trend is an unprecedented achievement of Tubman's administration. It was also during his administration that urbanization gained a new and special meaning for the Gbande people. They began leaving their homeland not only for other parts of Liberia and Africa but also for America, Asia, Canada, and Europe in search of higher education and for other similar purposes. The non-discriminatory policy of President Tubman resulted in an increase in the number of Gbandes settling in the coastal cities of Liberia for the first time in the history of Liberia. This phenomenon is also true for most other hinterland peoples, and there is no reason to believe that this trend will diminish.

Tribal Enclaves

Let me return to the idea that "the Gbandes are now more or less urban dwellers without being urbanized." It is true that whenever Gbandes gather in significant number in cities, they usually tend to cluster in pockets, forming enclaves within the urban milieu to such an extent that their original homogeneity is nearly maintained. However, the formation of tribal enclaves within the cities holds true for other similar groups. The fact is that the very enclaves in which the Gbandes and other hinterland peoples live are created by the nature of urbanization. Urbanization makes the Gbandes aware of themselves as Gbandes, and being Gbandes, they must live together in a particular area of the city. Likewise, other migrants to the city form similar patterns of settlement. It becomes, therefore, inevitable that this type of dispersion exerts an enormous influence upon the participants. Some of these influences may be classified as positive while others can be classified as negative, depending on which side of the fence one is on. This is a subtle problem because urban living does not permit the type of internal or in-group interaction which is so much a part of traditional Gbande life. In the urban contact situations there may be many alternatives available to the Gbandes in adjusting to urban life. Only two of these alternatives will be described here; they are the most obvious and are in frequent use. One alternative is to make friends with strangers regardless of their regional affiliation, although it is much easier to associate with strangers who live close to one's region. This type of association reduces one's ethnocentrism. The second alternative is to associate only with friends and kinsmen. The choice of either of these alternatives over the other depends largely upon the type of reception the participants receive from each other: rejection or acceptance. Rejection would reinforce their prejudices and ethnocentrism, whereas a cordial reception would lead to a reduction in prejudices and perhaps greatly alter such ethnocentrisms.

Life in the urban milieu offered the Gbandes unprecedented opportunities to live and mix with the other peoples who are their traditional neighbors. It made it possible for them to have frequent interactions with non-Gbandes under various conditions. Despite the opportunities for greater frequency of interaction with others on new terms, with many of the interactions favorable to all parties, they were reluctant to form new friendships. This reluctance was due to the traditional belief which haunts all Gbandes—the belief that their ancestor spirits, whose justice is always certain, will punish them for associating with strangers in a manner not prescribed by Gbande traditional rules. This restriction placed the Gbandes in a dilemma. It had several consequences for the Gbande urban dwellers. First, as had been noted elsewhere, when the Gbandes found themselves among strangers, especially in town, a new requirement emerged—a diffuse obligation to assist one another in need whenever and wherever possible, simply because one was a fellow Gbande rather than (as before) a kinsman. This fact may explain why in urban settings, recognition of common kinship fades almost imperceptibly into recognition of the ethnic bond between those of the same tribe, in this case between those who are Gbandes. There is a tendency to extend the concept of brotherhood metaphorically to include all fellow tribesmen. Though corporate kinship groups fail to survive, corporate associations based on tribal affiliation are being created. This is the case particularly for communities in the industrial areas in which tribesmen usually live together in a ghetto. The creation of such a ghetto is not possible in the urban milieu. In the first place, at this time there are not enough Gbandes in the urban areas to form a ghetto. In the second place, migration to the urban areas has not been as rapid and abrupt as to the industrial communities. In the urbanized areas one finds Gbandes with different urban backgrounds and experiences. The only thing these individuals have in common is their culture of primary socialization. Even this, as a cohesive factor, tends to be stronger for newcomers than for those who have lived longer in the city. The newcomer is at the mercy of those who are long-term residents of the city. He depends on them to give him a place to stay, to feed him, to get a job for him, and to teach him city behavior. He has complete confidence in their judgment and follows their advice closely. Because they are Gbandes, he considers them kinsmen even though this may not be the case. He subordinates himself to them in every conceivable way. As a result, he leaves himself open for exploitation at the hands of the older urban dwellers. This was almost a standard practice which all recent arrivals to the city were expected to experience. It was a practice which formed a vicious circle; each succeeding arrival was treated in a similar manner by those who preceded him. It was a process difficult for any recent arrival to escape.

A second consequence of urban living was the emergence of new patterns of relationships which contained the elements of cooperation and competition. Such cooperation and competition worked on three different levels. All the peoples of the hinterland, including the Gbandes, tend to have more empathy for one another than for those who are not from the hinterland. They show greater cooperation and less competition with each other, and greater competition and less cooperation with all non-hinterland peoples. This same phenomenon exists on the tribal level; that is, there is greater inter-tribal cooperation and less competition, but greater intra-tribal competition and less cooperation. Thus the Gbandes do cooperate as a cultural group and compete with all non-Gbandes such as the Loma and Gissie. The final

level is the case in which individuals compete with each
other in the accumulation of the cash and goods necessary
for them to help their families and kinsmen back in the
village. Cooperation and accompanying competition at these
three levels were necessary for the Gbandes and the rest of
the interior peoples to achieve their ends in the city. Although Gbandes and all the other peoples of the hinterland
are commonly referred to together as "country people," in
contrast to the Americo-Liberians and other indigenous
peoples who live down the coast, they differ widely and significantly from one another. The indiscriminant lumping-
together of these peoples into one category by the Americo-
Liberians, without regard to their cultural differences, led
them to take note of their common status despite their cultural differences. This awareness left the Gbandes little or no
choice but to cooperate with those non-Gbandes who were
thus designated as related. However, this does not mean the
erasing of tribal differences, nor does it mean the death of in-
dividuality within a tribe or tribes. What it means is that in
times past the descendants of the emancipated American
Negro slaves (founders of Liberia), who were city dwellers
par excellence, referred to all other groups as "country peoples," meaning uncivilized peoples. From this point of view,
it became expedient for those designated as country people
to initiate friendships—friendships of a new type. It became
equally necessary for individual members of various groups
to initiate friendships.

A third result of urban dwelling was the development of
cohesiveness of the Gbandes as a group. Anything unpleas-
ant involving a Gbande and any other country person would
quickly mobilize each group into concerted action against
the other. Táygili, a Gbande boy of about fourteen, had a
dispute with a Mano man about forty years old, a country
person from the eastern hinterland. The dispute concerned a
sixpence piece which Táygili found and which the Mano
man said was his. Táygili maintained that the money did not

have a name on it to indicate its ownership but the Mano man insisted that the money belonged to him. The Mano man then attempted to take it away from Táygili This action prompted members of each tribe to back their fellow tribesman without regard to who was right or wrong. In this case, Táygili kept the sixpence because there were more Gbandes than there were Manoes. But this competitive type of relationship between country peoples in the city leaves them at the mercy of the city or "civilized" peoples. Disagreement between country peoples, unless settled quietly and quickly by traditional methods is often subject to exploitation which in the end becomes costly to both sides. One result of inter-tribal or intra-tribal disputes is that an intended short-term visit to the city usually becomes a timeless one which, more often than not, stretches into permanent residence. If such a dispute—however insignificant—is not settled by traditional means, it is usually escalated by the jobless lawyers of the
· city. Until recent times, lawyers outnumbered cases because about 95% of the graduates of the Liberian College (now Liberia University) were lawyers. A lawyer had to find his own client if he was to be hired. The only other alternative for a lawyer was to be hired by the government. This situation made it necessary for these lawyers to encourage and intensify inter-tribal as well as intra-tribal disputes by telling their clients to take their grievances to court. Needless to say, such lawsuits were both costly and time-consuming. Once the clients were shoved into the jaws of the city's legal system, to which they were unaccustomed and in which they were unable to maneuver their own way around, they were at the mercy of the lawyers, who must then represent and guide them. In many instances, the parties involved had little or no intention of pursuing matters beyond traditional means of reconciliation, but the city did not recognize any standard except its own. Therefore, the country peoples (in this case the Gbandes) had little or no choice other than to do what the city lawyers told them to do, once they were in-

volved in a dispute. It did not matter whether the dispute
was inter-tribal or intra-tribal; the court proceedings were
long, expensive, and tedious legalistic processes which sometimes lasted for months or even years without yielding a
decision. But as long as the case was pending, the clients
remained at the mercy of their lawyers.

Inter- and Intra-Tribal Disputes

Examples of inter-tribal and intra-tribal disputes follow. In
the first case, Kēmba, a Gbande, had a quarrel with Kohínē,
another Gbande, about eating his cassava and palm oil.
Kohínē admitted using the cassava and palm oil but added
that he had every intention of replacing them in a day or
two. Kēmba contended that Kohínē had no business using his
cassava and palm oil without his permission. Mr. Ford, a
lawyer who lived in the vicinity, overheard them and immediately called Kēmba aside. Mr. Ford told Kēmba that he
had a good case against Kohínē and that he, Mr. Ford, was
willing to take the case to court for Kēmba if Kēmba wished.
Kēmba agreed and the matter was taken to the City Court of
Monrovia, Mesurado County. This act forced Kohínē to hire
Mr. Campbell to represent him. Once the case was properly
entered into the city court register, it mattered little whether
it was ever called. The lawyers were continually asking their
clients for favors ranging from money to services. After six
months, Kēmba wanted to withdraw the case from court but
was unable to do so. Finally, both Kēmba and Kohínē got jobs
with the Firestone Plantation Company and both of them
left Monrovia. This ended the case without a trial.

The second example is of an intra-tribal case, involving
Sēlé, a Gbande man, and Kagbáwōlō, a Kpelle man. Sēlé
made his living selling foodstuffs. Since Kagbáwōlō received
pay once a month, he usually borrowed foodstuffs from Sēlé
and paid him at the end of the month. This particular month,
Kagbáwōlō did not receive what he was expecting because

he missed a few days from work. Therefore, he was unable to pay Sēlé the full amount owed him. Sēlé insisted that he must get the full amount or his business would be ruined. Mr. Lewis, a lawyer, offered his services to help Sēlé recover his money from Kagbáwōlō. The matter was taken to court and Kagbáwōlō hired Mr. Thomas to represent him. After two years of the two clients' doing favors for these lawyers, the matter was terminated without a trial by the fact that Kagbáwōlō left town for an unknown destination without telling anyone that he was leaving. What these two cases illustrate is the fact that Gbandes who had come to the city to find new types of employment, money, and goods within relatively short periods now found themselves overwhelmed and captured in a new kind of poverty brought about by city living. Yet many of them would rather remain and die in the city than go back home empty-handed.

Industrial Camps

Perhaps the most dramatic aspect of Gbande migration does not involve those who are directed to the cities but those who go to the new industrial sites—the industrial sites set up by companies other than the Firestone Plantation Company. These sites (similar to company towns) are of special interest because they represent a sort of melting pot, more so than the cities. Here one finds representatives of many ethnic (tribal) groups, not only from Liberia but from West Africa in general. Because of the ethnic heterogeneity of these sites, they offer new challenges which are unparalleled in Gbande experience. They are unlike the cities in the following ways. There is neither a dominant group nor a site dominated by a given people, since the workers are assigned to a site by the entrepreneurs without regard to ethnic affiliation. Consequently, the workers are not free to select their place of residence as they do in the cities. These sites are considered by the African indigenous workers, including the

Gbandes, as temporary places of residence where quick material gains can be made, resulting in a quick return to the
homeland—in this case, Gbandeland. But, as it usually turns
out, this is seldom the case; many Gbandes do remain longer,
sometimes permanently, on the premises of these industries.
At one time, these companies or industries were as
capricious as the cities in many respects. For example, the facilities they offered were numerous. Their general stores
carried almost everything one can imagine. Credit was easy
for the employees to obtain from these stores. Gambling,
prohibited in the city, was permitted and even encouraged
in these camps. Gambling was considered one of the ways in
which fast economic gains could be made. All these facilities
were attractive enough to seduce the Gbandes into the arms
of a new kind of economic octopus of the industrial system
with its profit motives. This economic octopus operated on
two levels. The first level involves conditions the Gbande
workers imposed on themselves. (The second level involves
two conditions imposed on the Gbande workers by the companies.) The term "octopus" is used to emphasize the fact
that certain conditions were frequently cited as reasons for
not returning home as planned. For instance, the African
workers had to buy almost everything, including food, on
credit from the company stores; since they were illiterate
and did not know how to keep accurate records, over-
drawing their monthly earnings became one of the leading
causes of continued captivity. Most of the Gbandes were per-
petually engaged in (or accused of being engaged in)
diminishing their monthly cash income while increasing
their indebtedness to the company. The following were
among the most frequently cited causes of their indebtedness
to the company store: too much food; too much tobacco; too
many singlets and drawers; too many head-ties (headgear);
too many *lappas* (dresses for women); and high interest on
debts incurred. The quality of materials in the company
stores was very often second-, third-, or even fourth-rate.

(The Gbandes lacked discrimination in their selection of goods; hence the colorful but inferior materials often appealed to them.) As a result, the Gbandes were constantly buying additional goods to replace these things bought on credit. (Let me interject that in the case of Gbande workers who owed others from Gbandeland, a much better system was worked out; for lack of a better term, I call it the "pooling system." All pooled their resources to pay one debtor at a time. It worked as follows. The workers agreed that every pay day, each of them would give a certain sum to one debtor; the next pay day another debtor would be paid, and so forth. In this way, each was able to settle his debts and to send tax money home.) Gambling, the final condition on this first level on which the economic octopus operated, played an important role in these labor camps. The nature of the gambling games always turned winners into losers, because those who won were never content with their lot until they had lost everything.

This brings us to the second level on which the octopus operated. It involves two steps. First, the company charged for loss and breakage of any company property including the equipment issued to the workers; that is, each worker was responsible for any tool issued to him and had to account for it to his headman whenever requested to do so. A worker might be requested to account for his tools at any time, but usually he was asked to do so at the end of every month, at least a week or two before pay day. Checking tools at this particular time meant that the headman could report any loss in time for the necessary deduction to be made from the monthly earnings of the worker who was responsible. Tardiness and fines constitute the second factor on this level. Both tardiness and fines usually meant a reduction or deduction of already earned money. A worker had to be present at the time of roll call—that is, when his name was called—if he was to be credited for a full day's work. Fines were imposed upon a worker for a number of things. They might be imposed for failure to follow instructions, insubordination, carelessness, or anything which the headman considered undesirable. These factors constitute the arms of the economic octopus. The list could easily be extended but the result would be the same: many workers ended up with overdrawn accounts and became indebted to the company.

The result of these conditions in the economic sphere is clearly indicated by the decline of young people, particularly young men, in the population of Gbandeland. This decline of young men is a general trend throughout the Liberian hinterland. Such a trend is, in part, responsible for the drop in indigenous production of subsistence foods. This generalization refers to the serious shortages of staple foodstuffs (rice) which have become a problem in recent years. As a result of the shortages, rice has been imported from Nationalist China, as have Chinese methods of rice cultivation. The importation of staple foodstuffs by Liberia is a new phenomenon. By this I do not mean to imply that food was never imported by Liberia. Indeed, Liberia has always imported foods from both America and Europe, but these foods can be classed, by Liberian standards, as prestige foods (canned goods, ham, bacon, butter, and so on). Aside from these, almost all Liberians, whether city or country peoples, depended entirely upon indigenous cultivated foodstuffs, such as rice, cassava, and eddo (a starchy root). The drastic reduction in the production of indigenous foodstuffs can be attributed to the new industries. Since the establishment of these industries, they have attracted a constant flow of migrants from Gbandeland who are of an age when they would be most useful for indigenous farm work. Gbande young people, both male and female, have become restless and discontented with the monotonous routine of Gbande ways of life, because these industries have introduced to them a new way of life and have augmented their wants. In their quest for quick gain and for material acquisition with minimum work, they are drawn into more numerous and deeper debts. When I talked to these people, most of them expressed feelings of emptiness, worthlessness, and helplessness because of their failure to achieve any of the goals which brought them to the industries. For instance, a middle-aged Gbande man who called himself K>ño told me that he came to the industry with great hopes. Having worked for six years without realizing any of his dreams, he does not have any more hope. He feels worthless because he has failed not only himself but all of his kinsmen back in the village, and in addition he can do absolutely nothing about his failure. This is true of most of the Gbandes in these industries. The longer they stay in these industrial sites, the poorer they become and the more guilty they become about their failure to achieve the desired goals. Likewise, the poorer they are, the deeper their captivity becomes and the more they are alienated from their homeland. There is no doubt in my mind that this is a general pattern which holds true for other groups from the Liberian hinterland and for Africans in general. More peoples are leaving their hinterland villages for the industrial sites, and yet they are not making enough of anything to satisfy themselves or their kinsmen who stay at home. The industries afflict both migrants and non-migrants with anxiety and frustration. For instance, the non-migrant Gbandes are always uncertain of the fate of their migrant relatives. Many offerings of sacrifices are made to the ancestral spirits in behalf of the migrants in order to insure their well-being. The migrants anxious to make good in order to fulfill kinship obligations, become frustrated when the means to this end are blocked. While this kind of causal analysis is important in itself, the change in the Gbande way of life and attitudes about traveling is the issue here. As indicated elsewhere, the Gbandes were, for all practical purposes, a stay-at-home people. For them, Gbandeland was a land in which one lived all one's life and died in, to join the community of the ancestral spirits. The policies and practices of the new industries made it impossible for the Gbandes to return home as quickly as they desired. The number of Gbandes living permanently in the industrial areas is increasing substantially every year. Therefore, the migration of the Gbandes not only to the cities but also to the various industrial sites is important to any study of socio-cultural change. It is socio-cultural change par excellence, without the use of a conscious change agent to direct it. This type of condition-producing socio-cultural change may legitimately be assumed to hold true for the continent of Africa.

Another important factor to be considered in cultural change is the Western type of education. Western education is one of the keys which can unlock doors to new types of opportunities and to a partial emancipation from exploitation. For this reason, every Gbande is anxious to have this new education even at a great sacrifice. As a result of education, Gbandes have jobs now which were not previously open to them. These new job opportunities apply to both male and female. It has now become possible for Gbandes to go to foreign countries for higher education. Truly, education is one of the strongest vehicles of social and cultural change and socio-cultural reorganization. It is obvious that these factors are very much interdependent and interrelated. Urbanization and industrialization minimized barriers between groups in Liberia as well as between Liberians and those from foreign lands, thereby promoting better understanding. But it takes education to achieve tolerance and the understanding of one's fellow man.

Appendix

Phonology

THE FOLLOWING ANALYSIS suffers linguistically because of the lack of an extensive corpus and the inclusion of words from several dialects. (The /s/-/z/ contrast, for example, might well be an over-distinction when only one dialect is being analyzed.) The analysis was made using the usual field methods.

The transcription, then, is a broad phonetic one rather than a phonemic one, but it should give the reader a close approximation of the pronunciation of the words.

Except as noted below, the consonants have values close to those of most European languages.

Vowels

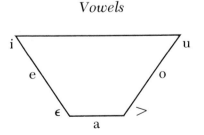

A set of seven vowels is used, which may be pronounced short in some words, long in others. English speakers will

need to take care not to glide /i/, /e/, /u/, and /o/ as we do in
the words *see, say, sue,* and *so.* Rather, vowel qualities are
very close to the corresponding vowels of French and may
be described as follows:

/i/   as in Fr. *si* (Eng. *see* glides)
/e/   as in Fr. *thé* (Eng. *say* glides)
/ɛ/   as in Fr. *sept* (Eng. *set*)
/a/   as in Sp. *casa* (This is a low mid vowel, about
      midway in quality between /a/ and /a/ in French
      patte and *pâte*. It is close to midwestern American
      /a/ in *pot*.)
/>/   as in Fr. *robe* (Eng. *rub* with lip rounding added)
/o/   as in Fr. *beau* (Eng. *bow* glides)
/u/   as in Fr. *vous* (Eng. *do* glides)

Vowel Length
      Vowel length is significant, with long vowels being
transcribed as a double vowel. A long vowel is not necessarily held twice as long as a short, but is held enough to be distinctive. Compare /kal ī/ 'hoe' and /kaal ī/ 'snake.'

Vowel Nasalization
      Vowels following a nasal consonant are nasalized. In ad-
dition, the final nasal consonant /n/ is produced by nasalizing
the preceding vowel. Vowel nasalization is not distinctive in
Gbande, however, as it is in French and Portuguese (e.g.,
/moan/ is pronounced [mõã]).

Tones
      Four pitch tones are posited: low, high, rising, and fall-
ing. Low tones are not marked; a high tone is transcribed as
a macron (l>̄ma), a rising tone as an acute accent (moán),
and a falling tone as a grave accent (falèy). Not all the pitch
tones can be regarded as phonemically significant. Some
may be due to mechanical linkages, the number of syllables
in a word, or other higher level constraints. (For example,

compare the tones of *hon* 'town' in G>́nd>lahon 'Gondo's town' and n͡ggolahón 'Forest town.') However, in the environments in which they are used, any substitution of one tone for another is regarded by the author-informant as a mispronunciation.

To the ear of an English speaker, the rising tone sounds like the stress and rising pitch of the final syllable *home* in the question, "Are you going home?". The falling tone sounds like the falling pitch on the same word in the answer, "Yes, I'm going home."

Consonants

	Labial	Dento-alveolar	Palatal	Velar	Labio-velar	Glottal
Stops	p	t		k	/k͡p/	
	b	d	j	g	/gb/	
	mb	nd		n͡g g		
	ß			k'		
Fricatives	f	s		g (γ)		h
	v	z				
Nasals	m	n	ñ	n͡g		
Sonorants	w	l	y			

Affricates
The only significant affricate is /j/ as in Eng. *jet*.

Stops
The stops /mb/, /nd/, and /n͡gg/ are each regarded as unit phonemes. In initial position, the nasal element is barely audible. Words and syllables may begin with any of these segments, but they do not nasalize a following vowel as the nasal consonants do.

The stop /ß/ is a voiced bilabial flap. Air pressure is built up behind the lips until they begin to puff out. On release they make a single outward flap.

The stop /k'/ is a voiceless velar ejective. Air pressure builds up behind the closure at the velum and on release explodes as a distinct egressive click. The author-informant pronounces the corresponding Mende words with an ingressive click.

The stops /k͡p/ and /g͡b/ are implosive unit phonemes with double articulation; i.e., they are made with a simultaneous closure at the lips and velum. There is a downward movement of the jaw and a backward movement of the point of contact of the back of the tongue and the soft palate. The pressure in the mouth lowers so that when the lips release, they pop inwards with an ingressive velaric air stream.

Fricatives

The fricative /g̶/ is a voiced velar fricative usually phonetically written [γ]. It is pronounced like Sp. *g* in *luego* or Danish *g* in *koge*.

Nasals

A vowel following any of the nasal consonants is strongly nasalized. In addition, word-final /n/ is always realized as nasalization of the preceding vowel. Any of the nasals may occur in word-initial or syllable-initial position. The nasals are:

/ñ/ like Fr. or It. *gn* or Sp. *ñ*
/n͡g/ like Eng. *ng* in *sing*

Sonorants

The sonorants /w/ and /y/ have values close to the corresponding segments in Eng. *wet* and *yet*.

In the case of / l / the point of articulation changes to accommodate to the following vowel. Before the high back vowels, /u/ and /o/, it is a retroflex prepalatal [l]; before front vowels it is alveolar, close to word-initial [l] in English.

Glossary

Terms

alligator	dapeñgī	
animal	suwáy	
arrow	dagbay	
aunt	tēna	father's sister only
bag	sīlō	
bananas	miyáñggi	
bark, special	ndɛndēy	
basket	kambày	
basket	kas>y	cylindrical
basket	kembāñgī	round, rigid, rattan
big thing	ñggali walāy	
bird	ñggolíi	
bird, wild	tutùy	
bitter leaves	kɛmbáy	a kind of greens similar to spinach
bowl	kālwī	
brother-in-law	dēmēna	
Bundoe	bondūy	female educational institution
bush's mother	d>b>njee	
cassava	jowí	

child   do
child, small   dulalày

Cities in Liberia
  Belleyallah   Gbeleyíala
  Boawolahum   Gb>āwólōhōn   hum-town
  Cigesuech   Sigésū
  Dangalahum   Dāñggālāhon
  Dianbough   Dāāmbū
  Gbageehilbah   Gbañggéhèmba
  Gbololahum   Gbōlōlāhon
  Gondolahum   G>nd>lahon
  Hailahum   Háylahon
  Kamalahum   Kamálahon
  Kialahum   K'aylahón
  Kololahum   Kolólahon
  Masambolahum   Māsāmbōlāhon
  Ngandolahum   Ñgg>nd>lahon   same as
                                           Gondolahum
  Nyeanwalahum   Ñɛ welehon
  Populahum   Pōpālāhon
  Somalahum   Sómalahon
  Vahum   Vāhōn
  Vorjamine   V>njama

Cities in Sierra Leone
  Bo   Gbō
  Pendembu   Pendémbu
  classmates   sāv>l>
  cloth, country   koluí
  cloth, piece of   lapā   wrapped around
                                           the waist
  cook (to cook)   gundēñggī
  cooking   g>nd>
  cooking stick   kambāñggī
  corn   ñ>ñggī
  cow   nikáy

dancer	lánib>géy	
deer	dupòy	
doctor	sowì	Gbande word for
doctor	zowī	Loma word for
doctor, woman	ß>tu	in mask or a Sande leader
dog	kēke	
drum	sagbay	regular drum
drum	fañggày	talking drum
drum	taaniñggí	another talking drum
eggplant	ßōlōñggi	
ethnic group	mandéñggo	of West Africa
fan (to fan)	gafē̄	
fan	dafē̄	
farm, our	ni balày	
father	kɛké	
fiber	dahay	from a vine
fiber	balúwi	of the rattan family
fortune teller	towōñgbē	
frog, spring	gbɛgbɛy	
frog, toe	dohóy	
Gbande	Gbāndi	group of people of Liberia (Word means "human beings" in their language.)

Gbande people subdivisions

Tahamba	Tāhāmbā
Goolahum or Ngoolahum	N̄ggolahón
Wawoma or Waoma	Wawomā
Hasala	Haasala
Vasala	Vaasala

Yawuyahum	Yāwíāhon	
Hembe	Hɛmbɛ	
God	Galā	
God of creation	Gew>l>n͡ggala	
good-for-nothing	kāāfōh̄	
good-for-nothing	suwáy	person or animal of lowest degree
gourd	tɛ̄jɛ̄	
gragra bush	glegle buz	
grandma	mamā	
grandpa	k'ɛwāla	
grass	tutuí	soft, fine, used for hut building
hammock	bowáin	
hoe	kalī	
hog	ndundéy	
hooks	dōlɛ̄njī	
husband, my	nihīɛngi	
iron, one	koluyīla	unit of exchange
kernel of palm nut	tuwì	
Kiahala	K'áyhala	a river of Liberia
kitchen	gbɛbèy	temporary hut
knife	ßowain	
kola nut	towolòy	
learned person	kamān	professor
leopard	k>l̄ī	
Liberia	Lābɛ̄lā	country in West Africa, home of the Gbande
lima beans	k>l>t>w>y	sweetheart beans
Lofa	Lōfā	a county of Liberia
logs, large	k>vi botòy	
Loma	Gbalūwi	Gbande word for

machete	ßolobáy	
mano	mānō	
mat	sabày	
meat	suwāy	
medicine	salèy	
medicine	gafwén	ordeal
Mende people	Hēgāwèn	Gbande word for
Mende people	Gūma	a district of
Moah	Moán	a river of Liberia
monkey	ñggīlī	
mortar, wooden	kondày	
mother	ndē ndè	
mourning	w>l>hày	
mushrooms	falèy	
Muslim	M>le	a Mende word for

names of men
Aigūjiamá
Āmā
Dagb>̄
Gb>le
Gbēse
Haalē
Kagbáwōlō
Kelénde
Kēmba
Kēsukēkula
K>̄lī
K>̄ño
Kohíné̄
Kpēle
Māsā gb>̄le
M>m>̄lu
M>m>̄lu Táygili
Momóluñgguyàn
Monlū
Nagbày

Sēlé
Sōmā
Táygili
Váni

neck	gbōlō	
Neighbors of the Gbandes		
Belle	Bēlɛ	south of the Gbandes
Loma	L⁻>ma	north of the Gbandes
	Būzī	another name for Lomas
Gissie	Gīsi	north of the Gbandes
Mende	Mēnde	west of the Gbandes
Kpelle	Kpēlɛ	south of the Belles
net	bowáin	
net	tuwī	Gbande word for
nieces or nephews	jāagbɛ	
October	Vōndōngī	Track-leaver
okra	gb>nd>y	
opossum	kuȟi	
palm kernel oil	toluwúl>y	
palm nut kernel	tuwì	
palm tree	t>gb>y	
peppers	kīhēn̂ggī	
pestle	gɛtey	
piassava tree	duhúi	
pineapples	kɛhéy	
porcupine	gbála	
Poro	p⁻>l⁻>	
Poro initiate, first	dōlēnje	of current session
Poro leader	gafùi	

Poro leader	lāneboge	tall, dancer
Poro leader	landáy	super
Poro leader, lesser	ñagbày	
Porogee	p⫽l⫽ngī	
potatoes	gb>wìi	
pots, large	fɛ̄	
raccoon	kōvā	
rats	jēɛn̂ggī	
rattan	balwī	
rice	mbáy	
roast	ma	
rock	k>tū	
rooster	tɛhenày	
rope	gesáy	
sale	salē	male educational institution
salts—see *units of exchange*		
Sande	sānde	female educational institution
Sande initiate, first	gbanā	of current session
Sande initiate, last	k⫽po	of current session
sibling	ndīa	older
sibling	ndēgē	younger
sibling	ni ndīa	our older
sibling	ni ndēgē	our younger
snail	kalúy	
snake	kalíi	
sorcery	kala	
spears	balay	
spoon	mitáy	
spirit	gaf>wɛ̄n	
squirrel	gbɛsɛn̂ggī	
sticks, dry	k⫽vī	
strangers	sotān̂ggī	

strangers	wīīkōlē	light-skinned Westerners
strangers	wīngī	Westerners
stringed instrument	mbakáy	
stringed instrument	gbɛkày	used for communication
stupid	gbōlōwā	
stupid person	bōlōwā mòin	
sugarcane family	sabày	weed of this family
sweetheart beans	k>l>t>w>y	lima beans
town	hon	
turtle	kɛsèy	
twine	gesáy	from palm fibers
uncle	kēɛn	

units of exchange:

one iron	koluyīla
one salt	gboloyīla
two salts	gbolofɛ̄le
three salts	gbolosāwa
ten salts	gbolopū

village or town	tɛ̄i	
vine	duwì	soft, used as a bath brush and bath soap
water, cold	jaw>lèy	
wife, my	niyáhay	
witch	kɛ̄lēn̂ggī	
witchcraft	kalān̂ggī	
wives, our	yahāīn ti	
wrestling	dapī	game of

xylophone	kēlēn͡ggī	
xylophone	mbakēlēn͡ggī	another form of
xylophone-like instrument	kēlēn͡ggē	
yams	kalúngi	

Phrases and Sayings

Ah! This is indeed a circumcision, it feels funny, but man! The thing can hurt.
Ya ya gbōlō lēn͡gga kē n͡gg>i waya n͡gal ī a gba lē.

An empty bag cannot stand up (or: A bag that is emptied will crumble).
Kɛsúi si n͡gali á su ey h>mβō ⁻>lo.

Breaking of the grave (a ritual).
Ka mbày wolonga.

Death! Death!
Sāy say!

Come, let's eat rice!
Vāmōbàyɛn!

Do you love him?
Ilūn͡gg> lɛ n͡gga n͡ggiē?

He who is wise is one who listens to his wives.
Nuisī kelegele n͡ggo āl> a w>l īl>⁻ n͡ggi ñáhày wan.

He who steals is one who is also capable of killing and lying.
Nwi áa n͡gui yá w> āl> aa nu và aa ndɛ le.

I apologize (or: I beg you).
Yī velene kày.

If I have always shown enthusiasm about other's joys, how
much more about my own kinsmen?
Gaagē nu n͡ggāāi dày wan njenje ke la wén nindāi ye.

I will do as you want me to.
Kɛgɛ siāndɛ.

Look! See? Yen͡ggbē and Mānjō have made me beautiful
leather jewels.
Yen͡ggbē gbēlē Manjō gbēlē kolo gbā tea ndā wān.

May the couple be blessed with good health and with many
children.
Sīña ta gehēn ti dolē tulahōn iwa.

May the relationship between these two and between us be
as strong and good as this iron money.
*Domān͡ggi ihiti tilūn͡gga n͡ggi age ni lōahon kɛ kōlawez
hambān͡gga.*

May this request be granted by our ancestors in the name of
God, the maker of all things.
*Sētanden͡ggā ēgano kɛɛ gafoēn n͡gga tēlua gelev>l>n͡ggala
hawɛn.*

My father, permit me to demonstrate my humility as abject
submission to you. Let me be your footstool.
Kɛgɛ yī vɛlɛni belēn͡ggī i w>w> hò.

My hand is under but let me hang my head. (Your words are

well spoken, but let me have a conference with the other relatives of my kinship group.)
Tokol>mbu bɛlɛn̂ggĩwu hũtɛ.

Oh! Sun, let me know before you disappear (or: Oh! Sun, tell me good-bye before you disappear).
O yāveli yāveli yaa gbombō folo ya l ĩ ve li mà.

One who has many children, his name will never die.
Nui ā ndoolé dahée n̂ggi ēhà.

Our hands are on your request.
Ni lōko lōma.

Pulling the sticks out of the rice.
Gulu wūla mbáy hon.

The blacksmith has gone wild because I am blowing the fire for him, but he keeps putting it out with water.
N̂Gge mōy l ĩt ĩ n̂ggā ay ya n̂gga fō n̂ggāy yā jāā vō n̂gga.

The decision is entirely yours (or: Whatever you say).
Sĩn> yāndɛ.

The leader's most beautiful wife has a mouth which smells worse than half-dry crayfishes.
M>le n̂ā hai n̂a nde jū man̂ggi lái gu n̂gg>y pɛpēy ma.

The razor has come down.
Welekē gbek'áy hítia.

The woman has called my name.
Ñahày dāwōn̂ggā.

What kind of tree shall we climb in order to be ourselves for a moment so that we can just sit down and look at each

other?
Ai lai ndèe na lɛ ñggulu bɛ̄gɛ̄lēhon na golēa ge na lɛ ñggu
begelehon.

When I am grown and have my own girl children, I will
first give many to Jī M>lé as he wants for wives, and if
there are more girls than he wants, I will give the rest to
G>̄nd> Bala.
Na ñggaandoole ñggāā fee Jī M>̄lē yɛ̄ ma tái aa lo gā fe
G>nd> Bala da nai na.

Where there are young ladies, there will the young men go.
Gbey nda ña hā poi ti ta gɛ̄ na, na l> si ɛn ndō poi
ti ta lī na.

Bibliography

Beattie, John, *Other Cultures*. New York: Free Press, 1964.

Bohannan, Paul, *Social Anthropology*. New York: Holt, Rinehart and Winston, Inc., 1966.

Davidson, Basil, *The African Past: Chronicles from Antiquity to Modern Times*. Boston: Little, Brown, & Company, 1964.

Galwash, A., *Introduction to the Koran*. Cairo, Egypt: Oxford University Press, 1961.

Herskovits, Melville J., *The Human Factor in Changing Africa*. New York: Alfred A. Knopf, 1962.

Kahl, Joseph, "Some Concomitants of Industrialization and Urbanization." *Human Organization* 18, no. 2 (Summer 1959).

Kenyatta, Jomo, *Facing Mt. Kenya,* London: Mercury Books, 1961.

Murdock, George P., *Africa: Its Peoples and Their Cultural History*. New York: McGraw-Hill Book Company, 1959.

Ottenberg, Simon and Phoebe, *Cultures and Societies of Africa*. New York: Random House, Inc., 1964.

Shinnie, Margaret, *Ancient African Kingdoms*. London: Edward Arnold Ltd., 1965.

Timasheff, Nicholas S., *Sociological Theory: Its Nature and Growth*. New York: Random House, Inc., 1957.

Townsend, E. Reginald, *Liberia, Story of Progress*. Monrovia, Liberia: Liberian Information Service, 1965.

Uchendu, Victor C., *The Igbo of Southeast Nigeria*. New York: Holt, Rinehart and Winston, Inc., 1965.

United Nations, Department of Economic and Social Affairs, *The Future Growth of World Population*. New York: 1958.

Index

Government (*continued*)
  50, 154–55, 249–63, 291,
  293–95
Grandparents, 93–94, 95–96,
  107, 110, 113, 120, 171
Guma District, 12

Hailahum, 12
Harmattan wind, 4, 143
Hasala, 10, 12, 179, 255
Headman, 71, 133, 163, 251,
  253–55, 256
Horns, 44, 155–56, 159, 207,
  209
Hunting, 3, 10, 25, 34–44, 60,
  138, 195, 231, 232, 235
Huts, 4, 28, 31, 33, 49, 68–75,
  93, 140, 149, 167, 170,
  175, 213, 215, 217, 222–
  23, 234, 235, 237, 255,
  256, 270, 275, 282, 291
Hygiene, 19, 25, 33, 236, 239–
  45, 247. *See also* Sanitation

Industrialization, 289–291,
  301–6
Initiation, 129–34, 145
Insults, 237
Islam, 3, 12, 13, 18, 178–79,
  182, 245

Jail, 281–82, 293
Jewelry, 60, 62, 75, 82, 187,
  195, 196, 202, 213
Jokes, 28, 205, 234–38, 273
Kamalahum, 12

Kenyatta, Jomo, x
Kiahala River, 5
Kinship, rules of, 89–96, 101–
  8
Kola nut, 52–53, 75, 79, 123
Koloahum, 5, 10, 63, 148, 149,
  180, 266, 273, 291
Koran, 18, 182
Kpelles, 21, 300

Landay, 52, 138–39, 140,
  189–90
Language, 12, 13, 14, 15, 19,
  20–22, 153–54, 158, 173,
  179, 185, 196, 307–10
Law, 63, 168, 264, 270–75,
  277, 281, 291, 299–301
Laziness, 18, 19, 28, 149, 272,
  280–81
Leather, 63, 82, 186, 195–196,
  202
Legends, 159, 212, 213–16
Liberia, xi, 4, 7, 22, 54, 147,
  148, 250–51, 253–55, 258,
  260–62, 274, 289, 291,
  292, 293–96, 298, 301,
  304, 306
Life after death, 177–78
Literacy, 8, 9, 18, 149, 153,
  179, 302
Lofa River, 5
Lomas, vii, 1, 5, 10, 13, 14–17,
  19, 20, 21, 143, 215, 297
Love, 17–18, 20, 78–79, 120,
  182
Lying, 272, 274, 275–76, 280,
  281